Managerial
Excellence

The Harvard Business Review Book Series

Designing and Managing Your Career, Edited by Harry Levinson

Ethics in Practice: Managing the Moral Corporation, Edited with an Introduction by Kenneth R. Andrews

Managing Projects and Programs, With a Preface by Norman R. Augustine

Manage People, Not Personnel: Motivation and Performance Appraisal, With a Preface by Victor H. Vroom

Revolution in Real Time: Managing Information Technology in the 1990s, With a Preface by William G. McGowan

Strategy: Seeking and Securing Competitive Advantage, Edited with an Introduction by Cynthia A. Montgomery and Michael E. Porter

Leaders on Leadership: Interviews with Top Executives, Edited with a Preface by Warren Bennis

Seeking Customers, Edited with an Introduction by Benson P. Shapiro and John J. Sviokla

Keeping Customers, Edited with an Introduction by John J. Sviokla and Benson P. Shapiro

The Learning Imperative: Managing People for Continuous Innovation, Edited with an Introduction by Robert Howard

The Articulate Executive: Orchestrating Effective Communication, With a Preface by Fernando Bartolomé

Differences That Work: Organizational Excellence through Diversity, Edited with an Introduction by Mary C. Gentile

Reach for the Top: Women and the Changing Facts of Work Life, Edited with an Introduction by Nancy A. Nichols

Global Strategies: Insights from the World's Leading Thinkers, With a Preface by Percy Barnevik

Command Performance: The Art of Delivering Quality Service, With a Preface by John E. Martin

Manufacturing Renaissance, Edited with an Introduction by Gary P. Pisano and Robert H. Hayes

The Product Development Challenge: Competing through Speed, Quality, and Creativity, Edited with an Introduction by Kim B. Clark and Steven C. Wheelwright

The Evolving Global Economy: Making Sense of the New World Order, Edited with a Preface by Kenichi Ohmae

Managerial Excellence: McKinsey Award Winners from the *Harvard Business Review,* **1980–1994,** Foreword by Rajat Gupta, Preface by Nan Stone

Fast Forward: The Best Ideas on Managing Business Change, Edited with an Introduction and Epilogue by James Champy and Nitin Nohria

First Person: Tales of Management Courage and Tenacity, Edited with an Introduction by Thomas Teal

Managerial Excellence

McKinsey Award Winners from the *Harvard Business Review,* 1980–1994

Foreword by
Rajat Gupta
Managing Director,
McKinsey & Company, Inc.

Preface by
Nan Stone
Editor,
Harvard Business Review

A Harvard Business Review Book

The *Harvard Business Review* articles in this collection are available as individual reprints. Discounts apply to quantity purchases. For information and ordering contact Customer Service, Harvard Business School Publishing, Boston, MA 02163. Telephone: (617) 495-6192, 9 a.m. to 5 p.m. Eastern Time, Monday through Friday. Fax: (617) 495-6985, 24 hours a day.

The paper used in this publication meets the requirements of the American National Standard for Permanence of Paper for Printed Library Materials Z39.48-1984

Library of Congress Cataloging-in-Publication Data

Managerial excellence : McKinsey award winners from the Harvard
   Business Review, 1980–1994 / forward by Rajat Gupta ; preface by Nan
      Stone
         p.   cm.—(A Harvard business review book)
      Includes index.
      ISBN 0-87584-670-X
      1. Management.   2. Industrial management.   I. Series.
II. Series: Harvard business review book series.
HD31.M293934   1996
658—dc20   95-36267
                                                                 CIP

Contents

Foreword   xiii
Rajat Gupta

Preface   xvii
Nan Stone

1980
  Managing Our Way to Economic Decline   1
  Robert H. Hayes and William J. Abernathy
  Too often Americans blame the weakened U.S.
  economy on inflation, the effects of government
  regulation and tax policy, or price escalation by OPEC.
  Arguing that responsibility lies not only with these
  general economic forces but also with American
  managers' failure to keep their companies
  technologically competitive, the authors offer their
  own prescriptions for nursing American business back
  to health.

1981
  The New Industrial Competition   25
  *William J. Abernathy, Kim B. Clark, and Alan M.
  Kantrow*
  U.S. manufacturers have long felt pressure from their
  European and Japanese competitors. Using the
  automobile manufacturing industry as a case example,
  the authors show how Japanese carmakers' success
  secrets—namely, their superior manufacturing
  plants—have changed the rules of the game. The

challenge for U.S. companies in endangered industries is to recognize the new worldwide industry rules, adjust to them, and learn to manage change.

1982

Managing As If Tomorrow Mattered   51
Robert H. Hayes and David A. Garvin
Attempting to apply greater rationality to investment decisions, American managers have turned increasingly to sophisticated analytic techniques for evaluating proposed investments. The authors assert, however, that such actions often lead to a serious underinvestment in the capital stock (production capacity, technology, and worker skills) on which their companies rest. Managers need to be wary of certain techniques that may be profoundly biased against investment.

1983

Quality on the Line   67
David A. Garvin
Drawing on his multiyear study of production operations at all but one of the manufacturers of room air conditioners in the United States and Japan, the author documents the immense variation in levels of quality performance along the spectrum of competitors. His analysis reveals that superior performance levels come not from cultural advantage and national traits but from the systematic implementation of sound management practices.

1984

Wrestling with Jellyfish   89
Richard J. Boyle
Changing office culture and management style within a large corporation is a challenging task with an often uncertain outcome. Here the author recounts his own experience with such organizational changes as vice president and group executive at Honeywell, Inc. He chronicles the efforts of employees in one division to

relax the company's traditional militaristic style of management and implement instead a more participative approach.

1985

Managing Innovation: Controlled Chaos   **107**
James Brian Quinn
The innovative process is rarely marked by order and rigidity. Exceptionally innovative companies in fact thrive in conditions of chaos and uncertainty, succeeding over those companies that stifle innovation with detailed planning and bureaucratic procedures. The authors draw on a multiyear research project and many case studies to examine patterns in successful large companies' approaches to technological innovation, starting with their initial acceptance of the essential chaos of development.

1986

The Productivity Paradox   **127**
Wickham Skinner
While American manufacturers have often turned to cost-cutting programs to improve their productivity and thereby enhance their international competitiveness, the author argues that these cost-cuttings are not always the best resort for achieving real productivity improvement. Though attention to costs is important, manufacturers need to direct their focus away from straight cost-cutting toward strategy, quality enhancement, and process technology—looking beyond quick fixes toward improved world competitiveness.

1987

From Competitive Advantage to Corporate Strategy   **137**
Michael E. Porter
Strategies of diversification have failed in the majority of large U.S. companies. Whether through acquisitions, joint venture, or start-up efforts,

diversification has not generally produced the profitability or competitive edge sought by executives. To ensure better results from future diversification attempts, companies must steer away from hands-off strategies like portfolio management toward more collaborative efforts that capitalize on the interlocking strengths of the organization's diverse units.

1988

Time—The Next Source of Competitive Advantage   171
George Stalk, Jr.

Progressing since the 1940s from a strategic focus on low labor costs to the outbreak of variety wars in the 1980s, leading Japanese companies today recognize that time is now the most critical factor in maintaining a competitive advantage. Time-based approaches allow companies to implement faster new product introductions, more efficient manufacturing, and swifter sales and distribution. Drawing on examples of time-focused Japanese companies, the author concludes that while conventional companies are occupied with cost and size issues, today's cutting-edge competitors derive their competitive advantage from time.

1989

Strategic Intent   193
Gary Hamel and C.K. Prahalad

For many executives of Western companies, efforts to regain competitiveness will require rethinking many of the basic concepts of strategy. New global competitors approach strategy from a fundamentally different perspective than traditional management thought. The new competitors emphasize strategic intent and competitive innovation and focus on a company's resourcefulness rather than the resources it controls. The authors propose a new approach toward strategy, emphasizing overambitious goals and relentless market probing.

1990

**Motorola U: When Training Becomes
an Education** **219**
William Wiggenhorn
When Motorola began a new skills training program
in 1980, its modest goal was to educate its work force
on quality improvement techniques like statistical
process control. As the program evolved, it became
apparent that many employees lacked more basic
business skills yet were often unreceptive to the
education Motorola offered them. The author tells the
fascinating story behind what would become
Motorola University, the company university he now
heads, chronicling how it grew from a limited training
program into a company's broad commitment to
education.

1991

The Computerless Computer Company **241**
Andrew S. Rappaport and Shmuel Halevi
By the year 2000, the competitive advantage will lie
with "the computerless computer company," the
computer company that competes on how computers
are used, not how they are built. As long as
companies have reliable supplies of adequate
hardware, not necessarily the most advanced
hardware, there are few advantages to building
computers. The authors outline new rules for
competing in this changing arena, identifying how to
survive—and achieve market power through—the
transformation of the computer industry.

1992

**Balancing Corporate Power: A New
Federalist Paper** **265**
Charles Handy
As chief executives in some of today's largest
corporations attempt to manage their increasingly
complex organizations, they are turning to one of the
world's oldest political philosophies—federalism. The

author asserts that given the growing view of organizations as minisocieties, the idea of applying political principles to management is a logical connection. Federalism breaks through paradoxes of power and control, balancing power among those in the center of the organization, those in the center of the expertise, and those in the center of the action—essentially avoiding the risks of autocracy and the overcontrol of a central bureaucracy—and succeeding because independent bits know that they are part of a greater whole.

1993

Predators and Prey:
A New Ecology of Competition   281
James F. Moore

Most managers view competition as a head-to-head battle within an industry, a relentless struggle for market share. Here the author proposes a new metaphor for competition drawn from the study of biology and social systems, suggesting that a company be viewed not as a member of a single industry but as part of a "business ecosystem" that crosses a variety of industries. In such an environment companies "co-evolve" around a new innovation, working competitively yet cooperatively to generate new products and meet customer needs—*together* fueling today's industrial transformation.

1994

Good Communication That Blocks Learning   303
Chris Argyris

Today's new but now familiar corporate communication techniques, such as focus groups and surveys, can often block organizational learning even while generating solutions for certain problems. Though these practices do gather simple, single-loop information, the author points out that they can also discourage the kind of organizational self-scrutiny that

is so critical in today's business environment.
Managers need to encourage and value employees
who think constantly and creatively about the
organization's needs.

About the Contributors   **319**

McKinsey Award Second Place Winners   **325**

Index   **327**

Foreword

Rajat Gupta

A recent article in the *Financial Times* described how one company was struggling with the question of whether to structure its international organization around products or markets. I had a feeling of déjà vu and I asked myself, how long will companies doing business in several countries debate this or other perennial questions relating to market segmentation, sales force management, span of control, the role of the corporate center, or channel selection? Despite all the management fads and new techniques for fixing problems, the fundamental questions of strategy and organization have outlasted the answers.

Not only do the problems remain, but they now occur in a context of uncertainty and unpredictability. With world markets changing so fast, one must ask, can advice and theory about management really be helpful to leaders who must make decisions in real time? It's interesting, then, that the first article in this book is entitled "Managing Our Way to Economic Decline." Published in 1980, it attacks what it characterized as an MBA-dominated approach to management—an overly analytical, technologically illiterate, and control-oriented mindset among managers that the authors believed was hurting the performance of American companies.

The article had a big impact on many of us, especially those of us with newly minted MBAs who believed that our problem-solving and analytical skills would lead to success. Even those who didn't read it soon realized through their experiences that two-dimensional thinking is of little use in a multidimensional world. And yet there were many students of management whose research and findings insisted on a simpler world.

In *The Reflective Practitioner*, Donald Schon argued that professionals lost their credibility during the seventies when they acted as if the world was certain, simple, and susceptible to a body of knowledge and tools. But "problems are interconnected, environments are turbulent, and the future is indeterminate just in so far as managers can shape it by their actions. What is called for, under these conditions, is not only the analytic techniques which have been traditional in operations research, but the active, synthetic skill of designing a desirable future and inventing ways of bringing it about."[1]

Schon was describing the need for what has been a fundamental change in the perspective of management thinking and research. Rather than dissecting the past, delineating cause and effect, and modeling the results, the study of management now looks forward, focusing on aspirations, empowerment, the creation of new products for new markets, and ways of probing an ill-defined future. More and more, the study of management reflects, or needs to reflect, a description of management proposed by Russell Ackoff: "Managers are not confronted with problems that are independent of each other, but with dynamic situations that consist of complex systems of changing problems that interact with each other. I call such situations messes. Problems are abstractions extracted from messes by analysis; they are to messes as atoms are to tables and charts. . . . Managers do not solve problems: they manage messes."[2]

How do we get better at managing "messes"? "Do it, try it, fix it,"[3] wrote the authors of *In Search of Excellence*, building on James Brian Quinn's arguments for "logical incrementalism." But the world seems to be changing too fast to appear logical or to tolerate incrementalism. Clearly managers should recognize the need and develop the ability to experiment with not only implementing but also conceiving strategy through interactive action and analysis. We experiment to discover and invent. In his analysis of the new professional, the "reflective practitioner," Schon described various experiments undertaken in order to both understand situations and improve them. "When the practitioner reflects-in-action his experimenting is at once exploratory, move testing, and hypothesis testing."[4]

Given Schon's arguments and the environment in which management operates today, it is not surprising that the roles of academics, consultants, and managers have begun to blur. Consultants do more research (McKinsey invests $50 million to $100 million per year) to help clients make real-time decisions; academics do more consulting to test the usefulness of their observations; and managers, much more aware of the theory behind their practice, do more willing experimentation with new approaches. All of us need to "reflect in action."

So why read this book? Because, unlike other books, these essays search for understanding rather than proselytize new answers to solve all problems. The articles that won the McKinsey Award between 1980 and 1994 reflect years of turmoil, waves of acquisitions and divestitures, lessons learned the hard way, and the emergence of a truly powerful and humbling global marketplace.

For younger managers this collection provides a good opportunity to scan some of the best thinking about management over the past 15 years and to determine what to pursue as part of their own development. For more seasoned managers, it offers a chance to return to relatively solid ground from the heights of management fads that seem to change yearly. And for the chief executive, this book serves as a reminder of the crucial task of developing people by exposing them to new management challenges and experiences.

Notes

1. Donald Schön, *The Reflective Practitioner* (New York: Basic Books, 1983), p. 16.

2. Richard Ackoff, "The Future of Operational Research Is Past," *Journal of Operational Research Society* 30, no. 2 (1979), 93–104.

3. Thomas J. Peters and Robert M. Waterman, Jr. *In Search of Excellence* (New York: Harper and Row, 1982).

4. Schön, p. 147.

Preface

Nan Stone

For more than 70 years, the *Harvard Business Review* has occupied a unique niche among publications, unlike any business magazine or scholarly journal. *Harvard Business Review* was founded in 1922 by Dean Wallace Donham of Harvard Graduate School of Business Administration to create a body of management knowledge and experience that would prove as useful to business leaders as the common law was to jurists. From the outset, therefore, *Harvard Business Review*'s readers and authors have shared a commitment to practice and to ideas, to the belief that effective management ends in action but begins with thought.

To support this commitment, the *Harvard Business Review* has always sought articles from a wide range of contributors—executives, academics, management consultants, and specialists of all kinds. Whatever the authors' backgrounds, however, the hallmarks of their articles are the same: intellectual integrity and managerial relevance. The best *Harvard Business Review* articles are distinguished by the fact that they develop new concepts *and* speak to pragmatic managerial concerns. By that standard, the McKinsey Award–winning articles collected in this volume are truly the best of the best.

Since 1959, the McKinsey Foundation for Management Research has awarded prizes annually for the two best articles published in the *Harvard Business Review*. Determination of the winners rests with an independent panel of executives, academics, and government or social sector leaders chosen each year by the editors. An article's contribution to existing knowledge, ability to stand conventional wisdom on its head, analytic depth, sound logic, and clear style all figure prominently among the criteria the judges apply. But in the end, what matters most is whether an article is relevant to the real work that managers do and to the important issues they face. Put simply, can the content provoke both thought and action?

Over the years, prizewinning articles have addressed many subjects. Nevertheless, three broad themes stand out. The first, and by far the largest, group of winning articles focuses on effective business management and, more particularly, the work of senior managers. The second cluster of articles looks at the role of business and its relation to society. The third and last set of articles centers on competitiveness. Recently, however, the lines that distinguish those categories have become increasingly blurred, as readers of this volume will discover.

As a representative example, consider the most recent prizewinner, "Good Communication That Blocks Learning" by Chris Argyris. The article's thesis is provocative and counterintuitive: the communications techniques with which senior managers are most familiar (techniques such as employee surveys, management-by-walking-around, and focus groups) undermine the ends they are intended to achieve. Instead of building individual commitment and organizational effectiveness, they foster passivity and discourage change because, in Argyris's words, "they do not get people to reflect on their work behavior."

Argyris's article draws on a lifetime of path-breaking work in social psychology. At first glance, the concepts he develops seem remote from the manager's daily round (as well as being just plain hard to work through). Double-loop learning, defensive reasoning, espoused theories versus theories in use, the dangers of positive thinking: the ideas are complex. Busy executives might be forgiven for wondering whether they are truly worth the investment of time. The answer, unambiguously, is yes. Engaging with these concepts and applying them can literally transform the way that readers—and organizations—think and behave.

On this dimension, also, Argyris's article is a representative McKinsey Award winner. From first to last, the articles collected in this volume have stimulated thought and provided a catalyst for action, in companies throughout the United States and around the globe. Readers today will find—or rediscover—that they retain all their power to provoke, inspire, and instigate change.

Managerial Excellence

1
Managing Our Way to Economic Decline

Robert H. Hayes and
William J. Abernathy

During the past several years American business has experienced a marked deterioration of competitive vigor and a growing unease about its overall economic well-being. This decline in both health and confidence has been attributed by economists and business leaders to such factors as the rapacity of OPEC, deficiencies in government tax and monetary policies, and the proliferation of regulation. We find these explanations inadequate.

They do not explain, for example, why the rate of productivity growth in America has declined both absolutely and relative to that in Europe and Japan. Nor do they explain why in many high-technology as well as mature industries America has lost its leadership position. Although a host of readily named forces—government regulation, inflation, monetary policy, tax laws, labor costs and constraints, fear of a capital shortage, the price of imported oil—have taken their toll on American business, pressures of this sort affect the economic climate abroad just as they do here.

A German executive, for example, will not be convinced by these explanations. Germany imports 95% of its oil (we import 50%), its government's share of gross domestic product is about 37% (ours is about 30%), and workers must be consulted on most major decisions. Yet Germany's rate of productivity growth has actually increased since 1970 and recently rose to more than four times ours. In France the situation is similar, yet today that country's productivity growth in manufacturing (despite current crises in steel and textiles) more than triples ours. No modern industrial nation is immune to the problems

and pressures besetting U.S. business. Why then do we find a disproportionate loss of competitive vigor by U.S. companies?

Our experience suggests that, to an unprecedented degree, success
in most industries today requires an organizational commitment to
compete in the marketplace on technological grounds—that is, to
compete over the long run by offering superior products. Yet, guided
by what they took to be the newest and best principles of management, American managers have increasingly directed their attention elsewhere. These new principles, despite their sophistication and
widespread usefulness, encourage a preference for (1) analytic detachment rather than the insight that comes from "hands on" experience
and (2) short-term cost reduction rather than long-term development
of technological competitiveness. It is this new managerial gospel, we
feel, that has played a major role in undermining the vigor of American industry.

American management, especially in the two decades after World
War II, was universally admired for its strikingly effective performance. But times change. An approach shaped and refined during stable
decades may be ill suited to a world characterized by rapid and unpre-
dictable change, scarce energy, global competition for markets, and a
constant need for innovation. This is the world of the 1980s and,
probably, the rest of this century.

The time is long overdue for earnest, objective self-analysis. What
exactly have American managers been doing wrong? What are the
critical weaknesses in the ways that they have managed the technological performance of their companies? What is the matter with the
long-unquestioned assumptions on which they have based their managerial policies and practices?

A Failure of Management

In the past, American managers earned worldwide respect for their
carefully planned yet highly aggressive action across three different
time frames:

- *Short term*—using existing assets as efficiently as possible.
- *Medium term*—replacing labor and other scarce resources with capital
  equipment.
- *Long term*—developing new products and processes that open new markets or restructure old ones.

The first of these time frames demanded toughness, determination, and close attention to detail; the second, capital and the willingness to take sizable financial risks; the third, imagination and a certain amount of technological daring.

Our managers still earn generally high marks for their skill in improving short-term efficiency, but their counterparts in Europe and Japan have started to question America's entrepreneurial imagination and willingness to make risky long-term competitive investments. As one such observer remarked to us: "The U.S. companies in my industry act like banks. All they are interested in is return on investment and getting their money back. Sometimes they act as though they are more interested in buying other companies than they are in selling products to customers."

In fact, this curt diagnosis represents a growing body of opinion that openly charges American managers with competitive myopia: "Somehow or other, American business is losing confidence in itself and especially confidence in its future. Instead of meeting the challenge of the changing world, American business today is making small, short-term adjustments by cutting costs and by turning to the government for temporary relief. . . . Success in trade is the result of patient and meticulous preparations, with a long period of market preparation before the rewards are available. . . . To undertake such commitments is hardly in the interest of a manager who is concerned with his or her next quarterly earnings reports."[1]

More troubling still, American managers themselves often admit the charge with, at most, a rhetorical shrug of their shoulders. In established businesses, notes one senior vice president of research: "We understand how to market, we know the technology, and production problems are not extreme. Why risk money on new businesses when good, profitable low-risk opportunities are on every side?" Says another: "It's much more difficult to come up with a synthetic meat product than a lemon-lime cake mix. But you work on the lemon-lime cake mix because you know exactly what that return is going to be. A synthetic steak is going to take a lot longer, require a much bigger investment, and the risk of failure will be greater."[2]

These managers are not alone; they speak for many. Why, they ask, should they invest dollars that are hard to earn back when it is so easy—and so much less risky—to make money in other ways? Why ignore a ready-made situation in cake mixes for the deferred and far less certain prospects in synthetic steaks? Why shoulder the competitive risks of making better, more innovative products?

Exhibit I.   Growth in labor productivity since 1960 (United States and abroad)

	Average annual percent change	
	Manufacturing 1960–1978	All industries 1960–1976
United States	2.8%	1.7%
United Kingdom	2.9	2.2
Canada	4.0	2.1
Germany	5.4	4.2
France	5.5	4.3
Italy	5.9	4.9
Belgium	6.9*	—
Netherlands	6.9*	—
Sweden	5.2	—
Japan	8.2	7.5

*1960–1977.

Source: Council on Wage and Price Stability, *Report on Productivity* (Washington, D.C.: Executive Office of the President, July 1979).

In our judgment, the assumptions underlying these questions are prime evidence of a broad managerial failure—a failure of both vision and leadership—that over time has eroded both the inclination and the capacity of U.S. companies to innovate.

Familiar Excuses

About the facts themselves there can be little dispute. Exhibits I-IV document our sorry decline. But the explanations and excuses commonly offered invite a good deal of comment.

It is important to recognize, first of all, that the problem is not new. It has been going on for at least 15 years. The rate of productivity growth in the private sector peaked in the mid-1960s. Nor is the problem confined to a few sectors of our economy; with a few exceptions, it permeates our entire economy. Expenditures on R&D by both

Exhibit II.   Growth of labor productivity by sector, 1948–1978

Time sector	Growth of labor productivity (annual average percent)		
	1948–65	1965–73	1973–78
Private business	3.2%	2.3%	1.1%
Agriculture, forestry, and fisheries	5.5	5.3	2.9
Mining	4.2	2.0	−4.0
Construction	2.9	−2.2	−1.8
Manufacturing	3.1	2.4	1.7
Durable goods	2.8	1.9	1.2
Nondurable goods	3.4	3.2	2.4
Transportation	3.3	2.9	0.9
Communication	5.5	4.8	7.1
Electric, gas, and sanitary services	6.2	4.0	0.1
Trade	2.7	3.0	0.4
Wholesale	3.1	3.9	0.2
Retail	2.4	2.3	0.8
Finance, insurance, and real estate	1.0	−0.3	1.4
Services	1.5	1.9	0.5
Government enterprises	−0.8	0.9	−0.7

Source: Bureau of Labor Statistics.

Note: Productivity data for services, construction, finance, insurance, and real estate are unpublished.

business and government, as measured in constant (noninflated) dollars, also peaked in the mid-1960s—both in absolute terms and as a percentage of GNP. During the same period the expenditures on R&D by West Germany and Japan have been rising. More important, American spending on R&D as a percentage of sales in such critical research-intensive industries as machinery, professional and scientific instruments, chemicals, and aircraft had dropped by the mid-1970s to about half its level in the early 1960s. These are the very industries on which we now depend for the bulk of our manufactured exports.

Investment in plant and equipment in the United States displays the

Exhibit III.   National expenditures for performance of R&D as a percent of GNP by country, 1961–1978*

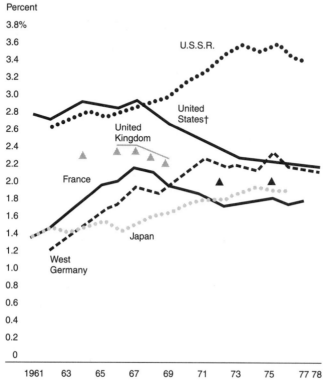

*Gross expenditures for performance of R&D including associated capital expenditures.

†Detailed information on capital expenditures for R&D is not available for the United States. Estimates for the period 1972–1977 show that their inclusion would have an impact of less than one-tenth of 1% for each year.

Source: *Science Indicators—1978* (Washington, D.C.: National Science Foundation, 1979), p. 6.

Note: The latest data may be preliminary or estimates.

same disturbing trends. As economist Burton G. Malkiel has pointed out: "From 1948 to 1973 the [net book value of capital equipment] per unit of labor grew at an annual rate of almost 3%. Since 1973, however, lower rates of private investment have led to a decline in that growth rate to 1.75%. Moreover, the recent composition of investment [in 1978] has been skewed toward equipment and relatively short-term projects and away from structures and relatively

Exhibit IV.   Industrial R&D expenditures for basic research, applied research, and development, 1960–1978 (in $ millions)

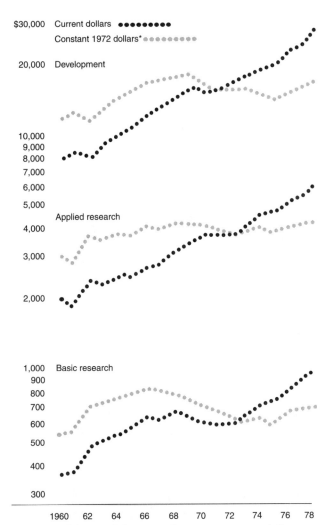

*GNP implicit price deflators used to convert current dollars to constant 1972 dollars.
Source: *Science Indicators—1978,* p. 87.
  Note: Preliminary data are shown for 1977 and estimates for 1978.

long-lived investments. Thus our industrial plant has tended to age. . . ."³

Other studies have shown that growth in the incremental capital equipment-to-labor ratio has fallen to about one-third of its value in the early 1960s. By contrast, between 1966 and 1976 capital investment as a percentage of GNP in France and West Germany was more than 20% greater than that in the United States; in Japan the percentage was almost double ours.

To attribute this relative loss of technological vigor to such things as a shortage of capital in the United States is not justified. As Malkiel and others have shown, the return on equity of American business (out of which comes the capital necessary for investment) is about the same today as 20 years ago, *even after adjusting for inflation.* However, investment in both new equipment and R&D, as a percentage of GNP, was significantly higher 20 years ago than today.

The conclusion is painful but must be faced. Responsibility for this competitive listlessness belongs not just to a set of external conditions but also to the attitudes, preoccupations, and practices of American managers. By their preference for servicing existing markets rather than creating new ones and by their devotion to short-term returns and "management by the numbers," many of them have effectively forsworn long-term technological superiority as a competitive weapon. In consequence, they have abdicated their strategic responsibilities.

The New Management Orthodoxy

We refuse to believe that this managerial failure is the result of a sudden psychological shift among American managers toward a "super-safe, no risk" mind set. No profound sea change in the character of thousands of individuals could have occurred in so organized a fashion or have produced so consistent a pattern of behavior. Instead we believe that during the past two decades American managers have increasingly relied on principles which prize analytical detachment and methodological elegance over insight, based on experience, into the subtleties and complexities of strategic decisions. As a result, maximum short-term financial returns have become the overriding criteria for many companies.

For purposes of discussion, we may divide this *new* management orthodoxy into three general categories: financial control, corporate portfolio management, and market-driven behavior.

FINANCIAL CONTROL

As more companies decentralize their organizational structures, they tend to fix on profit centers as the primary unit of managerial responsibility. This development necessitates, in turn, greater dependence on short-term financial measurements like return on investment (ROI) for evaluating the performance of individual managers and management groups. Increasing the structural distance between those entrusted with exploiting actual competitive opportunities and those who must judge the quality of their work virtually guarantees reliance on objectively quantifiable short-term criteria.

Although innovation, the lifeblood of any vital enterprise, is best encouraged by an environment that does not unduly penalize failure, the predictable result of relying too heavily on short-term financial measures—a sort of managerial remote control—is an environment in which no one feels he or she can afford a failure or even a momentary dip in the bottom line.

CORPORATE PORTFOLIO MANAGEMENT

This preoccupation with control draws support from modern theories of financial portfolio management. Originally developed to help balance the overall risk and return of stock and bond portfolios, these principles have been applied increasingly to the creation and management of corporate portfolios—that is, a cluster of companies and product lines assembled through various modes of diversification under a single corporate umbrella. When applied by a remote group of dispassionate experts primarily concerned with finance and control and lacking hands-on experience, the analytic formulas of portfolio theory push managers even further toward an extreme of caution in allocating resources.

"Especially in large organizations," reports one manager, "we are observing an increase in management behavior which I would regard as excessively cautious, even passive; certainly overanalytical; and, in general, characterized by a studied unwillingness to assume responsibility and even reasonable risk."

MARKET-DRIVEN BEHAVIOR

In the past 20 years, American companies have perhaps learned too well a lesson they had long been inclined to ignore: businesses should be customer oriented rather than product oriented. Henry Ford's famous dictum that the public could have any color automobile it wished as long as the color was black has since given way to its philosophical opposite: "We have got to stop marketing makeable products and learn to make marketable products."

At last, however, the dangers of too much reliance on this philosophy are becoming apparent. As two Canadian researchers have put it: "Inventors, scientists, engineers, and academics, in the normal pursuit of scientific knowledge, gave the world in recent times the laser, xerography, instant photography, and the transistor. In contrast, worshippers of the marketing concept have bestowed upon mankind such products as new-fangled potato chips, feminine hygiene deodorant, and the pet rock. . . ."[4]

The argument that no new product ought to be introduced without managers undertaking a market analysis is common sense. But the argument that consumer analyses and formal market surveys should dominate other considerations when allocating resources to product development is untenable. It may be useful to remember that the initial market estimate for computers in 1945 projected total worldwide sales of only ten units. Similarly, even the most carefully researched analysis of consumer preferences for gas-guzzling cars in an era of gasoline abundance offers little useful guidance to today's automobile manufacturers in making wise product investment decisions. Customers may know what their needs are, but they often define those needs in terms of existing products, processes, markets, and prices.

Deferring to a market-driven strategy without paying attention to its limitations is, quite possibly, opting for customer satisfaction and lower risk in the short run at the expense of superior products in the future. Satisfied customers are critically important, of course, but not if the strategy for creating them is responsible as well for unnecessary product proliferation, inflated costs, unfocused diversification, and a lagging commitment to new technology and new capital equipment.

Three Managerial Decisions

These are serious charges to make. But the unpleasant fact of the matter is that, however useful these new principles may have been initially, if carried too far they are bad for U.S. business. Consider, for example, their effect on three major kinds of choices regularly faced by corporate managers: the decision between imitative and innovative product design, the decision to integrate backward, and the decision to invest in process development.

IMITATIVE VS. INNOVATIVE PRODUCT DESIGN

A market-driven strategy requires new product ideas to flow from detailed market analysis or, at least, to be extensively tested for consumer reaction before actual introduction. It is no secret that these requirements add significant delays and costs to the introduction of new products. It is less well known that they also predispose managers toward developing products for existing markets and toward product designs of an imitative rather than an innovative nature. There is increasing evidence that market-driven strategies tend, over time, to dampen the general level of innovation in new product decisions.

Confronted with the choice between innovation and imitation, managers typically ask whether the marketplace shows any consistent preference for innovative products. If so, the additional funding they require may be economically justified; if not, those funds can more properly go to advertising, promoting, or reducing the prices of less-advanced products. Though the temptation to allocate resources so as to strengthen performance in existing products and markets is often irresistible, recent studies by J. Hugh Davidson and others confirm the strong market attractiveness of innovative products.[5]

Nonetheless, managers having to decide between innovative and imitative product design face a difficult series of marketing-related trade-offs. Exhibit V summarizes these trade-offs.

By its very nature, innovative design is, as Joseph Schumpeter observed a long time ago, initially destructive of capital—whether in the form of labor skills, management systems, technological processes, or capital equipment. It tends to make obsolete existing investments in both marketing and manufacturing organizations. For the managers concerned it represents the choice of uncertainty (about economic

Exhibit V.   Trade-offs between imitative and Innovative design for an established product line

Imitative design	Innovative design
Market demand is relatively well known and predictable.	Potentially large but unpredictable demand; the risk of a flop is also large.
Market recognition and acceptance are rapid.	Market acceptance may be slow initially, but the imitative response of competitors may also be slowed.
Readily adaptable to existing market, sales, and distribution policies.	May require unique, tailored marketing distribution and sales policies to educate customers or because of special repair and warranty problems.
Fits with existing market segmentation and product policies.	Demand may cut across traditional marketing segments, disrupting divisional responsibilities and cannibalizing other products.

returns, timing, etc.) over relative predictability, exchanging the reasonable expectation of current income against the promise of high future value. It is the choice of the gambler, the person willing to risk much to gain even more.

Conditioned by a market-driven strategy and held closely to account by a "results now" ROI-oriented control system, American managers have increasingly refused to take the chance on innovative product/market development. As one of them confesses: "In the last year, on the basis of high capital risk, I turned down new products at a rate at least twice what I did a year ago. But in every case I tell my people to go back and bring me some new product ideas."[6] In truth, they have learned caution so well that many are in danger of forgetting that market-driven, follow-the-leader companies usually end up following the rest of the pack as well.

BACKWARD INTEGRATION

Sometimes the problem for managers is not their reluctance to take action and make investments but that, when they do so, their action has the unintended result of reinforcing the status quo. In deciding to integrate backward because of apparent short-term rewards, managers often restrict their ability to strike out in innovative directions in the future.

Consider, for example, the case of a manufacturer who purchases a major component from an outside company. Static analysis of production economies may very well show that backward integration offers rather substantial cost benefits. Eliminating certain purchasing and marketing functions, centralizing overhead, pooling R&D efforts and resources, coordinating design and production of both product and component, reducing uncertainty over design changes, allowing for the use of more specialized equipment and labor skills—in all these ways and more, backward integration holds out to management the promise of significant short-term increases in ROI.

These efficiencies may be achieved by companies with commoditylike products. In such industries as ferrous and nonferrous metals or petroleum, backward integration toward raw materials and supplies tends to have a strong, positive effect on profits. However, the situation is markedly different for companies in more technologically active industries. Where there is considerable exposure to rapid technological advances, the promised value of backward integration becomes problematic. It may provide a quick, short-term boost to ROI figures in the next annual report, but it may also paralyze the long-term ability of a company to keep on top of technological change.

The real competitive threats to technologically active companies arise less from changes in ultimate consumer preference than from abrupt shifts in component technologies, raw materials, or production processes. Hence those managers whose attention is too firmly directed toward the marketplace and near-term profits may suddenly discover that their decision to make rather than buy important parts has locked their companies into an outdated technology.

Further, as supply channels and manufacturing operations become more systematized, the benefits from attempts to "rationalize" production may well be accompanied by unanticipated side effects. For instance, a company may find itself shut off from the R&D efforts of various independent suppliers by becoming their competitor. Similarly, the commitment of time and resources needed to master technology back up the channel of supply may distract a company from doing its own job well. Such was the fate of Bowmar, the pocket calculator pioneer, whose attempt to integrate backward into semiconductor production so consumed management attention that final assembly of the calculators, its core business, did not get the required resources.

Long-term contracts and long-term relationships with suppliers can achieve many of the same cost benefits as backward integration without calling into question a company's ability to innovate or respond to innovation. European automobile manufacturers, for example, have typically chosen to rely on their suppliers in this way; American companies have followed the path of backward integration. The resulting trade-offs between production efficiencies and innovative flexibility should offer a stern warning to those American managers too easily beguiled by the lure of short-term ROI improvement. A case in point: the U.S. auto industry's huge investment in automating the manufacture of cast-iron brake drums probably delayed by more than five years its transition to disc brakes.

PROCESS DEVELOPMENT

In an era of management by the numbers, many American managers—especially in mature industries—are reluctant to invest heavily in the development of new manufacturing processes. When asked to explain their reluctance, they tend to respond in fairly predictable ways. "We can't afford to design new capital equipment for just our own manufacturing needs" is one frequent answer. So is: "The capital equipment producers do a much better job, and they can amortize their development costs over sales to many companies." Perhaps most common is: "Let the others experiment in manufacturing; we can learn from their mistakes and do it better."

Each of these comments rests on the assumption that essential advances in process technology can be appropriated more easily through equipment purchase than through in-house equipment design and development. Our extensive conversations with the managers of European (primarily German) technology-based companies have convinced us that this assumption is not as widely shared abroad as in the United States. Virtually across the board, the European managers impressed us with their strong commitment to increasing market share through internal development of advanced process technology—even when their suppliers were highly responsive to technological advances.

By contrast, American managers tend to restrict investments in process development to only those items likely to reduce costs in the short run. Not all are happy with this. As one disgruntled executive told us: "For too long U.S. managers have been taught to set low priorities on mechanization projects, so that eventually divestment appears to be the best way out of manufacturing difficulties. Why?

"The drive for short-term success has prevented managers from looking thoroughly into the matter of special manufacturing equipment, which has to be invented, developed, tested, redesigned, reproduced, improved, and so on. That's a long process, which needs experienced, knowledgeable, and dedicated people who stick to their jobs over a considerable period of time. Merely buying new equipment (even if it is possible) does not often give the company any advantage over competitors."

We agree. Most American managers seem to forget that, even if they produce new products with their existing process technology (the same "cookie cutter" everyone else can buy), their competitors will face a relatively short lead time for introducing similar products. And as Eric von Hipple's studies of industrial innovation show, the innovations on which new industrial equipment is based usually originate with the user of the equipment and not with the equipment producer.[7] In other words, companies can make products more profitable by investing in the development of their own process technology. Proprietary processes are every bit as formidable competitive weapons as proprietary products.

The American Managerial Ideal

Two very important questions remain to be asked: (1) Why should so many American managers have shifted so strongly to this new managerial orthodoxy? and (2) Why are they not more deeply bothered by the ill effects of those principles on the long-term technological competitiveness of their companies? To answer the first question, we must take a look at the changing career patterns of American managers during the past quarter century; to answer the second, we must understand the way in which they have come to regard their professional roles and responsibilities as managers.

THE ROAD TO THE TOP

During the past 25 years the American manager's road to the top has changed significantly. No longer does the typical career, threading

Exhibit VI.   *Changes in the professional origins of corporate presidents (percent changes from baseline years [1948–1952] for 100 top U.S. companies)*

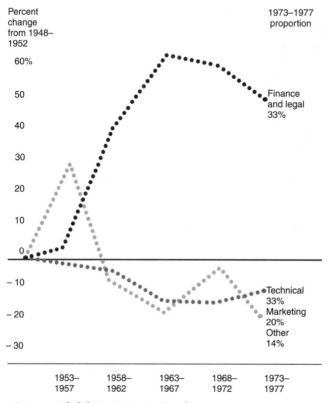

Source: Golightly & Co. International (1978).

sinuously up and through a corporation with stops in several functional areas, provide future top executives with intimate hands-on knowledge of the company's technologies, customers, and suppliers.

Exhibit VI summarizes the currently available data on the shift in functional background of newly appointed presidents of the 100 largest U.S. corporations. The immediate significance of these figures is clear. Since the mid-1950s there has been a rather substantial increase in the percentage of new company presidents whose primary interests and expertise lie in the financial and legal areas and not in production. In the view of C. Jackson Grayson, president of the American Productivity Center, American management has for 20 years "coasted off the great R&D gains made during World War II, and constantly rewarded executives from the marketing, financial, and legal sides of the business while it ignored the production men. Today [in business schools] courses in the production area are almost nonexistent."[8]

In addition, companies are increasingly choosing to fill new top management posts from outside their own ranks. In the opinion of foreign observers, who are still accustomed to long-term careers in the same company or division, "High-level American executives . . . seem to come and go and switch around as if playing a game of musical chairs at an Alice in Wonderland tea party."

Far more important, however, than any absolute change in numbers is the shift in the general sense of what an aspiring manager has to be "smart about" to make it to the top. More important still is the broad change in attitude such trends both encourage and express. What has developed, in the business community as in academia, is a preoccupation with a false and shallow concept of the professional manager, a "pseudo-professional" really—an individual having no special expertise in any particular industry or technology who nevertheless can step into an unfamiliar company and run it successfully through strict application of financial controls, portfolio concepts, and a market-driven strategy.

THE GOSPEL OF PSEUDO-PROFESSIONALISM

In recent years, this idealization of pseudo-professionalism has taken on something of the quality of a corporate religion. Its first doctrine, appropriately enough, is that neither industry experience nor hands-on technological expertise counts for very much. At one level, of course, this doctrine helps to salve the conscience of those who lack them. At another, more disturbing level it encourages the faithful to make decisions about technological matters simply as if they were adjuncts to finance or marketing decisions. We do not believe that the technological issues facing managers today can be meaningfully addressed without taking into account marketing or financial considerations; on the other hand, neither can they be resolved with the same methodologies applied to these other fields.

Complex modern technology has its own inner logic and developmental imperatives. To treat it as if it were something else—no matter how comfortable one is with that other kind of data—is to base a competitive business on a two-legged stool, which must, no matter how excellent the balancing act, inevitably fall to the ground.

More disturbing still, true believers keep the faith on a day-to-day basis by insisting that as issues rise up the managerial hierarchy for decision they be progressively distilled into easily quantifiable terms. One European manager, in recounting to us his experiences in a joint venture with an American company, recalled with exasperation that "U.S. managers want everything to be simple. But sometimes business situations are not simple, and they cannot be divided up or looked at in such a way that they become simple. They are messy, and one must try to understand all the facets. This appears to be alien to the American mentality."

The purpose of good organizational design, of course, is to divide responsibilities in such a way that individuals have relatively easy tasks to perform. But then these differentiated responsibilities must be pulled together by sophisticated, broadly gauged integrators at the top of the managerial pyramid. If these individuals are interested in but one or two aspects of the total competitive picture, if their training includes a very narrow exposure to the range of functional specialties, if—worst of all—they are devoted simplifiers themselves, who will do the necessary integration? Who will attempt to resolve complicated issues rather than try to uncomplicate them artificially? At the strategic level there are no such things as pure production problems, pure financial problems, or pure marketing problems.

MERGER MANIA

When executive suites are dominated by people with financial and legal skills, it is not surprising that top management should increasingly allocate time and energy to such concerns as cash management and the whole process of corporate acquisitions and mergers. This is indeed what has happened. In 1978 alone there were some 80 mergers involving companies with assets in excess of $100 million each; in 1979 there were almost 100. This represents roughly $20 billion in transfers of large companies from one owner to another—two-thirds of the total amount spent on R&D by American industry.

In 1978 *Business Week* ran a cover story on cash management in which it stated that "the 400 largest U.S. companies together have more than $60 billion in cash—almost triple the amount they had at the beginning of the 1970s." The article also described the increasing attention devoted to—and the sophisticated and exotic techniques used for—managing this cash hoard.

There are perfectly good reasons for this flurry of activity. It is entirely natural for financially (or legally) trained managers to concentrate on essentially financial (or legal) activities. It is also natural for managers who subscribe to the portfolio "law of large numbers" to seek to reduce total corporate risk by parceling it out among a sufficiently large number of separate product lines, businesses, or technologies. Under certain conditions it may very well make good economic sense to buy rather than build new plants or modernize existing ones. Mergers are obviously an exciting game; they tend to produce fairly quick and decisive results, and they offer the kind of public recognition that helps careers along. Who can doubt the appeal of the titles awarded by the financial community; being called a "gunslinger," "white knight," or "raider" can quicken anyone's blood.

Unfortunately, the general American penchant for separating and simplifying has tended to encourage a diversification away from core technologies and markets to a much greater degree than is true in Europe or Japan. U.S. managers appear to have an inordinate faith in the portfolio law of large numbers—that is, by amassing enough product lines, technologies, and businesses, one will be cushioned against the random setbacks that occur in life. This might be true for portfolios of stocks and bonds, where there is considerable evidence that setbacks are random. Businesses, however, are subject not only to random setbacks such as strikes and shortages but also to carefully orchestrated attacks by competitors, who focus all their resources and energies on one set of activities.

Worse, the great bulk of this merger activity appears to have been absolutely wasted in terms of generating economic benefits for stockholders. Acquisition experts do not necessarily make good managers. Nor can they increase the value of their shares by merging two companies any better than their shareholders could do individually by buying shares of the acquired company on the open market (at a price usually below that required for a takeover attempt).

There appears to be a growing recognition of this fact. A number of U.S. companies are now divesting themselves of previously acquired companies; others (for example, W.R. Grace) are proposing to break themselves up into relatively independent entities. The establishment of a strong competitive position through in-house technological superiority is by nature a long, arduous, and often unglamorous task. But it is what keeps a business vigorous and competitive.

The European Example

Gaining competitive success through technological superiority is a skill much valued by the seasoned European (and Japanese) managers with whom we talked. Although we were able to locate few hard statistics on their actual practice, our extensive investigations of more than 20 companies convinced us that European managers do indeed tend to differ significantly from their American counterparts. In fact, we found that many of them were able to articulate these differences quite clearly.

In the first place, European managers think themselves more pointedly concerned with how to survive over the long run under intensely competitive conditions. Few markets, of course, generate price competition as fierce as in the United States, but European companies face the remorseless necessity of exporting to other national markets or perishing.

The figures here are startling: manufactured product exports represent more than 35% of total manufacturing sales in France and Germany and nearly 60% in the Benelux countries, as against not quite 10% in the United States. In these export markets, moreover, European products must hold their own against "world class" competitors, lower-priced products from developing countries, and American products selling at attractive devalued dollar prices. To survive this competitive squeeze, European managers feel they must place central emphasis on producing technologically superior products.

Further, the kinds of pressures from European labor unions and national governments virtually force them to take a consistently long-term view in decision making. German managers, for example, must negotiate major decisions at the plant level with worker-dominated works councils; in turn, these decisions are subject to review by supervisory boards (roughly equivalent to American boards of directors), half of whose membership is worker elected. Together with strict national legislation, the pervasive influence of labor unions makes it extremely difficult to change employment levels or production locations. Not surprisingly, labor costs in Northern Europe have more than doubled in the past decade and are now the highest in the world.

To be successful in this environment of strictly constrained options,

European managers feel they must employ a decision-making appara-
tus that grinds very fine—and very deliberately. They must simply
outthink and outmanage their competitors. Now, American managers
also have their strategic options hedged about by all kinds of restrictions. But those restrictions have not yet made them as conscious as
their European counterparts of the long-term implications of their
day-to-day decisions.

As a result, the Europeans see themselves as investing more heavily
in cutting-edge technology than the Americans. More often than not,
this investment is made to create new product opportunities in advance of consumer demand and not merely in response to market-
driven strategy. In case after case, we found the Europeans striving to
develop the products and process capabilities with which to lead markets and not simply responding to the current demands of the marketplace. Moreover, in doing this they seem less inclined to integrate
backward and more likely to seek maximum leverage from stable,
long-term relationships with suppliers.

Having never lost sight of the need to be technologically competitive
over the long run, European and Japanese managers are extremely
careful to make the necessary arrangements and investments today.
And their daily concern with the rather basic issue of long-term survival adds perspective to such matters as short-term ROI or rate of
growth. The time line by which they manage is long, and it has made
them painstakingly attentive to the means for keeping their companies
technologically competitive. Of course they pay attention to the numbers. Their profit margins are usually lower than ours, their debt ratios
higher. Every tenth of a percent is critical to them. But they are also
aware that tomorrow will be no better unless they constantly try to
develop new processes, enter new markets, and offer superior—even
unique—products. As one senior German executive phrased it recently, "We look at rates of return, too, but only after we ask 'Is it a
good product?'"[9]

Creating Economic Value

Americans traveling in Europe and Asia soon learn they must often
deal with criticism of our country. Being forced to respond to such
criticism can be healthy, for it requires rethinking some basic issues of
principle and practice.

We have much to be proud about and little to be ashamed of relative to most other countries. But sometimes the criticism of others is uncomfortably close to the mark. The comments of our overseas competitors on American business practices contain enough truth to require our thoughtful consideration. What is behind the decline in competitiveness of U.S. business? Why do U.S. companies have such apparent difficulties competing with foreign producers of established products, many of which originated in the United States?

For example, Japanese televisions dominate some market segments, even though many U.S. producers now enjoy the same low labor cost advantages of offshore production. The German machine tool and automotive producers continue their inroads into U.S. domestic markets, even though their labor rates are now higher than those in the United States and the famed German worker in German factories is almost as likely to be Turkish or Italian as German.

The responsibility for these problems may rest in part on government policies that either overconstrain or undersupport U.S. producers. But if our foreign critics are correct, the long-term solution to America's problems may not be correctable simply by changing our government's tax laws, monetary policies, and regulatory practices. It will also require some fundamental changes in management attitudes and practices.

It would be an oversimplification to assert that the only reason for the decline in competitiveness of U.S. companies is that our managers devote too much attention and energy to using existing resources more efficiently. It would also oversimplify the issue, although possibly to a lesser extent, to say that it is due purely and simply to their tendency to neglect technology as a competitive weapon.

Companies cannot become more innovative simply by increasing R&D investments or by conducting more basic research. Each of the decisions we have described directly affects several functional areas of management, and major conflicts can only be reconciled at senior executive levels. The benefits favoring the more innovative, aggressive option in each case depend more on intangible factors than do their efficiency-oriented alternatives.

Senior managers who are less informed about their industry and its confederation of parts suppliers, equipment suppliers, workers, and customers or who have less time to consider the long-term implications of their interactions are likely to exhibit a noninnovative bias in their choices. Tight financial controls with a short-term emphasis will also bias choices toward the less innovative, less technologically aggressive alternatives.

The key to long-term success—even survival—in business is what it has always been: to invest, to innovate, to lead, to create value where none existed before. Such determination, such striving to excel, requires leaders—not *just* controllers, market analysts, and portfolio managers. In our preoccupation with the braking systems and exterior trim, we may have neglected the drive trains of our corporations.

Notes

1. Ryohei Suzuki, "Worldwide Expansion of U.S. Exports—A Japanese View," *Sloan Management Review*, Spring 1979, p. 1.

2. *Business Week*, February 16, 1976, p. 57.

3. Burton G. Malkiel, "Productivity—The Problem Behind the Headlines," *Harvard Business Review*, May–June 1979, p. 81.

4. Roger Bennett and Robert Cooper, "Beyond the Marketing Concept," *Business Horizons*, June 1979, p. 76.

5. J. Hugh Davidson, "Why Most New Consumer Brands Fail," *Harvard Business Review*, March–April 1976, p. 117.

6. *Business Week*, February 16, 1976, p. 57.

7. Eric von Hippel, "The Dominant Role of Users in the Scientific Instrument Innovation Process," MIT Sloan School of Management Working Paper 75–764, January 1975.

8. *Dun's Review*, July 1978, p. 39.

9. *Business Week*, March 3, 1980, p. 76.

2
The New Industrial Competition

William J. Abernathy, Kim B. Clark, and
Alan M. Kantrow

It is barely possible that in some remote corner of the United States
a latter-day Rip Van Winkle awoke this morning fresh with shining
images of American industry in the 1950s still fixed in his head. But
it is not very likely. Who, after all, during the past few years could
have slept undisturbed through the general chorus of lament about
the economy? Who could have remained unaware that much of U.S.
industry—especially the mature manufacturing sector—has fallen on
hard times?

And who did not have a surefire remedy? Born-again supply-siders
argued for the massive formation of capital; "new class" advocates of
a more systematic industrial policy, for better allocation of existing
capital; industrial economists, for enhanced productivity; organized
labor, for a coherent effort at reindustrialization; subdued (if unre-
pentant) Keynesians, for more artful demand management; boisterous
Lafferites, for a massive tax cut; congressional experts, for carefully
targeted tax breaks on depreciation and investment; Friedmanites, for
tight money; and Naderites, for an anticorporate economic democracy.

This loudly divided counsel on the best strategy for managing economic change reflects inadequacy in both perception and understanding: our current industrial malaise defies the usual interpretations and
resists the usual prescriptions. Managing change successfully has
proved difficult because policymakers in business and government,
trained in an old economic calculus, have found it hard to see the new
competitive realities for what they are—or to identify the best terms
in which to analyze them.

Policymakers fail to understand that the old rules of thumb and

worn assumptions no longer hold. Similarly, the traditional structural arrangements in many industries—the familiar relationship between, say, labor and management or producer and supplier—no
longer square with the facts of competitive life. As a result, decision
makers who continue to act as if nothing has happened are, at best,
ineffective and, at worst, inadvertent agents of economic disaster.

Levers of Change

What has happened? The two principal changes have been greater
exposure to international competition and technical advances that
alter competition. For a start, let's look at two basic major manufacturing industries that have experienced these forces.

One is color television:

- This industry was confronted with new competitors who emphasized
  high productivity, reliability, quality, and competent design (but not
  innovative design, except for Sony).

- Many competitors—Warwick, Motorola, and Admiral among them—did
  not survive the foreign thrust and were either taken over or went out
  of business.

- Foreign competitors' emphasis on manufacturing, a critical element, was
  transferred to their U.S. operations—witness Sanyo's management of
  the previously unsuccessful old Warwick plant, with many of the same
  employees and U.S. middle managers.

- Now technological changes have created a situation of potential renewal of the product life cycle—developments in videocassette record-
  ers; videodiscs; flat, high-resolution screens; telecommunications; and
  computers may combine to revolutionize the television business.

. . . And another is textile machinery:

- Before the 1960s a few U.S. manufacturers (for example, Draper) dominated this business. Conglomerates acquired them (e.g., Rockwell International took over Draper).

- The U.S. manufacturers began to lose business primarily because of
  deterioration in product performance relative to European and Japanese
  models and failure to remain at the cutting edge of new technology.

- Because of insufficient investment (conglomerates treated them as cash
  cows), the once-dominant U.S. manufacturers have lost technical and
  market leadership to the Swiss, Germans, and Japanese.

Now consider two other industries that are facing the new forces of international competition.

One of them is computers:

- Fujitsu has introduced a mainframe computer that attacks IBM where its strength is—service. Fujitsu is doing this by building a high-quality, reliable machine that can *guarantee* 99% uptime. In a test run of strategy, Fujitsu has taken on IBM in Australia with this approach and bested the U.S. giant in obtaining some mainframe contracts. The experience there to date: 99.8% uptime.

- In minicomputers and home computers the Japanese are entering the U.S. market. Producers like Mitsubishi, Nippon Electric, and Hitachi will soon offer high-quality products that are cost competitive.

. . . And another is machine tools:

- Japanese producers have entered this market with a strategy built around a very reliable, high-quality product. Recently, for instance, a U.S. auto producer ordered transfer lines from an established U.S. machine tool manufacturer and from Toyota. The lines arrived at the U.S. plant at the same time. Toyota sent two engineers who had the equipment running and fully debugged in two weeks, while the competitor's team of eight engineers spent several months getting its line operational.

- Developments in new technology—electronics, optical and tactile sensors, lasers, and robotics—are creating opportunities for improved metalworking operations and are opening up new applications in areas like assembly and inspection, where mechanization and automation have hardly played a role. Integration of these advances with computerized design and manufacturing could change the very concepts on which traditional machine tools are founded.

A number of other long-stable U.S. manufacturing industries no doubt will be shaken in the not-distant future by these pressures. One is the air compressor field, which a few companies have dominated. A Japanese producer, Hokuetsu, entered its domestic market five years ago and now rules it. Among the companies left in its wake is Ingersoll-Rand, whose market share in Japan plunged from well over 50% to zero. Hokuetsu offers a dependable, good-quality product at half the cost of the comparable U.S. compressor.

Still another field is major household appliances, which the Japanese have slated for heavy export activity in this decade. Sanyo, Toshiba, and other companies are setting up U.S. plants and distribution systems. General Electric, for one, is worried; GE has begun a program designed to improve greatly the quality and productivity of its Louisville appliance complex.

The list of endangered industries goes on: jet engines, commercial aircraft, small forklift trucks, steel, electric motors, lawnmowers, and chainsaws, to name just a few.

CHARACTER OF THE NEW COMPETITION

Let us focus on a single industry to show in detail the character of the conditions that the imperiled U.S. industries face. An inkling of these conditions has entered the consciousness of all Americans as they witnessed Japan's extraordinary success in capturing a large share of the automobile market from the entrenched Big Three domestic producers. In this article we go beyond the previously known facts and show exactly how the Japanese implemented their strategy on the plant floor, on the engineers' design boards, and in the executive offices.

Until recently, developments in the U.S. auto industry were determined mostly by government policies and economic forces peculiar to North America. The sheer extent of the U.S. market and its productive base had long guaranteed the industry a largely self-contained posture. Over the past 15 years, however, the competitive boundaries have expanded drastically until now they are virtually worldwide in scope.

Accompanying this expansion has been a rapid increase in the number of healthy competitors. These new international players, moreover, have quite a different approach from that of the U.S. Big Three; their plan consists of radically new strategies, modes of operation, and production experience.

More to the point, the novel competitive challenge they present cannot be overcome by the familiar responses U.S. companies have long used against each other. Strategically, the Big Three are well prepared to fight not this new war, but the last one.

Many observers believe that the perceived low quality of Detroit's vehicles is a simple function of lethargy and past practice. This view ignores the close connection between poor quality and a disadvantage in costs. The productive capacity of some new entrants, notably the Japanese, enjoys a significant cost advantage over that of the Americans. The Japanese have been especially skillful in exploiting this advantage by adding performance and quality to their cars. This combination of competitive price and high quality has proved tremendously successful in reaching consumers in the American market.

What makes this advantage particularly troublesome is that it does not represent primarily an investment problem; if it did, it would be far easier to remedy. Instead, it arises to some extent from differences in wage rates and, more significant, from differences in productivity and management of operations.

In 1973, when Lee A. Iacocca was asked about the competitive advantage of innovation as perceived by Ford, he responded simply, "Give them [American consumers] leather. They can smell it." In Ford's reading of the U.S. market, innovation did not pay; styling did. Things are quite different today: technology matters.

In the 1950s and 1960s, product technology was competitively neutral. No auto company sought a competitive advantage through significant innovation. In the 1980s, however, the necessity for advantage through innovation is steadily growing. In fact, consumer preference for small, fuel-efficient automobiles has developed faster in the United States than it did earlier in Europe or Japan. Beset by unfortunate decisions in the past, the continued absence of a workable long-term energy policy, conflicting regulatory requirements, and the massive financial demands posed by a retooling of production capacity, U.S. producers find themselves at a serious technological disadvantage.

But this is not all. The edge that U.S. companies have long enjoyed in mass production technology and in the resulting economies of scale—an edge long believed essential to competitive success—no longer obtains. Most of the standard U.S. technology is either already widely diffused or easily transferable. Moreover, the process technology for the new, smaller autos is subtly but significantly different from that now in place. In other words, changing market preferences and changing rates of technology diffusion have diluted, perhaps destroyed, the established scale economies of U.S. producers.

PREMIUM ON MANAGEMENT

Two main distinctions have largely provided the structure for discussions of manufacturing competitiveness. The first is the division between analysis and prescription of a "macro" sort (that is, having to do with such overarching questions of economic management as fiscal

Exhibit I.   Key elements in manufacturing competitiveness

	Macro	Micro
Hardware	**1.** **Government fiscal and monetary policies** Taxation Capital markets Savings	**2.** **Production capability** Plant Equipment
Software	**3.** **Socioeconomic environment** Work ethic Regulation Education	**4.** **Corporate management** Organization Administration Production systems

and monetary policy and tax incentives) and those of a "micro" sort (that is, having to do with issues relating to the management of particular companies). The second is the division between analysis and prescription based on "hardware" (equipment, buildings, and machinery) and those based on "software" (people management, organizational systems, and corporate strategies).

Considered together, these distinctions form the simple matrix shown in Exhibit I. Although the distinctions among these quadrants are rough, they are nonetheless useful. In practice, however, they are often neglected, which has left the unfortunate impression in some minds that the current industrial difficulties are composed equally— and indistinguishably—of problems in all the quadrants.

This impression has been mischievous, for these difficulties and their remedies are distributed unevenly about the matrix. In the auto industry the key measures for meeting the new competition fall primarily into Quadrant 4.

Japanese Micromanagement

The Japanese advantage in production costs and product quality in the auto industry, as well as many other established U.S. industries, is not only a fact defining the new competitive reality but also the result of a carefully honed approach to management—the stuff of Quadrant 4. Americans' talk of overregulation, underdepreciation, pervasive national culture, and markedly absent government support is misplaced.

COSTS OF PRODUCTION

Several estimates have placed the landed cost advantage in U.S. markets of Japanese-produced subcompact cars in the $400 to $600 range per vehicle. For example, Abraham Katz, then assistant secretary of commerce for international economic policy, testified last year that "the apparent cost advantage to Japanese producers may have been $560 per car in 1979."[1]

These estimates, in our view, seriously understate the advantage. In the first place, they fail to reflect both current rates of labor compensation and, perhaps more important, the great differences in productivity between Japanese and American manufacturers. Furthermore, they are often based on a narrow definition of the productive units to be compared, for they assume that the relevant comparison is between two original equipment manufacturers—say, Ford and Toyota—even though the really meaningful comparison lies between two productive systems, or "confederations"—that is, an OEM and its constellation of suppliers.

To get a truer picture of the Japanese cost advantage, we must therefore produce estimates that account for productivity differentials, labor costs, and industry structure.

The first step in developing these improved estimates is to update assessments of differential labor productivity. We know that in 1974 output per labor hour in the Japanese auto industry—OEMs and suppliers—was 88% of the level in the United States (that is, the ratio of Japanese to U.S. productivity was 0.88). Published data suggest that growth in labor productivity in the Japanese auto industry (motor vehicles and parts) averaged 8% to 9% in the 1970s; the comparable figure for the United States was 3% to 4%. Using a midrange estimate of the difference (5%), we arrive at a 1980 productivity ratio of 1.18.

This means that in 1980 Japanese producers operated at a productivity level almost 20% above that of their American competitors.

This rapid growth was offset in part by higher rates of wage increase: in 1974 Japanese hourly compensation rates were about 37% of those in the United States, while in 1980 they were roughly 50%. Dividing the compensation ratio (0.5) by the productivity ratio (1.18) yields a unit labor cost ratio of 0.424—a figure that has remained more or less constant during the entire 1974–1980 period.

Table A in the Appendix translates this steady labor cost ratio into a Japanese advantage of $1,673. Subtracting $400 for freight and tariff costs yields a landed cost advantage of $1,273 on a 1980 subcompact that sells in the American market for about $5,500—a cost advantage of 23%.

Although the calculations in Table A are based on a number of undocumented assumptions about cost structure and labor content, reasonable adjustment of these assumptions would not affect the order of magnitude of the Japanese cost advantage. Indeed, we were biased conservatively throughout in estimating that cost advantage. Moreover, inclusion of general administrative and selling expenses, as well as the costs of capital and salaried personnel, would leave the Japanese cost advantage intact. So we figure that Japanese producers enjoy a $1,200 landed cost advantage on every small vehicle sold in the United States.

We can to some extent check these numbers against information in the annual reports of major U.S. and Japanese producers. These reports yield data on the costs of nonlabor inputs and salaried personnel but none on the labor embodied in components or materials.

Getting at these data, however, presents several analytic problems. Perhaps the most serious is the great difference between U.S. and Japanese OEMs in their degree of vertical integration and in the nature of their relationships with suppliers. At Toyota, for example, purchases account for almost 80% of the value of sales; but because Toyota holds an equity interest in many of its suppliers, this figure is somewhat misleading. Comparable data for U.S. companies show much less reliance on suppliers; GM, for instance, has a purchase-to-sale ratio of less than 50%.

A second problem is the quite different product mix of U.S. and Japanese OEMs. The data we use come from 1979, when medium-size cars dominated the U.S. Big Three's product lines. The Japanese were producing a much narrower range of vehicles and, of course, were emphasizing the subcompact segment.

Table B in the Appendix shows estimates of total employee costs per vehicle in 1979 at Ford and Toyo Kogyo (Mazda). Our calculations suggest that assembly of the average Ford vehicle required 112.5 employee hours; a Toyo Kogyo vehicle, only 47. Employee costs in building the Ford vehicle were $2,464; for Toyo Kogyo, $491.

As already noted, this sizable cost gap reflects differences in product mix and vertical integration as well as in labor costs and productivity. Information on value added in the annual reports and discussions with industry sources suggest that the Toyo Kogyo results should be increased by 15% to 20% to adjust for vertical integration. Using these higher estimates yields a per-vehicle total of 56 hours instead of 47. (To correct for product mix, we have estimated the cost to Ford of producing the Toyo Kogyo product mix. These calculations are presented in Table C in the Appendix.)

Our analysis of annual report data suggests that in 1979 the difference between Ford and Toyo Kogyo employee costs per small vehicle was about $1,300. Updating this figure to 1980 might increase the absolute dollar amount somewhat, but the evidence we cited on relative growth rates in productivity and compensation implies that the percentage gap would not change much.

Adjustment for changes in exchange rates would also have a negligible effect. Using a rate of 200 yen to the dollar (the approximate rate at the end of 1980) instead of 218 would reduce the gap by only $50. And when we adjust this $1,300 to reflect the U.S. advantage in administrative and selling expenses, the 2.9% tariff with the relevant freight costs for Japanese imports, and the Japanese productivity edge at the supplier level, we emerge with a landed cost advantage for Japanese OEMs of about $1,400.

CONTRASTS IN PRODUCT QUALITY

It is, of course, true that the competitively important dimensions of auto quality are established not by experts but by the market. And many American consumers, who place a high value on quality of assembly workmanship (what the industry calls "fits and finishes"), on reliability, and on durability, seem to believe that Japanese cars are superior in each of these dimensions.

Exhibit II, which presents industry data on assembly quality, suggests that consumer perceptions are consistent with experience. Buy-

Exhibit II.   Evidence on assembly quality of U.S. autos vs. certain imports

	Vehicle category	Condition at delivery scale of 1–10; 10 is excellent		Condition after one month of service number of defects per vehicle shipped
	Aggregates	**Domestic**	**Imports**	
	Subcompact	6.4	7.9	
	Compact	6.2	7.7	
	Midsize	6.6	8.1	
	Standard	6.8	—	
Models	**Domestic**			
	Omni	7.4		4.10
	Chevette	7.2		3.00
	Pinto	6.5		3.70
	Rabbit(U.S.)*	7.8		2.13
	Horizon	7.5		N/A
	Imports			
	Civic	8.0		1.23†
	Fiesta	7.9		NA
	Colt	7.8		NA
	Corolla	7.8		0.71‡

*European Rabbit averages 1.42 defects per vehicle shipped.
†Honda average.
‡Toyota average.
Source: Aggregates—Rogers National Research, *Buyer Profiles,* 1979; models—industry sources.

Exhibit III.   Ratings of body and mechanical repair frequency (average = 10; maximum = 20; minimum = 0)

Make all models	Body 1980	Mechanical 1980
Domestic		
Buick	9.3	9.4
Chevrolet	8.4	8.9
Dodge	10.0	10.0
Ford	7.2	9.2
Lincoln	8.1	8.4
Oldsmobile	8.4	9.3
Volkswagen	11.3	8.6
Imports		
Datsun	15.3	10.8
Honda	16.0	11.1
Mazda	17.5	12.7
Toyota	16.9	12.4
Volkswagen	11.3	10.0
Volvo	11.9	10.5

Source: *Consumer Reports* annual auto issue, April 1981.

Note: The data cover repair frequency of mechanical systems, components, and body (structure and finish). Ratings are given in five categories: average, below average, far below average, above average, and far above average. Beginning with a score of zero for far below average, we have assigned values of 5, 10, 15, and 20 to the other categories. The sum of the scores on body and mechanical systems gives the total score.

ers rated the imports as a group superior in quality to the domestically produced cars, while the top Japanese models were ranked first and third among the nine rated. Japanese makes also had fewer defects after one month of service.

Similarly, subscribers to *Consumer Reports* gave high ratings to Japanese autos for reliability as measured by the incidence of repairs (see Exhibit III). Nevertheless, what little evidence exists indicates that U.S.-built vehicles have superior corrosion protection and longer-lived components and systems.

Exhibit IV.   Customer loyalty (percent who would buy same make/model again)

	Domestic	Imports	Total
Subcompact	77.2	91.6	81.2
Compact	74.2	91.4	72.4
Midsize	75.3	94.5	76.9
Standard	81.8	—	—
Luxury	86.6	94.6	87.2
Weighted average	78.7	91.8	—

Source: Rogers National Research, *Buyer Profiles*, 1979.

At any rate, American automobiles enjoy much less customer loyalty than do Japanese imports. Exhibit IV, which summarizes the data on loyalty, gives perhaps the clearest evidence of the differential customer perception of product value for each dollar spent.

Lessons of Quadrant 4

Most explanations of this Japanese advantage in production costs and product quality emphasize the impact of automation, the strong support of the central government, and the pervasive influence of national culture. No doubt these factors have played an important role, but the primary sources of this advantage are found instead in the Japanese producers' mastery of Quadrant 4—that is, in their execution of a well-designed strategy based on the shrewd use of manufacturing excellence.

It may seem odd to think of manufacturing as anything other than a competitive weapon, yet the history of the U.S. auto market shows that by the late 1950s manufacturing had become a competitively neutral factor. It was not, of course, unimportant, but none of the major American producers sought great advantage through superior manufacturing performance. Except perhaps for their reliance on economies of scale, they tended to compete by means of styling, marketing, and dealership networks.

The Japanese cost and quality advantage, however, originates in painstaking strategic management of people, materials, and equipment—that is, in superior manufacturing performance. This approach, in our view, arose from the Japanese pattern of domestic competition and the need for an effective strategy to enter the U.S. market.

At that time the Japanese realized it would be foolish to compete head-on with the established domestic producers' competence in making elaborately (and annually) styled large cars with a "boulevard ride." They lacked the experience, the manufacturing base, and the resources. Instead, taking a lesson from Volkswagen's success, the Japanese concentrated on producing a reliable, high-quality, solid-performance small automobile and on backing it up with a responsible network of dealers.

Exhibit V outlines the seven factors most responsible for successful productivity performance and compares the Japanese practice in each with the American. On the basis of extensive discussions with U.S. industry executives, engineers, and consultants, we have ranked these factors in the order of their importance in determining the current state of the industry and have given them approximate relative weights.

Surprisingly, the hardware associated with technology—new automation and product design—proves relatively insignificant in assessing the competitive difficulties of the U.S. manufacturers, although its importance for the future of the industry grows ever larger. Despite the publicity given Japan's experimentation with industrial robots and advanced assembly plants like Nissan's Zama facility, the evidence suggests that U.S. producers have so far maintained roughly comparable levels of process equipment. However appealing they may be, Quadrant 2 explanations cannot themselves account for U.S.-Japanese differentials in manufacturing productivity.

FOCUS ON 'PROCESS YIELD'

To the contrary, a valid explanation must start with the factor of "process yield," an amalgam of management practices and systems connected with production planning and control. This yield category reflects Japanese superiority in operating processes at high levels of efficiency and output over long periods of time. Although certain engineering considerations (machine cycles, plant layouts, and the like) are significant here, the Japanese advantage has far more to do

Exhibit V.   Seven factors affecting productivity: comparison of technology, management, and organization

Factor, with ranking and relative weights	Definition	Comparative practice, Japan relative to United States
Process systems		
Process yield 1(40%)	Output rate variations in conventional manufacturing lines; good parts per hour from a line, press, work group, or process line. Key determinants are machine cycle times, system uptime and reliability, affected by materials control methods, maintenance practices, and operating patterns.	Production-materials control minimizes inventory, reduces scrap, exposes problems. Line stops highlight problems and help eliminate defects. Operators perform routine maintenance; scheduling of two shifts instead of three leaves time for better maintenance.
Quality systems 5 (9%)	Series of controls and inspection plans to ensure that products are built to specifications.	Japanese use fewer inspectors. Some authority and responsibility are vested in production worker and supervisor; good relationship with supplier and very high standards lead to less incoming inspection.
Technology		
Process automation 4 (10%)	Introduction and adaptation of advanced, state-of-the-art manufacturing equipment.	Overall, state of technology is comparable. Japanese use more robots; their stamping facilities appear somewhat more automated than average U.S. facilities.

with the interaction of materials control systems, maintenance practices, and employee involvement. Exhibit VI attempts to make this interaction clear.

At the heart of the Japanese manufacturing system is the concept of "just in time" production. Often called *kanban* (after the cards or tickets used to trigger production), the system is designed so that materials, parts, and components are produced or delivered just before

Product design 6 (7%)	Differences in the way the car is designed for a given market segment; aspects affecting productivity: tolerances, number of parts, fastening methods, etc.	Japanese have more experience in small car production and have emphasized design for manufacturability (i.e, productivity and quality). Newer U.S. models (Escort, GM J-car) are first models with design/manufacturing specifications comparable to Japanese.

Work force management

Absenteeism 3 (12%)	All employee time away from the workplace, including excused, unexcused, medical, personal, contractual, and other reasons.	Levels of contractual time off are comparable; unexcused absences are much higher in United States.
Job structure 2 (18%)	Tasks and responsibilities included in job definitions.	Japanese practice is to create jobs with more breadth (more tasks or skill per job) and depth (more involvement in planning and control of operations); labor classifications are broader; regular production workers perform more skilled tasks; management layers are fewer.
Work pace 7 (4%)	Speed at which operators perform tasks.	Evidence is inconclusive; some lines run faster, some appear to run more slowly.

they are needed. Tight coupling of the manufacturing stages reduces the need for work-in-process inventory. This reduction helps expose any waste of time or materials, use of defective parts, or improper operation of equipment.[2]

Furthermore, because the system will not work if frequent or lengthy breakdowns occur, it creates inescapable pressure for maximizing uptime and minimizing defects. This pressure, in turn, supports a vigorous maintenance program. Most Japanese plants operate with only two shifts, which allows for thorough servicing of equipment during nonproductive time and results in a much lower rate of machine breakdown and failure than in the United States.

Exhibit VI.   Determinants of process yield

Rated machine speed total parts per hour	×	**Uptime** hours per year	×	**1-defect rate** good parts/ total parts	=	**Annual output of good parts**

Pressure for elimination of defects makes itself felt not in maintenance schedules but in the relationships of producers with suppliers and in work practices on the line. Just-in-time production does not permit extensive inspection of incoming parts. Suppliers must, therefore, maintain consistently high levels of quality, and workers must have the authority to stop operations if they spot defects or other production problems.

Worker-initiated line stoppages are central to the concept of *jidoka* (making a just-surfaced problem visible to everyone by bringing operations to a halt), which—along with kanban—helps direct energy and attention to elimination of waste, discovery of problems, and conservation of resources.

It is difficult, of course, to separate the effects of kanban-jidoka on process yield from the effects of, say, job structure and quality systems—factors given a somewhat lower ranking by the experts we consulted (see Exhibit V). It is also difficult to separate them from the benefits of having a loyal work force (Japanese factories have little unexcused absenteeism). Taken together, these aspects of work force management clearly account for much of the Japanese advantage in production.

It is sometimes argued, by the way, that the union-management relationship in the United States helps explain the superior Japanese performance in productivity and product quality. There is no doubt that the industrial relations system in the U.S. auto industry is a critical element in its performance. Nor is there any doubt that many aspects of that system do not square with the new facts of competitive life. Yet to lay these problems at the door of the union—and only there—is misleading.

Employment contracts and collective bargaining relationships do not just happen. Indeed, a contract provision that a company today finds dysfunctional often was initiated by management sometime in the past. Moreover, the production philosophy embodied in a contract may have had its origins in the very early days of the industry, long before unionization. Finally, many of the systems and practices that inhibit performance have little to do with a collective bargaining agreement.

Superior manufacturing performance, the key to the Japanese producers' competitive success, is therefore not the fruit of government policy, technical hardware, or national culture (Quadrants 1, 2, and 3). Instead it derives simply from the way people and operations are organized and managed (Quadrant 4).

Technological Renewal

Having looked at causes, we now turn our attention to cures. In a time of expensive energy, by their success in the marketplace Japanese producers have rekindled interest in the automobile—especially the small, fuel-efficient automobile—as a product and thus have opened the way for technology to become the relevant basis of competition in the American market. As one General Motors executive remarked, "We took a look at the Honda Accord and we knew that the game had changed."

But does the American auto industry—or, for that matter, do government bureaucrats, lenders, and suppliers—really understand that the game has changed? Our investigation indicates that it has not—yet. We often hear two interpretations of the current crisis, both of them deeply flawed. By extension, both of these interpretations can apply to other sectors of the U.S. industrial economy.

MISPERCEPTIONS OF CAUSES

The first of these interpretations, which we call "the natural consequences of maturity," holds that what has happened is the natural consequence of life cycle processes operating internationally on mature industrial sectors. Once an industry reaches the point where its production process has been embodied in equipment available for purchase—that is, once its mode of production is stable and well known—the location of factories becomes a simple matter of exploiting geographic advantages in the relative costs of production. In this view, it makes perfect sense to move these facilities out of the United States as lower cost opportunities become available elsewhere.

Many economists argue that rather than coming to the aid of threatened industries, government and management should follow the path of least resistance, so to speak, and let the life cycle work its will. They recommend a policy not of intervention but, in the phrase of Edward M. Graham, of "positive adjustment." "Government should not," he writes, "protect or subsidize industries that are threatened by imports or [are otherwise] noncompetitive internationally, but should take concrete steps to encourage the transfer of resources from less into more competitive industries.[3]

The question of who is sufficiently infallible to be entrusted with the nasty job of picking winners and losers is, of course, conveniently left unanswered. The evidence to date suggests that no one is.

The second line of interpretation, which we call "transient economic misfortune," is a considerably more optimistic point of view. It holds that the present difficulties with automobiles are temporary, the result of rapid changes in oil prices and consumer preferences. Cost or quality is not the problem, but inappropriate capacity: too many facilities for building big cars.

The forces needed to right the competitive balance are even now locked into place, their happy result merely a matter of time and of bringing the needed capacity on line. Understandably, this view of things appealed strongly to many in the Carter administration, who could use it to rationalize a firm policy of doing nothing.

Both of these interpretive schemes are inadequate—not only because they ignore differences in Quadrant 4 management but also because they count on future stability in technology. Adherents of the maturity thesis assume an irreversible tendency of products to become standardized—that is, technologically stable over time. Adherents of the misfortune thesis, assuming that all outstanding technological problems have been solved, see the industry as needing only to bring the requisite capacity on line to recapture its competitive standing.

Both groups of adherents argue from a set of familiar but outdated assumptions about the relation of technology to industrial development. Looking back on the years since World War II as a period of competition in autos based mainly on economies of scale, styling, and service networks, they persist in viewing the car manufacturers as constituting a typical mature industry, in which any innovation is incremental, never radical, and is thus—in marketing terms—virtually invisible.

FLUIDITY VERSUS STABILITY

Times have changed. Environmental concerns and the escalating price of oil have combined since the oil shock of 1979 to change the structure of market demand fundamentally. Technological innovation—in its radical as well as its incremental forms—again has vital competitive significance.

Changes in product technology have become at once more rapid and more extreme. Unlike most of the postwar period, recent technical advances have spawned a marked diversity in available systems and components. In engines alone, the once dominant V-8 has been joined by engines with four, five, and six cylinders, diesel engines, rotary engines, and engines with turbocharging and computer feedback control.

Moreover, these kinds of product innovation are increasingly radical in their effects on production processes. We have moved from a period in which product innovation focused on the refinement and extension of existing concepts to a period in which completely new concepts are developed and introduced. And this transition from a time of little change in production systems to a time of great turbulence in equipment, processes, skills, and organization is only beginning.

If our assessment is right, this shift in the nature of innovation will have far-reaching implications for the structure of the industry, the strategic decisions of companies, and the character of international trade. The supposedly mature auto industry now has the opportunity to embark on a technology-based process of rejuvenation in which the industry could recover the open-ended dynamics of its youth when competitive advantage was based largely on the ability to innovate.

Research has shown that manufacturing processes, no less than the products turned out, go through a life cycle evolution. As products evolve from low-volume, unstandardized, one-of-a-kind items toward high-volume, standardized, commoditylike items, the associated processes likewise evolve from individual job-shop production toward continuous-flow production. In other words, a product-process configuration, or productive unit that is initially fluid (relatively inefficient, flexible, and open to radical change), gradually becomes stable (relatively efficient, inflexible, and open only to incremental change).

This seemingly inexorable movement toward technological stability has long been the fate of the auto industry. Economies of scale on massive production lines have for more than a generation dictated the search for ever-greater product standardization and more stream-lined production. Radical change in the underlying technology of either became competitively dysfunctional; the production unit was too finely tuned to wring out the last increment of marginal cost reduction—and its management too focused on organizational coordination and control—to allow the entrepreneurially fertile disruptions caused by radically new technology.[4]

The new industrial competition, however, has dated this older logic by rewarding the ability to compete on technological grounds. It has precipitated a technological ferment, which has in turn been supported by the market's post-1979 willingness to pay a premium for vehicles boasting new technology.

Consider, for example, the rapid market adoption of General Motors' X-bodies with their transaxle and transverse mounted engines; the popularity of enhanced four-cylinder engines like Ford's compound-valve hemispherical head; or the appeal of such fuel-saving materials as graphite fibers, dual-phased steel, and advanced plastics. As a result, the industry has begun to revitalize itself in a movement back to a more fluid process-product configuration in the companies and a more lively technology-based competition among them.

TECHNOLOGY-DRIVEN STRATEGIES

Three factors are the prime elements in the renewal of the auto industry: (1) an increasing premium in the marketplace on innovation, (2) a growing diversity in the technology of components and production processes, and (3) an increasingly radical effect of factors 1 and 2 on long-established configurations in the productive unit as a whole. These developments, in turn, have begun to define the structure and competitive dynamics of the industry in the years ahead—and the corporate strategies best suited to both.

The conventional wisdom about industry structure and strategy accepts an implicit equation between concentration and maturity. When technology-based competition heats up, this logic runs, industry concentration loosens. In such a case, car manufacturers will know how to adjust their strategies accordingly.

To be sure, in a capital-intensive industry with great economies of scale, a period of ferment in product technology often allows manufacturers to offer an increasing variety of products at or below the cost of the old product mix. Especially when the production technology is well understood and easily procurable (in the form of equipment or human skills), companies on the fringe of the industry and fresh entrants can identify and exploit new market niches. Technological activity, market growth, and industry deconcentration usually go hand in hand.

When, however, the ferment in product technology is so extreme that it causes fundamental alterations in process technology, the same degree of activity may have very different results. In this case the immediate effect of a process-linked industry renewal may well be to *increase* the degree and the stability of concentration—that is, as many believe, to push industry structure apparently in the direction of *greater* maturity.

Where these observers go wrong is in failing to distinguish concentration from maturity or, said another way, in assuming that all evidence of frozen or rising concentration is evidence of movement toward maturity. This may, but need not, be the case.

In the auto field, for example, some corporate responses to the prospect of radical process innovation probably will take the industry farther along the road to maturity. Because truly radical product changes are still some years off and because commitments to existing process technology are large (especially in the standard model segment), it is reasonable to expect producers with experience in the older technologies to defend their positions through technical alterations that reduce costs or improve performance but do not make their processes obsolete.

Such a strategy requires the high volumes necessary for scale economies. As a result, the strategy may help concentrate production—either through greater use of joint ventures or, if the scale effects are great enough, through mergers and like forms of mature industry consolidation.

Other corporate responses to process-linked renewal may have the opposite effect. Major innovations in products that are linked to innovations in process technology often permit drastic reductions in production costs or improvements in performance, thus making possible the higher volumes necessary to expand market share. These innovations, however, usually involve large capital outlays as well as development of hard-to-acquire skills on the part of workers and management. So they require large increases in volume to offset the greater investment. As a result, only the leading producers may be able to profit from the process innovations and thus, temporarily at least, enhance their market share and reinforce industry concentration.

Though this pattern of concentration may appear identical to the one we have described, nothing could be further from the truth. Here a consolidation of the market serves to throw the industry into technological ferment that stimulates further technological competition—not to lock it into older process technology.

In time, this upheaval in process technology may even provide the competitive basis for new entrants to the field. Depending on the nature of process advances in auto production, companies in related industries (electronics, for example, or engines or energy) may find invasion of the market an attractive strategic option. But even if a decade from now these new entrants have not materialized, the forces that made their participation possible will have changed the competitive structure of the industry in two fundamental ways:

Whatever its immediate tendency, industry concentration will in the long run have become far less stable than at present.

The basis of competition will have changed to reflect the now-crucial importance of technology-driven strategies.

The Challenge to Management

Once U.S. auto manufacturers understand that energy prices and internationalization of competition have altered the industry's old competitive dynamics, they have to decide how they want to compete under the new rules of the game. It may be best for them to avoid duplicating the Japanese pattern of competition. At any rate, after decades of the maturing process, the basis for competing is in flux for U.S. producers and radical rethinking about strategy—not blind imitation—is in order.

The industrial landscape in America is littered with the remains of once-successful companies that could not adapt their strategic vision to altered conditions of competition. If the automobile producers prove unequal to the new reality that confronts them, their massive, teeming plants will become the ghost towns of late twentieth century America. The same, of course, holds true for all companies, large and small, in those old-line manufacturing industries exposed to assault from abroad. Only those able to see the new industrial competition for what it is and to devise appropriate strategies for participating in it will survive.

Managers must recognize that they have entered a period of competition that requires of them a technology-driven strategy, a mastery of efficient production, and an unprecedented capacity for work force management. They cannot simply copy what others do but must find their own way. No solutions are certain, no strategies assured of success. But the nature of the challenge is clear.

Henry Ford, as Alfred P. Sloan recalled him, was a man who had had ". . . many brilliant insights in [his] earlier years, [but] seemed never to understand how completely the market had changed from the one in which he had made his name and to which he was accustomed. . . . The old master failed to master change."[5] That is still the crucial challenge—and opportunity.

Notes

1. Statement before the Subcommittee on Trade of the House Ways and Means Committee, March 18, 1980.

2. See Robert H. Hayes, "Why Japanese Factories Work," *Harvard Business Review,* July–August 1981, p. 56.

3. Edward M. Graham, "Technological Innovation and the Dynamics of the U.S. Competitive Advantage in International Trade," in *Technological Innovation for a Dynamic Economy*, edited by Christopher T. Hill and James M. Utterback (Elmsford, N.Y.: Pergamon Press, 1979), p. 152.

4. For a discussion of the evolution toward industrial maturity, see James M. Utterback and William J. Abernathy, "A Dynamic Model of Process and Product Innovation," *Omega*, vol. 3, 1975, p. 639.

5. Alfred P. Sloan, Jr., *My Years with General Motors* (Garden City, N.Y.: Doubleday, 1964), pp. 186–187.

Appendix: The Japanese cost advantage

Table A. Calculation of U.S. and Japanese labor costs for a subcompact vehicle

	1	2	3	4	5	6 [4×5]	7 [6×.575]
	Share in OEM manufacturing costs	Average OEM hours per vehicle	Estimated OEM employee cost per hour	Estimated cost per vehicle	Labor content	Labor cost per vehicle	U.S.-Japan difference
OEM labor							
Hourly	.24	65	$18	$1,170	100%	$1,170	$ 673
Salaried	.08	15	21	315	100	315	181
Purchased components	.39	NA	NA	1,901	66	1,255	721
Purchased materials	.14	NA	NA	683	25	171	98
Total	—	—	—	**$4,875**	**NA**	**$2,911**	**$1,673**

Notes: OEM hourly labor is defined as total nonexempt and includes direct and indirect production workers. The calculations assume an exchange rate of 218 yen per dollar. The method of calculation and sources of data are as follows:

Column 1 contains estimates of the share of total manufacturing cost accounted for by direct and indirect production labor (at the OEM level), purchased components, and materials. These estimates do not reflect the experience of any one company but approximate an industry average. They are based on data prepared for the National Research Council's Committee on Motor Vehicle Emissions as well as on discussions with industry sources. The latter have also provided us with the data in columns 2, 3, and 5.

We made the calculation of U.S.-Japan cost differences in three steps. We first used the data in columns 2 and 3 to get an OEM labor cost per vehicle of $1,170, then extrapolated using the cost shares (column 1) to arrive at a total manufactured cost and the cost of purchased components and materials (column 4). We next multiplied the cost per vehicle in column 4 by an estimate of the labor content of the three categories presented in column 5. The data imply, for example, that $1,255 of the $1,901 cost of components is labor cost. Finally, we calculated the Japan-U.S. labor cost gap by multiplying the U.S. data in column 6 by 0.575, the adjustment factor derived from our estimate of the Japan-to-U.S. unit labor cost ratio.* Thus column 7 provides an estimate of the difference in the cost of producing a subcompact vehicle in the United States and Japan due to differences in unit labor costs, not only at the OEM level but also at the supplier level.

*Let C(US) and C(J) indicate unit labor costs in the United States and Japan. We estimate C(J)/C(US) = .425 We want to know C(US)−C(J). Column 6 gives us C(US). Thus, $C(US)-C(J) = (1 - \frac{c(J)}{c(US)}) \times$ column 6; this result is in column 7.

Table B. Ford and Toyo Kogyo's estimated per-vehicle employee costs in 1979

	Ford	Toyo Kogyo
Domestic car and truck production* in millions	3.163	0.983
Total domestic employment†		
Automotive	219,599	24,318
Nonautomotive	19,876	2,490
Total domestic employee hours‡		
Automotive in millions	355.75	46.20
Total employee cost§		
Automotive in millions	$7,794.50	$482.20
Employee hours per vehicle	112.5	47.0
Employee cost per vehicle	$2,464	$491

*Ford Figure includes 65,000 imported vehicles; Toyo Kogyo figure is adjusted for production of knock-down assembly kits.

†Data on automotive employment and costs were obtained by assuming that the ratio of automotive employment to total employment was the same as the ratio of sales. The same assumption was made to obtain Ford employment costs.

‡Ford hours were determined by assuming that each employee worked 1,620 hours per year; Toyo Kogyo hours assume 1,900 hours. These adjustments reflect vacations, holidays, leaves, and absences.

§Data include salaries, wages, and fringe benefits. Toyo Kogyo compensation data were derived by updating a 1976 figure using compensation growth rates at Toyota. An exchange rate of 218 yen/$ (1979 average) was used to convert yen.

Table C. Product mix adjustment

	Ford	Toyo Kogyo
1. Ratio of car to total vehicle production	0.645	0.652
2. Production shares by size		
Small	0.11	0.83
Medium	0.68	0.17
Large	0.21	—
3. Relative manufacturing cost by size		
Small	1.00	NA
Medium	1.35	NA
Large	1.71	NA
4. Weighted average of relative manufacturing cost small = 1.00	1.38	1.06
5. Production of Toyo Kogyo mix at Ford level of integration		
Employee cost per vehicle	$1,893	$589
Employee hours per vehicle	87	56

Notes: Line 2 for Ford assumes that only Pinto and Bobcat models are small; Mustang and Capri sales were placed in the medium category.

Line 5 for Ford is obtained by multiplying lines 6 and 7 in Exhibit B by (1.06/1.38).

Table B uses the data on manufacturing costs by vehicle size developed for the Committee on Motor Vehicle Emissions of the National Research Council in 1974. We derived estimates of the cost to Ford of producing the Toyo Kogyo mix by first computing a weighted average of the relative manufacturing cost indices with Ford's 1979 production shares by size as weights. The ratio of the comparable Toyo Kogyo weighted average (1.06) to the Ford weighted average (1.38) was used to adjust both costs and productivity as a means of estimating the effect of product mix on Ford's average cost and labor hours per vehicle. After these adjustments we estimate that Ford would require 87 employee hours to produce the average-size vehicle in the Toyo Kogyo product line, compared with 56 hours in the Japanese company. Labor cost per vehicle is just over $1,300 higher at Ford. These comparisons are based on the average-size vehicle at Toyo Kogyo. For a small vehicle (i.e., Pinto vs. Mazda GLC), the Ford estimate is 82 hours per vehicle, while the comparable Toyo Kogyo figure is 53; the corresponding costs per vehicle are $1,785 (Ford) and $566 (Toyo Kogyo). Even this adjustment may overstate costs and hours required to produce the Toyo Kogyo mix at Ford if the trucks and commercial vehicles produced by the two companies differ substantially.

3
Managing As If Tomorrow Mattered

Robert H. Hayes and
David A. Garvin

Few economic decisions are as difficult as those involving the choice between present and future consumption. Some people, unable to place much faith in the future, happily borrow to fund present pleasures; others, with longer time horizons, are wary of such "fly now, pay later" policies. They fear that the required payments, when viewed up close, will be much more burdensome than they appear from a distance.

Investments in plant and equipment are especially sensitive to such differences in outlook and perception. Ethical issues make these decisions more difficult still, for a company's approach to investments in long-lived capital stock says much about its sense of duty to future workers, managers, and stockholders.

Highly sophisticated analytic techniques now dominate the capital budgeting process at most companies. Rare is the manager who will make an important investment decision without first carefully calculating its net present value or internal rate of return. Although these methods have been around for years, managers are using them more and more today as aids to rational decision making. A 1971 survey of 184 large manufacturing companies showed that 57% used discounting techniques to evaluate investment projects; only 19% had done so in 1959. A 1975 survey of 33 major corporations indicated even wider acceptance, with 94% of the companies using discounting calculations.[1]

As these techniques have gained ever wider use in investment decision making, the growth of capital investment and R&D spending in this country has slowed. We believe this to be more than a simple coincidence. We submit that the discounting approach has contributed to a decreased willingness to invest for two reasons: (1) it is often based on misperceptions of the past and present economic environment, and (2) it is biased against investment because of critical errors in the way the theory is applied. Bluntly stated, the willingness of managers to view the future through the reversed telescope of discounted cash flow analysis is seriously shortchanging the futures of their companies.

A Decline in Reinvestment

Raw data on recent capital spending and R&D investment by the private sector tell a tale of modest but steady increase—until, that is, one adjusts for inflation or for changes in GNP and the size of the work force. Then the figures tell a different story. Although gross business investment as a percentage of GNP has remained roughly constant in real terms since the 1950s, the capital invested per labor hour and the share of GNP devoted to net new investment have both declined over the last decade.

Between 1948 and 1973, for example, the ratio of the net book value of capital equipment to the number of labor hours worked grew at about 3% per year. Since then it has increased at only about one-half that rate. Moreover, the growth in the ratio of net capital stock to the number of full-time equivalent employed workers—a figure that adjusts for changes in the hours per week worked by the average employee—reveals an even greater post-1973 decline.

Spending on R&D presents an equally disturbing picture. Viewed as a percentage of GNP, total U.S. investment in R&D fell steadily between 1967 and 1978. In basic research, which involves longer time horizons, the picture is even bleaker. Measured in constant dollars, investment peaked in the late 1960s, then dipped, and did not regain its earlier level until 1978. As a percentage of GNP, corporate spending on basic research is today only two-thirds of what it was in the mid-1960s.

American managers are also underinvesting in human resource development, especially in critical industrial skills. The average age of experienced tool and die makers, for example, is approaching 50 years. If present trends continue, within the next decade this vital reservoir of skills—necessary in a variety of industries and already in short supply—threatens to dry up. Similarly, the Department of Labor estimates an annual demand for 22,000 skilled machinists during the 1980s, yet only about 2,800 graduate each year from various apprenticeship programs. Much the same is true for skilled assemblers, forging-machine operators, and optical workers.

Taken together, this evidence suggests that business spending on many crucial activities has been lagging badly in recent years. What lies behind this dangerous slowdown in long-term investment?

SEARCHING FOR ANSWERS

There is no shortage of popular explanations. Most fall into one of three categories:

1. **Managerial theories,** which blame business itself for the emphasis on near-term profitability that now dominates managerial decision making. Observers attribute this myopia to a variety of causes: the shift to multidivisional organizations, which typically use short-term financial measures as the primary means for evaluating managerial performance; the desire of younger managers for rapid advancement, which tends to limit the time a person spends at any one job; and pressure from the financial community.
2. **Environmental theories,** which cite as culprits inflation, high income and capital gains taxes, rising energy prices, constrictive federal regulations, erratic shifts in public policy, and other features of the business environment.
3. **Financial theories,** which point to the recent increase in mergers and acquisitions as being responsible for the decline in direct investment. According to this view, managers are simply responding rationally to current economic conditions when they purchase inexpensive used assets rather than invest in more expensive—and risky—new assets.

Some of these theories are more persuasive than others. That American managers tend to be more concerned with short-term financial performance than their German and Japanese counterparts is, for example, now widely recognized. So, too, is the effect on investment of dramatic changes in the economic environment, although other developed countries have experienced similar shifts during the past decade without a corresponding slackening of investment.[2] Increases in merger activity and in the funds devoted to corporate acquisitions, however, do not explain this decline in capital spending.

Corporate acquisitions are neither a substitute for direct investment nor a cheap way of acquiring plant and equipment. The bargain-base-ment character of such activity is an illusion resulting from attention to the wrong set of figures. Typically, analysts cite data that compare the market value of U.S. companies (as measured by the sum of their outstanding debt and equity) with their replacement value to justify the claim that assets can be obtained more cheaply by acquisition than by direct investment.

Government figures do indeed show that market value, measured in this way, has been well below replacement cost in each year since 1972. Most mergers, however, involve acquisition prices substantially above supposed market value because some premium is generally required to entice managers and shareholders to approve the sale. Should a bidding war develop, the acquisition price can escalate dra-matically—often to more than double the company's market value.

Focusing only on acquisitions that have actually happened, rather than on the market value-to-replacement cost ratios of all compa-nies, gives a different perspective on the financial attractiveness of mergers. In the 1960s and early 1970s, actual acquisition prices aver-aged from 20% to 60% *more* than the estimated replacement costs of acquired companies. In recent years, this margin has declined some-what, but prices have still fallen only to a level about equal to replace-ment costs. Used assets may have become cheaper over the past few years, but they are not at all the bargain that many managers seem to think they are.

Indeed, even if these assets were underpriced, their attractiveness would not explain America's declining capital investment, for at the national level heightened merger activity does not substitute directly for stepped-up physical investment. Acquisitions, after all, are essen-tially transfers of funds between two business entities (except, of course, for the small percentage siphoned off by investment bankers, lawyers, and accountants). These transfers, therefore, should not di-minish total corporate investment, although they may affect the deci-sions of particular companies.

Nor can the problem be attributed to a lack of capital caused by inflation, reduced profitability, higher taxes, or government-mandated nonproductive expenditures. During the past 10 years, the inflation-adjusted aftertax return on equity for U.S. corporations has roughly equaled its level in the 1950s. The ratio of shareholder dividends to total corporate operating cash flow, however, was 11% higher in the late 1970s than in the late 1960s—and 30% higher in 1980. The ratio of investment in new capital equipment to corporate cash flow, on the other hand, has generally declined since the 1950s. The problem is not that U.S. business lacks the money to spend; it is simply not spending the money it has in the same ways that it used to.

Is this behavior evidence of a foolish, but unintentional, mistake on the part of American managers? Not necessarily. They appear to believe completely in the legitimacy of their investment decisions and in the techniques on which they are based. These methods, however, have profound conceptual weaknesses that are not always recognized, and the answers they provide depend on managers' perceptions of the current and future economic environment. This combination of theoretical blind spots and economic misjudgments can often lead a company to shortchange its future.

Discounting the Future

The theory is simple: a dollar received today is worth more than a dollar received tomorrow. How much more depends on the current uses to which the dollar can be put. If it can earn 5% interest, a dollar today will be worth $1.05 after a year; if 10%, $1.10. Conversely, at a 5% interest rate, a dollar received a year from now is worth only $1 \div \$1.05$, or 95.2 cents today; at a rate of 10%, 90.9 cents. This determination of a future dollar's present value is, according to accepted theory, the appropriate way to compare future benefits with present costs.

Extending the theory to capital investment is also simple: a company pays a certain amount of money to receive a series of returns stretching off into the future, each of which can be translated into an equivalent amount today. The difference between the amount invested and the sum of the discounted returns determines whether the proposed investment is more attractive than the best alternative use of the funds. Notice that this calculation requires several critical estimates: the size of the anticipated investment, the amount and timing of the resulting cash flows, and the rate of return that could be realized if the capital project were not approved and the funds were directed elsewhere. This last figure is generally termed the company's opportunity rate or, more prosaically, its hurdle rate.

Today such calculations have, because of their apparent rationality, gained the upper hand in the evaluation of new investment proposals. Yet these techniques are as subject to misperceptions and biases in application as are other, less formal methods. Consider the following example.

A company with a set of assets—its capital stock—worth $100 million generates an annual aftertax cash flow of $12 million. Here capital stock includes not only operating assets (the net value of plant and equipment, inventories, and accounts receivable) but also the productive value of such intangible assets as human skills and the residual value of the R&D and advertising expenditures that have built up over the years. Now, say this capital stock is deteriorating (that is, slowly losing its capacity to generate earnings) at a rate of 5% per year. Further, any cash not reinvested in the business can be invested in other activities—either directly by management or via dividend payments to stockholders—that will eventually generate cash flows equivalent to an 8% rate of return.

Please note that our use of the term *deterioration* is related to, but not precisely the same as, the usual accounting definition of *depreciation*. We are not concerned with the amortization of previous investments in fixed assets for the purpose of calculating taxes or reporting profits. Instead, we are interested in the rate of erosion in the earnings-generating power of the company's total capital stock, a rate that in practice is often highly irregular.

Skimping on reinvestment may therefore take other forms than not replacing equipment as it depreciates in value. Managers can, for example, allow the productivity of existing equipment to deteriorate faster than normal by using it more hours per week than before or by replacing it with less productive, and usually less expensive, equipment as it wears out. Or, more subtly, they can replace it with machinery based on dated technology. Similarly, managers can allow spending on R&D, advertising, and personnel development to fall below historical levels.

Back to our example. Simply to preserve the earnings-generating capacity of its capital stock, the company must reinvest $5 million (the annual deterioration, at a rate of 5%, of a $100 million capital base) of its yearly $12 million cash flow. Doing so ensures only that its capital stock will continue to be $100 million and that future earnings will stay at $12 million per year.

The remaining $7 million of cash flow can be invested outside the business, either directly or indirectly via dividends to shareholders. The discounted value of these annual outflows, assuming an opportunity rate of 8%, equals $7 million ÷ .08, or $87.5 million (see Exhibit I). This $87.5 million is, in a sense, the value today of a goose that will lay each and every year golden eggs that are worth $7 million—providing, of course, that the proceeds from these eggs can be invested in activities earning 8%.

Exhibit I.   The present value of different reinvestment rates: maintaining value of existing capital stock (in $ millions)

| | **Premise:** | | | |
| | Company reinvests $5 million every year (maintaining its earnings-generating capability) | | and invests the remaining $7 million each year outside its existing business. | |
Year	**Present value factor @ 8%**	**Invested in company**	**Invested outside**	**Present value of outside investment**
1	.926	$5	$7	$6.48
2	.857	5	7	6.00
3	.794	5	7	5.56
4	.735	5	7	5.15
5	.681	5	7	4.77
6	.630	5	7	4.41
7	.583	5	7	4.08
8	.540	5	7	3.78
9	.500	5	7	3.50
etc.	.	.	.	.
.	.	.	.	.
.	.	.	.	.
	Sum of present values			**$87.50**

In this simple case, we can calculate discounted present value directly: $\dfrac{\$7}{.08}$ = $87.5 million

Note: There is disagreement over the proper rate for discounting future payments. Some argue that it should be the company's opportunity rate (its average rate of return on alternative investments), while others prefer the company's cost of capital, the rate demanded by the stock market for those in the same risk class. Theoretically, in the long run the two rates should converge because the cost of capital will rise toward the opportunity rate as increasingly risky investments are undertaken. But the long run takes forever to arrive, and in the short run—where the cost of capital is usually less than the opportunity rate—most companies use the rate of return of the minimally acceptable investment (as determined by management) as the discount rate in present value calculations. We have followed this latter practice.

But is this the best way to manage the goose? Could the company raise the present value of these annual cash outflows either by taking more capital out of the business each year and thus cutting its earnings-generating capacity or by taking out less and building up its capital stock?

What would be the effect, for example, of increasing the cash throwoff from 58.3% ($7 million ÷ $12 million) to 70% of the annual cash flow? The first year $8.4 million would be available for outside investment instead of the previous $7 million. This figure could not, however, be sustained over time, for without adequate reinvestment the company's capital stock would gradually deteriorate and thus steadily reduce the value of the cash throwoff.

But what about the present value of the throwoffs resulting from this strategy of "more now, less later"? According to the calculations in Exhibit II, it actually rises from $87.5 million to $89.36 million.

In other words, present-value calculations support a decision to operate on the goose and remove some of its golden eggs prematurely, even though doing so impairs its future egg-laying ability. In fact, such calculations always justify a policy of progressive disinvestment as long as a company's net return on internal investment (the amount available, after deterioration, for the payment of capital charges and additions to earned surplus—12% minus 5% in our example) is less than its net return from external investment (8%).

The Theory's Wobbly Legs

Few managers, of course, view the reinvestment process in quite this stylized fashion. Their job is to evaluate specific investment proposals by discounting the estimated cash flows (after taxes and depreciation) from a proposed investment using a hurdle rate that reflects the minimum acceptable return for proposals of that type. Should a given project not promise to generate profits (after depreciation) equal to those available from investments outside the business, it will be rejected.

According to discounting theory, then, a pattern of progressive disinvestment might make perfect sense. Discounting techniques, however, rest on rather arbitrary assumptions about profitability, asset deterioration, and external investment opportunities. In fact, we believe that much of the decline in investment in capital stock is the result of misperceptions about the changes that have taken place in

Exhibit II. Gradual disinvestment (in $ millions)

Premise: Company reinvests only 30% of the cash throwoff each year (allowing its earnings-generating capability to gradually deteriorate) and reinvests the remaining 70% outside its existing business.

Year	Beginning-of-year capital stock	Cash generated during year	Deterioration during year	Reinvested in company	Invested outside	Present value of outside investment
1	$100.00	$12.00	$5.00	$3.60	$8.40	$ 7.78
2	98.60	11.83	4.93	3.55	8.28	7.10
3	97.22	11.67	4.86	3.50	8.17	6.48
4	95.86	11.50	4.79	3.45	8.05	5.92
5	94.52	11.34	4.73	3.40	7.94	5.40
6	93.19	11.18	4.66	3.35	7.83	4.93
7	91.89	11.03	4.59	3.31	7.72	4.50
8	90.60	10.87	4.53	3.26	7.61	4.11
9	89.33	10.72	4.47	3.22	7.50	3.75
etc.	.	.	.	.	.	.
.	.	.	.	.	.	.
.	.	.	.	.	.	.
Sum of present values						**$89.36**

We can calculate this discounted present value directly: $\dfrac{(1.0 - .30)(.12)100}{.08 + .05 - (.30)(.12)} = \$89.36$

these three critical variables over the past decade. American managers have acted as though these variables have been moving in such a way as to make direct reinvestment in their existing businesses less and less desirable. But how have these variables actually behaved?

CASH-GENERATING RATE

Many managers are convinced that the ability of their companies to generate earnings is less today than in the past. They blame global competition, industry maturation, and intrusive government for the decline; yet according to Burton Malkiel and other leading economists, the overall rate of return on equity for U.S. companies, *after adjustment for inflation*, has remained roughly constant for about 30 years.[3] Only during the mid-1960s, when the rate of return rose to double its historical level of about 4.5%, did this pattern change. Even then, the gains were short lived, and earnings soon fell back to their former levels.

Many executives, however, view the rates of return during the mid-1960s as the norm, rather than an aberration. By this standard, things have indeed worsened in recent years. But even though a company's profit margin may have dropped from, say, 10% in 1965 to 5% today, that 10% figure is not a reasonable reference point for historical comparison.

Nor, in fact, is the 5% figure always reliable. When managers attempt to net out the impact of inflation on the profitability of their businesses, they usually address only the asset side of the balance sheet. They reduce profits by the amount that inflation has increased the value of inventories and recalculate depreciation on the basis of the replacement cost, rather than the historical cost, of equipment. Rarely, however, do they acknowledge that their long-term debt also declines in value during an inflationary period. By ignoring the debit side of the balance sheet, many managers have overestimated—perhaps by as much as 50%—the decline in profitability attributable to inflation.[4]

DETERIORATION RATE

Even if the perception of a long-term decline in corporate profitability is illusory, there is good reason to believe that the rate of deterioration of capital stock has increased. Inflation is partly to blame, for the cost of many capital goods has risen faster than the prices of the products they make; consequently, it is more expensive to replace the fixed assets that a company employs in its business. Between 1970 and 1979, for example, the price of metal-forming machine tools almost tripled, but the price of all manufactured durables increased by little more than a factor of two. Such high prices often deter reinvestment or limit it to some fixed percentage of annual sales.

Also responsible, of course, are rising energy prices, which have so burdened operating costs that some production processes are no longer competitive. The rapid obsolescence of manufacturing equipment—whether because of high energy consumption, restrictive government regulations, or declining efficiency compared with the newer process technologies—can appear prohibitively expensive to remedy. When replacement costs are in the stratosphere, the need to reinvest in capital stock can easily paralyze, not galvanize, a manager's willingness to reinvest in existing businesses.

HURDLE RATE

Despite their perceptions of a decline in the profitability, and an increase in the rate of deterioration, of their companies' assets, American managers have not made a corresponding reduction in the hurdle rates they employ in capital budgeting.

These rates are typically quite high, often in the range of 25% to 40%, and there is some evidence that they have been rising over the past decade. A recent survey, for example, shows that about 25% of American manufacturing companies require expenditures for modernization and replacement of equipment to pay off within three years. Ten years ago only 20% had required that rapid a payoff. Shorter payback periods imply higher hurdle rates, just as higher hurdle rates imply a stronger emphasis on near-term benefits.

As with most of the arbitrary numbers that find their way into a company's systems and procedures, these hurdle rates are often used without question, even by executives who profess to be open-minded. The chairman of a leading American equipment manufacturer recently described himself as an executive who encouraged his managers to take risks; at the same time, he insisted that all new investments produce a 25% return during the first five years.

Such hurdle rates often bear little resemblance either to a company's real cost of capital (even after appropriate adjustment for differences in risk) or to the actual rates of return (net of deterioration replenishment) that the company can reasonably expect to earn from alternative investments. Again and again we have observed the use of pretax hurdle rates of 30% or more in companies whose actual pretax returns on investment were less than 20%.

How do managers normally defend this practice? First, they claim that an artificially high rate helps protect them from unforeseen reductions in cash throwoffs that are triggered by competitors' actions, unexpected inflationary increases in investment costs, and number fudging by subordinates anxious to have a project approved for personal reasons. Second, they argue that high hurdle rates increase motivation and that difficult-to-achieve targets tend to spur good performance.

As attractive as these explanations appear at first glance, their logic is faulty. Systematic adjustments for risk are quite appropriate when computing present values, but many of the hurdle rates that we have seen contain unreasonably high risk components. Moreover, using such rates as a motivational tool undermines their worth in evaluating investment opportunities. For one thing, they often discourage investment in existing businesses whose risks are known and direct it toward businesses whose risks are less understood.

Such behavior also reflects a growing preference among managers for acquisitions over internal investments. Despite considerable evidence to the contrary, American managers appear to believe that aggressive acquisition programs make possible both higher long-term growth rates and greater profitability. Many are so firmly convinced that the grass is greener in almost any industry other than their own that they are far less tough-minded in evaluating acquisition candidates than they are in assessing internal investment proposals.

The key assumptions in this approach for analyzing investment proposals—assumptions about rates of profitability, deterioration, and acceptable return—are highly unreliable and prone to individual bias. Managers may have an accurate sense of their businesses' past profitability, but their belief about future profitability depends heavily on their basic optimism and confidence in the economy. They may know to several decimal points the average depreciation rate for their industry, but they are less likely to know the real deterioration rate of their companies' total capital stock. Even more uncertain is their assessment of the profit opportunities and deterioration rates in businesses other than their own.

Bitten, perhaps, by the merger bug and unwilling to adjust their inflated hurdle rates, many American managers have found reinvestment in existing businesses less and less desirable. Under siege in a changing world, they recall the economic Camelot of the 1960s and believe that it still exists somewhere, waiting to be found outside their corporate bunker. Had they placed less faith in the misleading objectivity of their discounting techniques, they might instead be spending their time and resources reinforcing their own bunker's walls.

The Theory's Blind Spots

Discounting methods are biased against investment in new capital stock in still other ways. Present-value comparisons are especially difficult to make if the projects under review have different lifetimes: when projects are of equivalent length, present-value calculations favor those with shorter payback periods; when projects are of unequal length, those with longer lives often appear more attractive than those with shorter lives. Few investments, however, are intended as "doomsday projects" for which there is no successor. Managers usually assume that at the end of a current investment's lifetime, another, involving similar activities, will begin. Thus, unless corrected for, discounting's focus on the profitability of initial projects can lead to a series of absurd decisions.

Narrow use of the present-value criterion will, for example, almost inevitably argue for expanding facilities already in place rather than for building a new plant in a different location. The initial investment is normally much less, the returns more immediate. Over the long run, however, a series of such decisions—each backed by its own impeccable logic—can lead to ponderous, outmoded dinosaurs that are easy prey for the smaller, more modern, and better focused plants of competitors.

Consider the experience of one producer of large machinery that opened a simple assembly operation in the 1920s. As sales increased, the plant kept expanding both the size and number of its processes until today the company finds itself with a mammoth and uneconomical complex. Now it is trying to figure out how to break apart a manufacturing operation that appears to have grown like Topsy over the years, although each addition made sense at the time.

Another manufacturer, which recently focused attention on its home plant, discovered a collection of more than 40 multilevel buildings producing an extraordinary variety of low-demand items using equipment that dated back before World War II. Rather than undertake the immense task of modernizing this outmoded plant, whose condition was the result of a series of apparently rational investment decisions over a long period, the company reluctantly closed it down.

For similar reasons, the present-value criterion will often suggest delaying the replacement of a piece of equipment by another, more modern machine that performs roughly the same function. The economic benefit of delaying purchase for a year, say, is seldom offset by the efficiencies obtained from using the new machine on comparable activities. Less obvious benefits from increased worker skills and capabilities, new products, and a different cost structure are harder to document in advance and so do not fit neatly into a present-value analysis. In fact, to counteract this bias against modernization, some companies are experimenting with a "sunset law" for capital equipment, under which a piece of equipment is automatically replaced at the end of a predetermined period unless a special review process decides otherwise.

The Logic of Disinvestment

The threat implicit in discounting techniques is not limited to misperceptions, too short time horizons, or a bias against major modernization projects. It extends to the very ability—and willingness—of managers to ward off the attacks of aggressive competitors.

Consider, for example, two companies that share the market in a price-sensitive industry. Initially, both use the same production processes and have similar cost structures. A new manufacturing process, however, promises to reduce variable costs significantly. Company A, with a high hurdle rate, rejects the investment out of hand as being insufficiently profitable; Company B, with a lower hurdle rate, decides to buy the new equipment.

Both companies perform similar discounting calculations to weigh the advantages of the proposed investment. They arrive at opposite conclusions because of the differences in the hurdle rates employed and in the importance placed on maintaining competitive vigor. In theory, both should be satisfied with the results.

Company B, once its new equipment is in place, quite naturally proceeds to compete aggressively for market share by lowering prices. Its new manufacturing process, after all, gives it much lower variable costs and requires high production volumes for maximum efficiency.

Can Company A respond? Its outdated equipment places it at a distinct competitive disadvantage. Moreover, its competitor's price reductions have so reduced the profitability of its existing business that the investment required to upgrade its facilities looks even less attractive than before. At the least, Company A will lose market share; at the worst, it could be driven out of the business entirely and, perhaps, be forced to use its remaining capital to acquire another business, one apparently better able to meet its high hurdle rate.

Many American companies today find themselves in a position much like that of Company A. The problem is not that reliance on discounting techniques inevitably leads to inaccurate results but rather that managers can all too easily hide behind the apparent rationality of such financial analyses while sidestepping the hard decisions necessary to keep their companies competitive.

One reason companies so often become trapped in this sort of disinvestment spiral—deferred investment leading to reduced profitability, which further reduces the incentive to invest—is that discounting techniques make the implicit assumption that investment processes are reversible. That is, if one sells an asset, one can always buy it back; or if one delays an investment, one can always make it at some later date with no penalty other than that implied by the company's discount rate.

No company, however, can be sure of recovering lost ground quite so easily. To regain its position, a company may have to spend a good deal more than if it had made the investment when first proposed. As time passes, downward spirals become much more difficult to arrest. Moreover, as the experience of both Ford and Chrysler attests, postponed investments (in downsizing in the mid-1970s) may not be reversible; complete recovery may be impossible.

This irreversibility is partly rooted in the dynamics of human organizations. Companies are collections not simply of tangible assets but of people as well, and the bonds among them reflect understandings and commitments developed over a long time. Such bonds need constant support and reinforcement; once they begin to dissolve, an organization loses its sense of movement and often falls prey to a sense of resignation. Morale sags, performance suffers, and employees—generally the best ones—begin to leave. Faced with these circumstances, top management often concludes that a division or product line is unsalvageable and purposely continues the process of disinvestment.

REVERSING THE DISINVESTMENT SPIRAL

It is both difficult and costly for a company to extract itself from such a spiral, for usually no single investment can repair the damage.

Instead, simultaneous investments in several projects are often necessary to achieve an acceptable return. If managers evaluated each of these projects individually with no attention to the interactions among them, they might reject some as being insufficiently profitable. Unfortunately, the capital budgeting procedures that most companies follow today do not readily accommodate such interdependencies (what economists call "indivisibilities") among investment projects. The same logic that got a company into such a predicament can therefore impede its attempt to extract itself.

No company can break out of a disinvestment spiral by relying on the same financial logic that got it there. The only remedy is to understand the shape of that logic as well as the direction in which it leads—and then to take an opposite course. Managers must be willing to reinvest at the very time such action appears least attractive. They must stop pouring funds into refurbishing their images and upgrade their factories instead. They must resist the lure of unfamiliar businesses and mind their own.

Beyond all else, capital investment represents an act of faith, a belief that the future will be as promising as the present, together with a commitment to making that future happen. Modern financial theory argues that under certain "reasonable" assumptions disinvestment is a logical and appropriate course of action. Today, the future consequences of a disinvestment strategy, as seen through the reversed telescope of discounting, may appear inconsequential; but once tomorrow arrives, those who must deal with it are certain to feel differently.

Notes

1. See Thomas P. Klammer, "Empirical Evidence of the Adoption of Sophisticated Capital Budgeting Techniques," *Journal of Business*, July 1972, p. 393; and Eugene R. Brigham, "Hurdle Rates for Screening Capital Expenditure Proposals," *Financial Management*, Autumn 1975, p. 18.

2. Many of these points have been argued earlier in Robert H. Hayes and William J. Abernathy, "Managing Our Way to Economic Decline," *Harvard Business Review*, July–August 1980, p. 67.

3. See Burton G. Malkiel, "The Capital Formation Problem in the United States," *Journal of Finance*, May 1979, p. 291, and "Unraveling the Mysteries of Corporate Profits," *Fortune*, August 27, 1979, p. 90.

4. Franco Modigliani and Richard A. Cohn, "Inflation, Rational Valuation, and the Market," *Financial Analysts Journal*, March–April 1979, p. 24.

4
Quality on the Line

David A. Garvin

When it comes to product quality, American managers still think the competitive problem much less serious than it really is. Because defining the term accurately within a company is so difficult (is quality a measure of performance, for example, or reliability or durability), managers often claim they cannot know how their product quality stacks up against that of their competitors, who may well have chosen an entirely different quality "mix." And since any comparisons are likely to wind up as comparisons of apples with oranges, even a troubling variation in results may reflect only a legitimate variation in strategy. Is there, then, a competitive problem worth worrying about?

I have recently completed a multiyear study of production operations at all but one of the manufacturers of room air conditioners in both the United States and Japan (details of the study are given in Appendix A). Each manufacturer uses a simple assembly-line process; each uses much the same manufacturing equipment; each makes an essentially standardized product. No apples versus oranges here: the comparison is firmly grounded. And although my data come from a single industry, both that industry's manufacturing process and its managers' range of approaches to product quality give these findings a more general applicability.

The shocking news, for which nothing had prepared me, is that the

Author's note: I thank Professor Robert Stobaugh for his helpful comments on an earlier draft, the Division of Research at the Harvard Business School for financial support, and the Nomura School of Advanced Management in Tokyo for arranging and coordinating my trip to Japan.

failure rates of products from the highest-quality producers were between *500* and *1,000* times less than those of products from the lowest. The "between 500 and 1,000" is not a typographical error but an inescapable fact. There is indeed a competitive problem worth worrying about.

Measuring Quality

Exhibit I presents a composite picture of the quality performance of U.S. and Japanese manufacturers of room air conditioners. I have measured quality in two ways: by the incidence of "internal" and of "external" failures. Internal failures include all defects observed (either during fabrication or along the assembly line) before the product leaves the factory; external failures include all problems incurred in the field after the unit has been installed. As a proxy for the latter, I have used the number of service calls recorded during the product's first year of warranty coverage because that was the only period for which U.S. and Japanese manufacturers offered comparable warranties.

Measured by either criterion, Japanese companies were far superior to their U.S. counterparts: their average assembly-line defect rate was almost 70 times lower and their average first-year service call rate nearly 17 times better. Nor can this variation in performance be attributed simply to differences in the number of minor, appearance-related defects. Classifying failures by major functional problems (leaks, electrical) or by component failure rates (compressors, thermostats, fan motors) does not change the results.

More startling, on both internal and external measures, the poorest Japanese company typically had a failure rate less than half that of the best U.S. manufacturer. Even among the U.S. companies themselves, there was considerable variation. Assembly-line defects ranged from 7 to 165 per 100 units—a factor of 20 separating the best performer from the worst—and service call rates varied by a factor of 5.

For ease of analysis, I have grouped the companies studied according to their quality performance (see Appendix B). These groupings illustrate an important point: quality pays. Exhibit II, for example, presents information on assembly-line productivity for each of these categories and shows that the highest-quality producers were also those with the highest output per man-hour. On the basis of the number of direct labor hours actually worked on the assembly line,

*Exhibit I. Quality in the room air conditioning industry 1981–1982**

| | Internal failures | | | | External failures | | | |
| | Fabrication: coil leaks per 100 units | Assembly-line defects per 100 units | | | Service call rate per 100 units under first-year warranty coverage | | | |
		Total	Leaks	Electrical	Total	Compressors	Thermostats	Fan motors
Median								
United States	4.4	63.5	3.1	3.3	10.5†	1.0	1.4	.5
Japan	< .1	.95	.12	.12	.6	.05	.002	.028
Range								
United States	.1–9.0	7–165	1.3–34	.9–34	5.3–26.5	.5–3.4	.4–3.6	.2–2.6
Japan	.03–.4	.15–3.0	.0015–.5	.0015–1.0	.04–2.0	.002–.1	0–.03	.001–.2

*Although most companies reported total failure rates for 1981 or 1982, complete data on component failure rates were often available only for earlier years. For some U.S. companies, 1979 or 1980 figures were employed. Because there was little change in U.S. failure rates during this period, the mixing of data from different years should have little effect.

†Service call rates in the United States normally include calls where no product problems were found ("customer instruction" calls); those in Japan do not. I have adjusted the U.S. median to exclude these calls; without the adjustments, the median U.S. service call rate would be 11.4 per 100 units. Figures for the range should be adjusted similarly, although the necessary data were not available from the U.S. companies with the highest and lowest service call rates.

Exhibit II.   *Quality and productivity*

Grouping of companies by quality performance	Units produced per assembly-line direct labor man-hour actual hours*		Units produced per assembly-line direct labor man-hour standard output†	
	Median	Range	Median	Range
Japanese manufacturers	NA‡	NA	1.8	1.4–3.1
Best U.S. plants	1.7	1.7§	1.7	1.4–1.9
Better U.S. plants	.9	.7–1.0	1.1	.8–1.2
Average U.S. plants	1.0	.6–1.2	1.1	1.1–1.7
Poorest U.S. plants	.35	.35§	1.3	.8–1.6

*Direct labor hours have been adjusted to include only those workers involved in assembly (i.e., where inspectors and repairmen were classified as direct labor, they have been excluded from the totals).

†Computed by using the average cycle time to derive a figure for hourly output, and then dividing by the number of assembly-line direct laborers (excluding inspectors and repairmen) to determine output per man-hour.

‡NA = not available.

§In this quality grouping, man-hour data were only available from a single company.

productivity at the best U.S. companies was five times higher than at the worst.

Measuring productivity by "standard output" (see Exhibit II) blurs the picture somewhat. Although the Japanese plants maintain a slight edge over the best U.S. plants, categories of performance tend to overlap. The figures based on standard output, however, are rather imperfect indicators of productivity—for example, they fail to include overtime or rework hours and so overstate productivity levels, particularly at the poorer companies, which devote more of their time to correcting defects. Thus, these figures have less significance than do those based on the number of hours actually worked.

Note carefully that the strong association between productivity and quality is not explained by differences in technology or capital intensity, for most of the plants employed similar manufacturing techniques. This was especially true of final assembly, where manual operations, such as hand brazing and the insertion of color-coded wires, were the norm. Japanese plants did use some automated transfer lines

Exhibit III.   Quality and costs

Grouping of companies by quality performance	Warranty costs as a percentage of sales*		Total cost of quality (Japanese companies) and total failure costs (U.S. companies) as a percentage of sales†	
	Median	Range	Median	Range
Japanese manufacturers	.6%	.2–1.0%	1.3%	.7–2.0%
Best U.S. plants	1.8	1.1–2.4	2.8	2.7–2.8
Better U.S. plants	2.4	1.7–3.1	3.4	3.3–3.5
Average U.S. plants	2.2	1.7–4.3	3.9	2.3–5.6
Poorest U.S. plants	5.2%	3.3–7.0%	> 5.8%	4.4–>7.2%

*Because most Japanese air conditioners are covered by a three-year warranty while most U.S. units are covered by a warranty of five years, these figures somewhat overstate the Japanese advantage. The bias is unlikely to be serious, however, because second- to fifth-year coverage in the United States and second- to third-year coverage in Japan are much less inclusive—and therefore, less expensive—than first-year coverage. For example, at U.S. companies second- to fifth-year warranty costs average less than one-fifth of first-year expenses.

†Total cost of quality is the sum of all quality-related expenditures, including the costs of prevention, inspection, rework, scrap, and warranties. The Japanese figures include expenditures in all of these categories while the U.S. figures, because of limited data, include only the costs of rework, scrap, and warranties (failure costs). As a result, these figures understate total U.S. quality costs relative to those of the Japanese.

and packaging equipment, but only in compressor manufacturing and case welding was the difference in automation significant.

The association between cost and quality is equally strong. Reducing field failures means lower warranty costs, and reducing factory defects cuts expenditures on rework and scrap. As Exhibit III shows, the Japanese manufacturers incurred warranty costs averaging 0.6% of sales; at the best American companies, the figure was 1.8%; at the worst 5.2%.

In theory, low warranty costs might be offset by high expenditures on defect prevention: a company could spend enough on product pretesting or on inspecting assembled units before shipment to wipe out any gains from improved warranty costs. Figures on the total costs of quality, however, which include expenditures on prevention and inspection as well as the usual failure costs of rework, scrap, and warranties, lead to the opposite conclusion. In fact, the total costs of quality incurred by Japanese producers were less than one-half the failure costs incurred by the best U.S. companies.

The reason is clear: failures are much more expensive to fix after a unit has been assembled than before. The cost of the extra hours spent pretesting a design is cheap compared with the cost of a product recall; similarly, field service costs are much higher than those of incoming inspection. Among manufacturers of room air conditioners, the Japanese—even with their strong commitment to design review, vendor selection and management, and in-process inspection—still have the lowest overall quality costs.

Nor are the opportunities for reduction in quality costs confined to this industry alone. A recent survey[1] of U.S. companies in ten manufacturing sectors found that total quality costs averaged 5.8% of sales—for a $1 billion corporation, some $58 million per year primarily in scrap, rework, and warranty expenses. Shaving even a tenth of a percentage point off these costs would result in an annual saving of $1 million.

Other studies, which use the PIMS data base, have demonstrated a further connection among quality, market share, and return on investment.[2] Not only does good quality yield a higher ROI for any given market share (among businesses with less than 12% of the market, those with inferior product quality averaged an ROI of 4.5%, those with average product quality an ROI of 10.4%, and those with superior product quality an ROI of 17.4%); it also leads directly to market share gains. Those businesses in the PIMS study that improved in quality during the 1970s increased their market share five to six times faster than those that declined—and three times faster than those whose quality remained unchanged.

The conclusion is inescapable: improving product quality is a profitable activity. For managers, therefore, the central question must be: What makes for successful quality management?

Sources of Quality

Evidence from the room air conditioning industry points directly to the practices that the quality leaders, both Japanese and American, have employed. Each of these areas of effort—quality programs, policies, and attitudes; information systems; product design; production and work force policies; and vendor management—has helped in some way to reduce defects and lower field failures.

PROGRAMS, POLICIES, AND ATTITUDES

The importance a company attaches to product quality often shows up in the standing of its quality department. At the poorest performing plants in the industry, the quality control (QC) manager invariably reported to the director of manufacturing or engineering. Access to top management came, if at all, through these go-betweens, who often had very different priorities from those of the QC manager. At the best U.S. companies, especially those with low service call rates, the quality department had more visibility. Several companies had vice presidents of quality; at the factory level each head of QC reported directly to the plant manager. Japanese QC managers also reported directly to their plant managers.

Of course, reporting relationships alone do not explain the observed differences in quality performance. They do indicate, however, the seriousness that management attaches to quality problems. It's one thing to say you believe in defect-free products, but quite another to take time from a busy schedule to act on that belief and stay informed. At the U.S. company with the lowest service call rate, the president met weekly with all corporate vice presidents to review the latest service call statistics. Nobody at that company needed to ask whether quality was a priority of upper management.

How often these meetings occurred was as important as their cast of characters. Mistakes do not fix themselves; they have to be identified, diagnosed, and then resolved through corrective action. The greater the frequency of meetings to review quality performance, the fewer undetected errors. The U.S. plants with the lowest assembly-line defect rates averaged ten such meetings per month; at all other U.S. plants, the average was four. The Japanese companies reviewed defect rates daily.

Meetings and corrective action programs will succeed, however, only if they are backed by genuine top-level commitment. In Japan, this commitment was deeply ingrained and clearly communicated. At four of the six companies surveyed, first-line supervisors believed product quality—not producing at low cost, meeting the production schedule, or improving worker productivity—was management's top manufacturing priority. At the other two, quality ranked a close second.

The depth of this commitment became evident in the Japanese practice of creating internal consumer review boards. Each of the Japanese producers had assembled a group of employees whose primary function was to act as typical consumers and test and evaluate products. Sometimes the products came randomly from the day's production; more frequently, they represented new designs. In each case, the group had final authority over product release. The message here was unmistakable: the customer—not the design staff, the marketing team, or the production group—had to be satisfied with a product's quality before it was considered acceptable for shipment.

By contrast, U.S. companies showed a much weaker commitment to product quality. At 9 of the 11 U.S. plants, first-line supervisors told me that their managers attached far more importance to meeting the production schedule than to any other manufacturing objective. Even the best performers showed no consistent relationship between failure rates and supervisors' perceptions of manufacturing priorities.

What commitment there was stemmed from the inclusion (or absence) of quality in systems of performance appraisal. Two of the three companies with the highest rates of assembly-line defects paid their workers on the basis of total output, not defect-free output. Is it any wonder these employees viewed defects as being of little consequence? Not surprisingly, domestic producers with low failure rates evaluated both supervisors and managers on the quality of output— supervisors, in terms of defect rates, scrap rates, and the amount of rework attributable to their operations; managers, in terms of service call rates and their plants' total costs of quality.

These distinctions make good sense. First-line supervisors play a pivotal role in managing the production process, which is responsible for internal failures, but have little control over product design, the quality of incoming materials, or other factors that affect field performance. These require the attention of higher level managers, who can legitimately be held responsible for coordinating the activities of design, purchasing, and other functional groups in pursuit of fewer service calls or reduced warranty expenses.

To obtain consistent improvement, a formal system of goal setting is necessary.[3] Only three U.S. plants set annual targets for reducing field failures. Between 1978 and 1981, these three were the only ones to cut their service call rates by more than 25%; most of the other U.S.

plants showed little or no change. All the Japanese companies, however, consistently improved their quality—in several cases, by as much as 50%—and all had elaborate companywide systems of goal setting.

From the corporate level at these companies came vague policy pronouncements ("this year, let the customer determine our quality"), which were further defined by division heads ("reduced service call rates are necessary if we are to lower costs") and by middle managers ("compressor failures are an especially serious problem that must be addressed"). Actual quantitative goals ("improve compressor reliability by 10%") were often set by foremen or workers operating through quality control circles. The collaborative nature of this goal-setting process helped these targets earn wide support.

At the final—or first—level of goal setting, specificity matters. Establishing an overall target for an assembly-line defect rate without specifying more detailed goals by problem category, such as leaks or electrical problems, is unlikely to produce much improvement. A number of U.S. plants have tried this approach and failed. Domestic producers with the lowest defect rates set their overall goals last. Each inspection point along the assembly line had a target of its own, which was agreed on by representatives of the quality and manufacturing departments. The sum of these individual targets established the overall goal for the assembly line. As a result, responsibility for quality became easier to assign and progress easier to monitor.

INFORMATION SYSTEMS

Successful monitoring of quality assumes that the necessary data are available, which is not always true. Without specific and timely information on defects and field failures, improvements in quality are seldom possible. Not surprisingly, at the poorest U.S. companies information on defects and field failures was virtually nonexistent. Assembly-line defects and service call rates were seldom reported. "Epidemic" failures (problems that a large proportion of all units had in common) were widespread. Design flaws remained undetected. At one domestic producer, nearly a quarter of all 1979–1981 warranty expenses came from problems with a single type of compressor.

Other companies reported more extensive quality information—daily and weekly defect rates as well as quarterly and, occasionally, monthly service call rates. These variations in the level of reporting detail correlated closely with differences in quality performance.

Among average U.S. performers, for example, quality reports were quite general. Data on assembly line defects gave no breakdowns by inspection point; data on field failures were for entire product lines, not for separate models. Without further refinement, such data cannot isolate quality problems.

A 10% failure rate for a product line can mean a number of things: that all models in the line fail to perform 10% of the time, with no single problem standing out; that several models have a 5% failure rate and one a 30% rate, which suggests a single problem of epidemic proportions; or anything in between. There is no way of distinguishing these cases on the basis of aggregate data alone. What is true of goal setting is equally true of reporting systems: success requires mastering the details.

The best U.S. companies reported defect rates for each inspection point on the assembly line and field failure rates by individual model. The Japanese not only collected information that their U.S. counterparts ignored, such as failure rates in the later years of a product's life; they also insisted on extreme precision in reporting. At one company, repairmen had to submit reports on every defective unit they fixed. In general, it was not unusual for Japanese managers to be able to identify the 30 different ways in which Switch X had failed on Model Y during the last several years. Nor did they have to wait for such information.

Service call statistics in the United States took anywhere from one month to one year to make the trip from the field to the factory; in Japan, the elapsed time averaged between one week and one month. Differences in attitude are part of the explanation. As the director of quality at one Japanese company observed, field information reached his company's U.S. subsidiaries much more slowly than it did operations in Japan—even though both employed the same system for collecting and reporting data.

PRODUCT DESIGN

Room air conditioners are relatively standardized products. Although basic designs in the United States have changed little in recent years, pressures to improve energy efficiency and to reduce costs have resulted in a stream of minor changes. On the whole, these changes have followed a common pattern: the initiative came from marketing;

Exhibit IV. Quality and product stability

Grouping of companies by quality performance	Median number of design changes per year	Median number of models	Median number of design changes per model*	Median percentage that peak production exceeded low production†
Japanese manufacturers	NA‡	80	NA	170%
Best U.S. plants	43	56	.8	27
Better U.S. plants	150	81	1.9	63
Average U.S. plants	400	126	3.2	50
Poorest U.S. plants	133	41	3.2	100%

*Column 1 divided by column 2.

†The figures in this column were derived by dividing each plant's largest daily output for the year by its smallest (non-zero) output for the year.

‡NA = not available.

engineering determined the actual changes to be made and then pretested the new design; quality control, manufacturing, purchasing, and other affected departments signed off; and, where necessary, prototypes and pilot production units were built.

What did differ among companies was the degree of design and production stability. As Exhibit IV indicates, the U.S. plants with the lowest failure rates made far fewer design changes than did their competitors.

Exhibit IV conveys an important message. Variety, at least in America, is often the enemy of quality. Product proliferation and constant design change may keep the marketing department happy, but failure rates tend to rise as well. By contrast, a limited product line ensures that workers are more familiar with each model and less likely to make mistakes. Reducing the number of design changes allows workers to devote more attention to each one. Keeping production level means less reliance on a second shift staffed by inexperienced employees.

The Japanese, however, have achieved low failure rates even with relatively broad product lines and rapidly changing designs. In the room air conditioning industry, new designs account for nearly a third of all models offered each year, far more than in the United States. The secret: an emphasis on reliability engineering and on careful shakedowns of new designs before they are released.

Reliability engineering is nothing new; it has been practiced by the aerospace industry in this country for at least 20 years. In practice, it involves building up designs from their basic components, determining the failure probabilities of individual systems and subsystems, and then trying to strengthen the weak links in the chain by product redesign or by incorporating more reliable parts. Much of the effort is focused up front, when a product is still in blueprint or prototype form. Managers use statistical techniques to predict reliability over the product's life and subject preliminary designs to exhaustive stress and life testing to collect information on potential failure modes. These data form the basis for continual product improvement.

Only one American maker of room air conditioners practiced reliability engineering, and its failure rates were among the lowest observed. All of the Japanese companies, however, placed considerable emphasis on these techniques. Their designers were, for example, under tremendous pressure to reduce the number of parts per unit; for a basic principle of reliability engineering is that, everything else being equal, the fewer the parts, the lower the failure rate.

Japanese companies worked just as hard to increase reliability through changes in components. They were aided by the Industrial Engineering Bureau of Japan's Ministry of International Trade and Industry (MITI), which required that all electric and electronic components sold in the country be tested for reliability and have their ratings on file at the bureau. Because this information was publicly available, designers no longer needed to test components themselves in order to establish reliability ratings.

An emphasis on reliability engineering is also closely tied to a more thorough review of new designs before units reach production. American manufacturers usually built and tested a single prototype before moving to pilot production; the Japanese often repeated the process three or four times.

Moreover, all affected departments—quality control, purchasing, manufacturing, service, and design engineering—played an active role at each stage of the review process. American practice gave over the early stages of the design process almost entirely to engineering. By the time other groups got their say, the process had gained momentum, schedules had been established, and changes had become difficult to make. As a result, many a product that performed well in the laboratory created grave problems on the assembly line or in the field.

PRODUCTION AND WORK FORCE POLICIES

The key to defect-free production is a manufacturing process that is "in control"—machinery and equipment well maintained, workplaces clean and orderly, workers well trained, and inspection procedures suited to the rapid detection of deviations. In each of these areas, the Japanese were noticeably ahead of their American competitors.

Training of the labor force, for example, was extensive, even for employees engaged in simple jobs. At most of the Japanese companies, preparing new assembly-line workers took approximately six months, for they were first trained for all jobs on the line. American workers received far less instruction (from several hours to several days) and were usually trained for a single task. Not surprisingly, Japanese workers were much more adept at tracking down quality problems originating at other work stations and far better equipped to propose remedial action.

Instruction in statistical quality control techniques supplemented the other training offered Japanese workers. Every Japanese plant relied heavily on these techniques for controlling its production process. Process control charts, showing the acceptable quality standards of various fabrication and assembly-line operations, were everywhere in general use. Only one U.S. plant—the one with the lowest defect rate—had made a comparable effort to determine the capabilities of its production process and to chart the results.

Still, deviations will occur, and thorough and timely inspection is necessary to ferret them out quickly. Japanese companies therefore employed an inspector for every 7.1 assembly-line workers (in the United States the ratio was 1:9.5). The primary role of these inspectors was to monitor the production process for stability; they were less "gatekeepers," weeding out defective units before shipment, than providers of information. Their tasks were considered especially important where manual operations were common and where inspection required sophisticated testing of a unit's operating characteristics.

On balance, then, the Japanese advantage in production came less from revolutionary technology than from close attention to basic skills and to the reduction of all unwanted variations in the manufacturing process. In practice, this approach can produce dramatic results. Although new model introductions and assembly-line changeovers at American companies boosted defect rates, at least until workers became familiar with their new assignments, Japanese companies experienced no such problems.

Before every new model introduction, Japanese assembly-line workers were thoroughly trained in their new tasks. After-hours seminars explained the product to the work force, and trial runs were common. During changeovers, managers kept workers informed of the models slated for production each day, either through announcements at early morning meetings or by sending assembled versions of the new model down the line 30 minutes before the change was to take place, together with a big sign saying "this model comes next." American workers generally received much less information about changeovers. At the plant with the highest defect rate in the industry, communication about changeovers was limited to a single small chalkboard, listing the models to be produced each day, placed at one end of the assembly line.

The Japanese system of permanent employment also helped to improve quality. Before they are fully trained, new workers often commit unintentional errors. Several American companies observed that their workers' inexperience and lack of familiarity with the product line contributed to their high defect rates. The Japanese, with low absenteeism and turnover, faced fewer problems of this sort. Japanese plants had a median turnover of 3.1%; the comparable figure for U.S. plants was two times higher. Even more startling were the figures on absenteeism: a median of 3.1% for American companies and *zero* for the Japanese.

In addition, because several of the U.S. plants were part of larger manufacturing complexes linked by a single union, they suffered greatly from "bumping." A layoff in one part of the complex would result in multiple job changes as workers shifted among plants to protect seniority rights. Employees whose previous experience was with another product would suddenly find themselves assembling room air conditioners. Sharp increases in defects were the inevitable result.

VENDOR MANAGEMENT

Without acceptable components and materials, no manufacturer can produce high-quality products. As computer experts have long recognized, "garbage in" means "garbage out." Careful selection and monitoring of vendors is therefore a necessary first step toward ensuring reliable and defect-free production.

At the better U.S. companies, the quality department played a major role in vendor selection by tempering the views of the engineering ("do their samples meet our technical specifications") and purchasing ("is that the best we can do on price") departments. At the very best companies, however, purchasing departments independently ranked quality as their primary objective. Buyers received instruction in the concepts of quality control; at least one person had special responsibility for vendor quality management; goals were set for the quality of incoming components and materials; and vendors' shipments were carefully monitored.

Purchasing departments at the worst U.S. companies viewed their mission more narrowly: to obtain the lowest possible price for technically acceptable components. Site visits to new vendors were rarely made, and members of the purchasing department seldom got involved in the design review process. Because incoming inspection was grossly understaffed (at one plant, two workers were responsible for reviewing 14,000 incoming shipments per year), production pressures often allowed entire lots to come to the assembly line uninspected. Identification of defective components came, if at all, only after they had been incorporated into completed units. Inevitably, scrap and rework costs soared.

In several Japanese companies incoming materials arrived directly at the assembly line without inspection. New vendors, however, first had to pass rigorous tests: their products initially received 100% inspection. Once all problems were corrected, sampling inspection became the norm. Only after an extended period without a rejection were vendors allowed to send their products directly to the assembly line. At the first sign of deterioration in vendor performance, more intensive inspection resumed.

In this environment, inspection was less an end in itself than a means to an end. Receiving inspectors acted less as policemen than as quality consultants to the vendor. Site visits, for example, were mandatory when managers were assessing potential suppliers and continued for as long as the companies did business together. Even more revealing, the selection of vendors depended as much on management philosophy, manufacturing capability, and depth of commitment to quality as on price and delivery performance.

Closing the Gap

What, then, is to be done? Are American companies hopelessly behind in the battle for superior quality? Or is an effective counterattack possible?

Although the evidence is still fragmentary, there are a number of encouraging signs. In 1980, when Hewlett-Packard tested 300,000 semiconductors from three U.S. and three Japanese suppliers, the Japanese chips had a failure rate one-sixth that of the American chips. When the test was repeated two years later, the U.S. companies had virtually closed the gap. Similar progress is evident in automobiles. Ford's Ranger trucks, built in Louisville, Tennessee, offer an especially dramatic example. In just three years, the number of "concerns" registered by the Louisville plant (the automaker's measure of quality deficiencies as recorded at monthly audits) dropped to less than one-third its previous high. Today, the Ranger's quality is nearly equal that of Toyota's SR5, its chief Japanese rival.

But in these industries, as with room air conditioners, quality improvement takes time. The "quick fix" provides few lasting gains. What is needed is a long-term commitment to the fundamentals— working with vendors to improve their performance, educating and training the work force, developing an accurate and responsive quality information system, setting targets for quality improvement, and demonstrating interest and commitment at the very highest levels of management. With their companies' futures on the line, managers can do no less.

Notes

1. "Quality Cost Survey," *Quality*, June 1977, p. 20.
2. Sidney Schoeffler, Robert D. Buzzell, and Donald F. Heany, "Impact of Strategic Planning on Profit Performance," *Harvard Business Review*, March–April 1974, p. 137; and Robert D. Buzzell and Frederik D. Wiersema, "Successful Share-Building Strategies," *Harvard Business Review*, January–February 1981, p. 135.
3. For a summary of evidence on this point, see Edwin A. Locke et al., "Goal Setting and Task Performance: 1969–1980," *Psychological Bulletin*, vol. 90, no. 1, p. 125.

Appendix A

Research Methods

This article is based mainly on data collected in 1981 and 1982 from U.S. and Japanese manufacturers of room air conditioners. I selected that industry for study for a number of reasons; it contains companies of varying size and character, which implies a wide range of quality policies and performance; its products are standardized, which facilitates inter-company comparisons; and it employs a simple assembly-line process, which is representative of many other mass production industries.

Nine of the ten U.S. companies in the industry and all seven of the Japanese companies participated in the study. They range in size from small air conditioning specialists with total sales of under $50 million to large home appliance manufacturers with annual sales of more than $200 million in this product line alone. Taken together, they account for approximately 90% of U.S. industry shipments and 100% of Japanese industry shipments. I have collected data separately for each plant (two of the American companies operate two plants apiece; otherwise, each company employs only a single plant). Of the 18 plants studied, 11 are American and 7 Japanese.

Once U.S. companies agreed to participate in the study, I sent them a questionnaire requesting background information on their product line, production practices, vendor management practices, quality policies, and quality performance. I then visited them all in order to review the questionnaire results, collect additional data, tour the factories, and conduct interviews with key personnel. The interviews were open-ended and unstructured, although I posed similar questions at each company. A typical visit included interviews with managers in the quality, manufacturing, purchasing, engineering, and service departments, as well as several hours spent walking the production floor.

Preliminary analysis of the interviews and questionnaires showed that companies neither employed the same conventions in reporting data nor answered questions in the same degree of detail. I therefore sent each company its own set of follow-up questions to fill in these gaps and to make the data more comparable across companies. In addition, I requested each company to administer a brief questionnaire on quality attitudes to each of its first-line supervisors.

I followed a similar approach with the Japanese manufacturers, although time constraints limited the amount of information that I could collect. All questionnaires were first translated into Japanese and mailed to the participating companies. Six of the seven companies completed the same basic quality questionnaire as did their American counterparts; the same companies also administered the survey on quality attitudes to a small number of their first-line supervisors. With the aid of a translator, I conducted on-site interviews at all the companies and toured six of the plants.

Appendix B

Classifying Plants by Quality Performance

To identify patterns of behavior, I first grouped U.S. plants into categories according to their quality performance on two dimensions—internal quality (defect rates in the factory) and external quality (failure rates in the field).

Table A. *Field performance for U.S. plants in 1981*

Plant	Service call rate, first-year warranty coverage		Service call rate less "customer instruction" calls	
	Percentage	Rank	Percentage	Rank
I	5.3%	I	< 5.3%	I
2	8.7	2	< 8.7	2,3
3	9.2	3	5.6	2,3
4	10.5	4	9.8	5
5	11.1	5	9.3	4
6	11.4	6	10.5	6
7	12.6	7	10.5	6
8	16.2	8	11.8	8
9	17.5	9	13.8	9
10	22.9	10	< 22.9	10
11	26.5%	11	< 26.5%	11

	Ranking of plants on field performance external quality		
	Good	Average	Poor
Plant number	1,2,3	4,5,6,7,8	9,10,11

Table A presents the basic data on external quality. I measured field performance in two ways: by the service call rate for units under first-year warranty coverage (the total number of service calls recorded in 1981 divided by the number of units in the field with active first-year warranties) and by the service call rate for units under first-year warranty coverage less "customer instruction calls" (only those service calls that resulted from a faulty unit, not from a customer who was using the unit improperly or had failed to install it correctly).

The second measure was necessary because companies differed in their policies toward customer instruction calls. Some reimbursed repairmen for these calls without argument; others did their best to

Table B.   *Internal quality for U.S. plants in 1981*

Plant	Assembly-line defects per 100 units		Assembly-line defects per 100 units requiring off-line repair		Repairmen per assembly-line direct laborer	
	Number	Rank	Number	Rank	Number	Rank
1	150	9	34	5,6	.06	3
2	7	1	7	1	.05	2
3	10	2	10	3	.04	1
4	NA*	NA	NA	NA	.09	8
5	57	5	47	7	.13	9
6	70	6	67	8	.06	3
7	26	4	7	1	.08	6
8	18	3	11	4	.08	6
9	> 100	7	> 30	5,6	.16	11
10	165	10	165	10	.13	9
11	135	8	> 68	9	.07	5

*NA = not available.

	Ranking of plants on internal quality		
	Good	Average	Poor
Plant number	2,3,7,8	1,4(?),5,6	9,10,11

eliminate such calls completely. An accurate assessment of product performance required the separation of these calls from problems that reflect genuinely defective units.

I classified plants on the basis of their rankings on the second of the two measures in Table A, and then grouped them according to their actual levels of field failures. In most cases, the dividing lines were clear, although there were some borderline cases. Plant 8, for example, had a total service call rate well above the industry median, yet after subtracting customer instruction calls, its failure rate differed little from the other average performers. Because this second figure

Table C. Classification of plants on internal and external quality

		External quality			
		Poor	**Fair**	**Good**	**Excellent**
Poor U.S. plants ■	**Internal quality**				
Average U.S. plants ■	**Poor**	Plants 9, 10, 11			
Better U.S. plants ▢	**Fair**		Plants 4, 5, 6	Plant 1	
Best U.S. plants ▨	**Good**		Plants 7, 8	Plants 2, 3	
	Excellent				All Japanese plants

more accurately reflects the rate of product malfunction, I treated Plant 8 as having average, rather than poor, external quality. A number of companies with high failure rates did not break out customer instruction calls. I have treated them as having poor external quality because their customer instruction calls would have to have been two or three times as frequent as the highest rate recorded in 1981 for them to have warranted an average ranking.

I followed a similar procedure in classifying plants on internal quality. Because companies differed in how they defined and recorded defects (some noted every single product flaw; others were interested only in major malfunctions), I employed several indexes to ensure consistency. The results are displayed in Table B. I ranked companies first by their total assembly-line defect rates (every defect recorded at every station along the assembly line divided by the number of units produced) and then by the number of defects requiring off-line repair. The second index compensates for the different definitions just noted, for it more accurately reflects the incidence of serious problems. Minor adjustments and touch-ups can generally be made without pulling a unit off the line; more serious problems normally require off-line repair. Measured on this basis, the high total defect rates of Plants 1 and 9 appear to be much less of a problem.

Because several companies had to estimate the off-line repair rate, I used a third index, the number of repairmen per assembly-line direct laborer, to measure defect seriousness. The proportion of the work force engaged in repair activities, including workers assigned to separate rework lines and to rework activities in the warehouse, is likely to correlate well with the incidence of serious defects, for more serious problems usually require more time to correct and necessitate a larger repair staff. This measure provides important additional information, confirming the conclusions about Plant 1 (its high total defect rate appears to include a large number of minor problems) but contradicting those about Plant 9 (its large number of repairmen suggests that defects are, in fact, a serious problem, despite the small proportion of units requiring off-line repair).

I assigned plants to groups using much the same procedure as before. I first computed a composite ranking for each plant by averaging together the three rankings of Table B. Dividing lines between groups followed the absolute levels of the indexes for each plant. Once again, some judgment was involved, particularly for Plants 4, 5, and 9. Plants 5 and 9 were borderline cases, candidates for ranking as either average or poor internal quality. I classified the former as average, even though its overall rank was low, because its absolute scores on the first two measures were quite close to the median. I classified the latter as poor because its absolute scores on both the first and the third measures were so high. Plant 4 presented a different problem, for it provided no information at all on assembly-line defects. Rather than classifying the plant on the basis of the third index alone, I employed supplementary data. Based on its defect rate at the end-of-the-line quality audit and its rework and scrap costs as a percentage of sales, both of which were quite close to figures reported by other companies with average internal quality, Plant 4 showed up as an average performer.

Table C combines the results of the previous two tables. Overall quality rankings appear for each plant. In most cases, success on internal quality implied success on external measures, although the correlation is not perfect, as Plants 1, 7, and 8 demonstrate. The Japanese plants are in a category of their own, for on both internal and external measures they are at least twice as good as the best U.S. plant.

5
Wrestling with Jellyfish

Richard J. Boyle

Many organizations today want to break out of the beat-'em-up school of management and move toward a more participative management style. Managers raised in a less enlightened manner may have difficulty operating under a new set of rules.

At Honeywell, we have been working to change from what I call the Patton style of management to a more collaborative way of operating. We are still in the midst of this process. The way we manage people is still less than perfect. But now our employees can have a real share of the action rather than feeling blocked or frustrated by a rigid bureaucracy. And the results, both in quantifiable terms of productivity improvement and in less measurable terms of work climate and quality of innovation, have been extremely positive.

I'd like to share my observations about the changing of Honeywell's management style, the difficulties we encountered along the way, and the solutions we employed to bring us where we are today. Understanding our mistakes is crucial to understanding our story, because some of the mistakes were an integral part of our evolution. In other words, making participation an organic way of working had to come about through an organic process—at least in our organization. Taking a cookbook approach or bringing in executive quick-change artists would not have achieved the same results. On the other hand, I don't

Author's note: I would like to recognize the many valuable contributions of Rosabeth Kanter of Yale University and of Goodmeasure, Inc. particularly for her insights into the new demands of management in the 1980s. I would also like to thank Charlie Quimby of Honeywell and Tana Pesso of Goodmeasure who were very helpful in making the article so readable.

believe others must repeat our mistakes to share our central discovery—that the participative process must be managed.

We made this discovery between 1980 and 1982 in a division of Honeywell now called the Defense and Marine Systems Group (then the Defense Systems Division). That division has since expanded and reorganized as a group of divisions, in part because of the success it has achieved in the past several years. The group has about 8,000 employees concentrated in Minnesota, California, and Washington. It represents roughly 10% of Honeywell's people and 12% of Honeywell's $6 billion in revenues. About half of the group's population is in the Minneapolis area, where Honeywell has its corporate headquarters and several other large operations.

The group's defense business includes making torpedoes, ammunition, and other weapons for the U.S. military as well as designing computer-based training systems. Our commercial business is aimed at the offshore oil and maritime industries, for which we provide services and produce drilling vessel stabilization systems and undersea robots and television cameras. We also offer engineering services, primarily in water resource management. Our work force is a highly educated, highly motivated group of people. About one in five is an engineer. The group's 1,600 factory employees in Minneapolis are unionized. It is common to find employees with 20 years' tenure in the older divisions.

Patton-style Management

When I began my career at Honeywell in the late 1950s and as I advanced to more senior positions, steely, no-nonsense executives were the norm. Many examples of their autocratic management are permanently blazed in corporate legend. One "productivity initiative" from those days (long since reversed) was the removal of bathroom stall doors to discourage reading on company time. Today's middle and upper managers were trained during that period, and getting them to commit themselves to a new management style was no simple matter. After all, why should they trade their pearl-handled revolvers for a copy of *The One Minute Manager* when a swift, Patton-like kick took only a few seconds?

Employees had seen many management improvement programs come and go. Honeywell's paternalistic organization had taken care of its employees, who were only sporadically encouraged to demonstrate initiative. And when they did so, urged on by some program or other, they often found that the system set up to exhort them to excellence wasn't really equipped to tolerate innovation. The suggestion system was used primarily in the factory, and its success was due more to a handful of prolific suggesters than to broad-based participation. In general, employees greeted management efforts to improve productivity with a fair amount of cynicism. People just did their jobs. To be sure, not all employees hesitated to come forward with ideas, and not all managers were Pattons. But the management culture generally encouraged a dominant-passive relationship between superiors and subordinates.

Several factors dissuaded me from following the Patton role model. Certainly one was that I hadn't enjoyed my own exposure to autocratic managers. But two others were more significant.

From 1974 to 1981 I headed a unit that grew from about 70 employees to 1,000. We didn't consciously choose a management style during that period of rapid growth. We didn't start from a set of assumptions that said, "This is the right way to manage our business." We experimented with all kinds of ideas. We kept the things that worked and discarded those that didn't. During those years I began to see that an ad hoc style of management could work. Perhaps we selected people who would be effective under a less rigid style of operating. For whatever reasons, the unit was very successful, and people liked working there.

Raising four children and watching them grow also influenced my thinking about participative management. I learned a great deal from my family about what people need to develop and feel happy. My family also helped me understand what values are important and showed me that a more open management style could support many of the human relations goals that I believe are important in organizational life.

Beginnings of Change

These experiences persuaded me that a new management style could work in a large and complex organization. In early 1981, when I became vice president and general manager of the Defense and Marine Systems Group, I got the chance to find out for sure.

My predecessor at the group, Matt Sutton, who is now group vice president of Honeywell's other aerospace and defense group, had already made a commitment to greater employee involvement to increase productivity and improve the work climate in the organization. Quality circles of unionized hourly employees had been in place since 1978. In 1980 Matt had identified seven principles that summarized for him the way the business ought to be conducted in a people-centered management culture (see "Honeywell's New Way of Managing"). Knowing that expressing the principles was only a first step, Matt instructed his staff to translate them into practice. The project was organized under the name "Managing Today's Workforce," and a task team composed of salaried employees from all levels of the organization was formed to address each principle.

Honeywell's New Way of Managing: Seven Principles

Productivity is a responsibility shared by management and the employee.

Broadened employee participation in decision making will be fostered.

Teamwork, mutual respect, and a sense of ownership will be promoted at all levels of the division.

Good performance is expected, and achievement will be rewarded.

A positive climate for career growth will be supported throughout the division.

The best affordable equipment and facilities required to meet job and employee needs will be provided.

Work life and personal life have interacting needs that will be recognized.

The task teams produced a rather hefty set of conditions that defined what the principles would look like in reality. But between the theory and its implementation lay a great deal of uncharted territory. There was no action plan, no sense of how we would get there from here. The findings of the seven teams had four areas in common: performance appraisal, career development, communications and involvement, and quality of work life. In 1980 we formed four teams that corresponded with these areas of concern. Simultaneously but independently, two other teams came into being, one responsible for pay and the other for equal employment opportunity and affirmative action.

Each new team was instructed to use the earlier teams' findings as a base from which to recommend specific actions. In some cases, teams' implied charters were straightforward: design a new pay system that rewards excellence and encourages high achievement; reverse the high turnover and dissatisfaction among minority employees; formalize a career development process. Other teams, however, faced ill-defined or impossibly large challenges: improve communication and employee involvement; promote quality of work life.

That some teams had to deal with issues that were overwhelming is evident only in hindsight. At the time I came into the picture, things seemed to be moving in the right direction. Within six months, many problems with this way of managing (or rather not managing) participation had become apparent. Meanwhile, we had some operational problems that needed attention as well.

For instance, we had been experiencing substantial losses in one major program that were related in part to the management culture we had developed. Over the years, we had generally stomped on the bearers of bad tidings. Naturally, no one was enthusiastic about being the messenger, so employees adapted by controlling and shaping the project information that management received. A certain amount of frenzy went on behind the scenes at lower levels to solve problems, and some serious matters were hidden from top management. The messengers were more concerned about their own survival than the survival of the project.

We quickly found that it would be in everybody's interest to develop a less confrontational management style. And people were hungry for more involvement. As the Managing Today's Workforce initiatives spread through the organization, task teams began to proliferate. Hopes were high.

Participation Amok

It soon became apparent that we had no idea how many task teams we had, what problems they were addressing, how much they cost, and whether they were worth it.

In 1981 we did an inventory of the task teams, and the results gave us our first clue that the whole affair might be running amok. We counted about 200 "task teams" in existence. Some of these were actually quality circles, and we may have missed others because the people responding didn't share a common understanding of what a task team was.

Two hundred seemed a lot of teams, but we had no idea what the right number should be. Many of the teams seemed to be addressing real problems, about a third were investigating problems in the category of "interesting, but so what?" and a few teams looked like a total waste of everybody's time and effort. We had a variety of computer committees. Each building had a parking committee. Task teams and committees with overlapping jurisdictions for safety and hazardous materials abounded. No attempts to regulate duplication were made, and there was very little communication among teams.

At one point, we conducted a random survey of 39 groups and discovered that one-quarter of the participants on these teams were middle managers or above and that supervisors and managers accounted for more than half the committee time per month. Nearly half the team members came from the engineering department. Without even pulling out a calculator, we could see that the costs were enormous. We had not been managing the process at a grass-roots level. Anyone could start a task team for any reason, commandeer any combination of people, and spend any amount of time reinventing the wheel.

Nor, we soon learned, had we done an adequate job of managing the six officially sanctioned task teams. What had originally seemed like clear marching orders turned out for some teams to be equivocal. Some teams had no clear reporting relationship to the formal organization, and their charters and operating procedures were vague. Questions arose that had no clear answers. Do we make recommendations only? Or do we go ahead and implement our plans? If we don't implement them, who will? When do we report? How will we know when we've completed our work? What approvals do we need for what actions? Do we define the issue we are addressing, or must we accept the definition implicit in the work of the previous task teams? Do we have any responsibility to monitor ongoing activities that result from our recommendations? What if top management doesn't like what we recommend?

Although the task teams nominally reported to an advisory committee headed by the director of employee relations, this body had not established consistent guidelines either. Like the task teams, the advisory committee never clarified its own functions and authority or the proper direction for the general effort to increase participation.

Looking back on those early days, the following mistakes seem critical:

- We had set no ground rules for task teams and their chairs.
- We failed to clarify—to the task team managers and to the committee itself—the functions and role of the advisory committee.
- We did not establish accountabilities, standards, timetables, and deadlines for the task teams.
- The overall activity was too isolated from the main business of the division. Teams had little visibility, and employees regarded them with considerable skepticism.
- No common committee or mechanism linked the task teams. Attempts to avoid overlapping tasks and to communicate among teams were atypical, not part of an overall strategy.
- Some task team chairpersons developed too strong a sense of project ownership. "Their" programs seemed to become the team's reasons for being, and the team members were regarded as subordinates.
- Some teams forgot that they were supposed to represent the entire organization and that other parties had a stake in what they were doing.
- Some task team members complained that the time and effort absorbed by the teams seemed totally out of proportion to the impact they were having.

Two different but related problems, then, emerged from our failure to manage the new wave of participation. Teams dealing with operational issues were forming spontaneously, and many of them were out of control. We lacked what I call a coupling mechanism—we had no way to know whether teams' initiatives had an impact on the organization. For example, a task team might make terrific recommendations about new career paths, but if actually creating the paths was beyond their scope, nothing would change. In general, we didn't know if the teams were working on the right things that supported our overall business objectives, and we had no good way of finding out.

Teams working on the strategic issues had been told they were working on important issues, but they had problems: they lacked coupling mechanisms, ways of connecting what the teams did to the daily operations of the business. Working for a task team, said one member, was like wrestling with jellyfish. There was no firm substance or structure to grab onto. (See "A New Way of Managing: Defining 'It.'")

A New Way of Managing: Defining 'It'

In 1982 Honeywell's Defense Systems Division struggled to define its new approach to management. The following excerpt appeared in a company publication:

"Other companies refer to these activities and processes by names such as QWL (quality of work life), productivity improvement, employee involvement, or participative management. But the more we thought about *all* aspects of our new way of managing, the less adequate seemed any single phrase.

"Our approach is not simply a productivity improvement program, because attention to employee needs is also important; neither is it simply a QWL effort, because we fully expect bottom-line results. Participative management is important to us, but as a *method* for achieving results, not simply as an end in itself. And all of this leaves out important ideas like 'quality' and 'innovation.'

"We used 'it' so often to stand for all these ideas that we finally decided to call it 'it.'

"This is a total way of managing our business to benefit the company, its managers, and all other employees. 'It' encompasses more than a set of particular programs. It starts with how we are organized, with a flexible structure, continually appraised for its capacity to enable people to be involved in a variety of ways and to learn and contribute from a variety of perspectives. Some areas are functionally organized, while others involve project teams from various disciplines that can work on large-scale programs.

"Cutting across the whole division is another, parallel organization for policy development and employee problem solving: the 'it' steering committee, managing a series of cross-department task teams. The 'it' steering committee consists of the divisional general manager, some members of his staff, and other key executives. The task teams it manages focus on issues such as appraisal and pay, career development, communications, quality of work life, equal employment opportunity and affirmative action, and community relations. New cross-department task teams are created periodically from employee proposals submitted to the 'it' steering committee."

We had succeeded in shaking some of the rigidity out of the organization. What we needed, we decided, was to put some discipline back in, to manage this activity with the same care and attention we give other tasks.

Putting Structure in the Jellyfish

The realization that we needed more structure was a real turning point for us. With the help of a consultant, we developed the concept of the parallel organization led by a steering committee. And we also decided that good business principles should apply to our participative management activities—including setting goals, defining accountabilities, and using a strategic planning approach. We began with a single steering committee for the entire business unit, which included two separate operations in Minnesota and one in Seattle. Later, after the group reorganized into divisions, we set up steering committees at each division.

The steering committee gave us a coupling mechanism, the link between the formal, hierarchical organization that carries out routine, ongoing operations and the flatter, more flexible parallel organization that seeks to stimulate employee participation. The steering committee, composed of senior managers who represent the major functions of the conventional organization, ensures that concerns of the ongoing operations are reflected in the parallel organization activities and that the results of the participative problem-solving teams are incorporated into ongoing operations.

The steering committee helped overcome our previous difficulties by setting limits, objectives, and accountability for the teams; requiring the teams to make formal plans and schedules; and recognizing and rewarding the teams when their work is finished.

The employee relations department serves as staff to the steering committee; it acts as a liaison with the task teams, prepares them to make presentations to the steering committee, points out pitfalls, and answers routine questions and concerns. The staff also prepares briefing books for our meetings that include synopses of topics to be covered, pertinent background data, and other information that will help members use the meeting productively.

Although the steering committee meets once a month for about three hours, it may schedule longer meetings to hear task team reports. The committee also holds a daylong self-assessment about every nine months. On these occasions, outside facilitators are present to help us review our objectives and progress, examine the appropriateness of what we've done in the last period, and set priorities for the future. In short, the steering committee follows a strategic planning process with all the questions and tools that normally appear in planning for other aspects of our business.

The composition of the steering committee itself serves more than one purpose. I chair the committee because I think it's important to show that participation is not limited to the shop floor. Restricting participative management to the lower levels of the organization sends the message that this is another program to keep the natives from getting too restless, one that doesn't really reflect on "important" business. Instead, what we should be saying is "What's good for one level is good for all."

The interaction between the steering committee and the task teams has been critical to our success. Traditional taboos about who can make presentations to upper management have been removed. In relaxing our bureaucratic norms, we have increased communication between functions and levels that rarely had contact in the past. A striking illustration is a factory worker whose presentation to the steering committee eventually brought her an invitation to address the Honeywell board of directors.

Because the steering committee's role is crucial, it is important to choose the right members. They not only represent functional areas but they also play other roles. I do the selecting myself for three reasons: to signal management commitment, to facilitate the process itself, and to convert skeptics.

Because converts often become the most persuasive supporters, I chose to put skeptics on the steering committee. At first the idea threatened to backfire. Resistance was not overt, but some members could never seem to make the meetings. Partly to undercut this passive resistance, I decided to chair the committee. I could demonstrate my commitment and, at the same time, learn how the process was working and see where it needed change.

I hoped that my presence on the committee would counter the protests of other members who claimed to be too busy to attend. In a few cases, however, there was always a big business deal or customer crisis brewing somewhere else. Finally, I said, "Look, we will be meeting at this time on this day. We know you'll hate to miss the meeting, so we will arrange a teleconference. Surely you can find a telephone and participate in the meeting for an hour?" After a few teleconferences, the alternative of actually attending the meeting became much more attractive.

Attendance at steering committee meetings has become crucial because the committee provides linkages that do not exist in the formal organizational structure. Indeed, the steering committee has taken over some of the functions of traditional staff meetings, which have been abolished.

Like many organizations, the Defense and Marine Systems Group was accustomed to holding regular staff meetings, normally each Monday from 8:30 A.M. to noon. The typical format was a series of one-on-one status reports. Each staff member reported while the others sat and listened—or at least sat. I didn't believe that this was a productive use of executives' time, nor did I think that staff meetings provided an effective forum for raising important issues. Since staff meetings were regularly scheduled, people tended to hold agenda items for the meetings, and the trivial and the momentous got lumped together. In addition, people may have been reluctant to demand the general manager's time, even when such a demand was called for, if they could see him at regular meetings.

By dispensing with required staff meetings and stressing the importance of the steering committee, I think we signaled to our people that they have greater autonomy, more trust, and freer access. By breaking down the formal reporting relationship, I'm getting better reporting, while my people are getting better at handling what they need to handle and consulting when they need to consult.

The steering committee in its new form, with a clear mandate and explicit lines of authority, has proven invaluable in directing the participative effort to produce the greatest benefit to the group, its managers, and employees. We now have procedures for starting up task teams and for measuring their progress. We have means of disbanding teams once their work is done. And we have fewer task teams now.

Cost is no longer a major concern because we know teams are working on important issues and will not outlive their usefulness.

Relaxing Our Style

Not all the efforts at changing the management culture were formally planned and executed. Many other factors contributed to a management climate more receptive to change. One of the more effective methods, I discovered, is irreverence toward some company traditions. By deliberately disregarding some habits and practices that had become entrenched in our group over the years, I think I was able to speed the transition to a more participative style.

We had to shake things up somehow. By signaling in various ways that certain traditional practices would no longer hold, we helped prepare people to accept the next idea: that they could continue to look to management to define appropriate objectives and results but they could start looking to themselves for ways of achieving them. To paraphrase our vice chairman, Jim Renier, management's role would be to set the goals and then manage the environment so people could achieve those goals. People would manage themselves.

Irreverence toward tradition can help knock down barriers to effectiveness that an organization has built up over its history. The "company way" may often obstruct productive relationships between people. One way of attacking the company way without seeming to attack the company is to demonstrate an irreverent attitude toward some hallowed customs.

One aspect of the company way at Honeywell was an excessive formality. In parts of the organization, a precisely structured chain of command was the only accepted avenue for getting things done. If a section chief had a dispute with a technical editor, he might report the incident to the chief engineer, who reported to the director of engineering, who talked with the director of marketing, who talked with the communications manager, who talked with the editorial supervisor, who talked with the technical editor, who in turn sent his response back up the chain.

We wanted to change that convention. Early on we emphasized that anyone could talk to anyone by simply dropping by the office. Then I started paying visits. At first my appearances disturbed some people who weren't used to seeing the boss unless there was bad news, but I think few people are bothered now.

I found that making ostensibly trivial adjustments to organizational life could have major repercussions. For example, soon after my arrival at the group, an issue was made of assigned parking spaces. The reorganization of which I was part increased the ranks of management. An unanticipated result was that we ended up with more managers than could be accommodated in our parking garage. When I learned that two members of my staff had flipped a coin to see who won the last available spot, I told the loser that he could have mine. Now, indoor parking may have symbolic importance in many companies, but in Minnesota in January, the symbol carries more than the usual weight.

My action sent a ripple through the executive ranks—Boyle had given up his garage space! By failing to exercise my executive prerogative, I put people on notice that we would not be operating business as usual. (Later, when a garage space did open up, I took it. But even then I did not take the number-one stall next to the door. This was another chance to send a signal that power was being used differently.)

Another manifestation of our company way was our dress habits. Although Honeywell had no strict policy on dress, house rules regarding office attire, including "mandatory" neckties, were in force throughout the organization. In the summer of 1982 I issued a memo to employees announcing a "relaxed" policy on neckties during the summer. Although I really did nothing more than restate the existing Honeywell policy, an editorial in the employee newsletter poked fun at the memo. Nonetheless, the editorial agreed that exercising common sense over arbitrary rules could be healthy for the organization in many areas. But only when I actually showed up at the office without a tie did people begin to believe that the new dress code was really OK.

There was little overt resistance to such changes in our organizational customs since most managers could sense which way the wind was blowing. At the corporate level, Jim Renier's emphatic support of cultural change gave our efforts added strength. However, some managers in other parts of the company and some of our customers who had entrusted us with large projects expressed strong reservations about what we were doing. They were not sure that an irreverent management could be a serious and effective management. The company way held that schedule and cost control resulted from bearing down on people and not letting up until they screamed. Customers were concerned with results, not symbols. But when we were able to demonstrate performance improvement—in some cases, remarkable improvement in quality, yields, and learning curves—our customers came around.

Return on the Investment

I don't mean to suggest that we have solved every problem. Sometimes we accept solutions that are less than optimal or we live through the protracted birth of something that could have been handled quickly and simply by one person. On the other hand, our new system is more likely to produce answers that seemed totally out of reach in the past. Let me offer some examples.

Our career development task team took two-and-one-half years to generate a career development program for employees. We could have brought in a consultant for the money we spent internally and probably have had a similar program in one-fifth the time. But having a program isn't sufficient. Once it's in place, supervisors and employees must understand it, accept it, and be willing to use it. Putting up with contending factions agonizing over a solution was worth the quick and full acceptance of the result later on.

One of the hardest things about becoming a more participative manager is the occasional need to sacrifice the best solution or approach to a problem to sustain employee involvement. People who are always turned down will eventually become turned off. For example, our pay task team introduced a new salary program based on performance improvement and tied to specific markets. The new method of determining pay raises eliminated many inequities from the old system, clarified when and how raises would be delivered, and rewarded people fairly based on their improved performance. The team's ongoing role included monitoring the system and fine-tuning it as we learned how well it was working.

After one year both the team members and supervisory personnel felt that the program worked very well, except for one problem: How should we deal with experienced employees whose work was unlikely to improve in the future? These employees, primarily senior engineers, were important contributors; nevertheless, they were ineligible for merit salary increases because the system rewarded performance improvement, not performance level. The lack of merit pay was discouraging people we didn't want to discourage, the team argued, because we seemed to be saying that their work was not valuable. The task team wanted to add a feature to the system called "lump-sum merit." This would enable supervisors to reward these steady but valued workers.

At the time, I disagreed with the task team and argued that the steady employees were already highly paid for their competence, that lump-sum merit would open up a whole new range of problems, and that the team was applying a Band-Aid to avoid reexamining the entire system. The steering committee rejected the proposal on two occasions. Yet the team presented a third refinement of the lump-sum merit scheme. This time team members were adamant, and they were also beginning to grumble that participative management would be condoned only as long as it produced what top management was looking for. The compensation team was one of the best we had, and I was alienating its members from the process through which they had performed so well. Eventually I decided that it would be better to support the proposal and deal with the consequences later than to further alienate them—and probably many others with whom they had contact.

The proposal had one more hurdle to clear. Because numerous Honeywell divisions are located in the Minneapolis area, corporate approval is required for compensation programs to ensure consistency among these operations. In the end, corporate staff rejected our lump-sum merit proposal. Although they lost, the team members achieved a moral victory. The process worked. The process, in this case, was more important than the product.

The limited numbers of women and minority people in our group was another problem that concerned many of us. Our EEO data were unambiguous: whatever we might claim about our organization, we had limited success in hiring and retaining minority employees and we couldn't seem to find better answers. We had EEO standards in our contracts and in our division and departmental objectives, but we were having difficulty reaching our goals. Our retention rate highlighted the problem. In 1980, we lost seven minority employees for every ten we hired. Simply issuing an order to hire minorities was not having the desired effect.

An EEO task team composed of middle managers was formed to attack the problem. To their credit, the members looked around the table and saw nothing but white, middle-aged male faces, and they began to see the situation in a new light. The team voted to add minority members, and the original group received an eye-opening education in race relations. One manager admitted that he didn't know that blacks weren't calling themselves negroes anymore. The team learned firsthand about the difficulties that face young black engineers from southern schools who move to predominantly white Minnesota and find the weather, the culture, and the company un-friendly.

To deal with such problems, the team eventually developed a comprehensive EEO affirmative action plan, a training program in cultural awareness for supervisors, a minority scholarship program, a career development program, and an appeals process.

We still need to improve opportunities for minorities, women, and handicapped workers at Honeywell Defense and Marine Systems. But the climate of our operations has improved dramatically, and the minority retention rate has improved threefold to be in line with the rate for the work force generally.

Finally, the participative process can pay off by solving problems beyond the ones addressed directly. Recently I was faced with a management decision that in the past I would have made on my own. Two of the group's major units had cooperated to win a very large contract. The project would require the skills of both units, but the production could take place in only one. Thus, one unit would receive a very large flow of revenues. This unit would also receive a large amount of capital improvement funds. To make matters worse, the two units had been extremely competitive with each other over the years. The capital investments flowing to one of them would give it an edge for years to come.

Rather than deciding between the units myself, I involved both units in the decision. Over six months, I met with the directors of the units and their staffs periodically to discuss alternative approaches and the implications of winning and losing. Members of both units had the opportunity to argue their case, and each side heard the other's views and concerns. Getting these units to share data was an accomplishment in itself in light of their long-standing rivalry.

In the end, we concluded that the winning unit might have to subsidize the losing unit for some time. During these discussions, members of both units began to develop a clearer vision of long-range corporate goals and began to see these as distinct from the goals of their own units.

Each unit still favored its own case. But when I made the final decision in favor of one, the losing side did not go into a blue funk. Everyone understood the reasons for the decison. The winning team was also smart enough not to gloat. The project proceeded smoothly because we had anticipated many of the potential snags. Finally, the two units developed a cooperative relationship for the first time that really benefits the group as a whole. In fact, a few months ago I discovered that one of the units had voluntarily relinquished control over a project to the other without involving me in the decision.

With participative management yielding such benefits, I am able to work on other management concerns. Although I spend more time managing participation, I spend less time refereeing internal squabbles or soothing irate customers. Our employees are solving little problems before they become big problems. Many more decisions are made at lower levels of the organization. Anything they want to keep out of my office is fine with me.

Participative management does require a greater commitment of time compared with traditional management intervention, at least in the short term. But the long-term rewards of *managed* participative management are abundant. Not the least of them is the fun I'm having doing my job.

6
Managing Innovation: Controlled Chaos

James Brian Quinn

Management observers frequently claim that small organizations are more innovative than large ones. But is this commonplace necessarily true? Some large enterprises are highly innovative. How do they do it? Can lessons from these companies and their smaller counterparts help other companies become more innovative?

This article proposes some answers to these questions based on the initial results of an ongoing 2 1/2 year worldwide study. The research sample includes both well-documented small ventures and large U.S., Japanese, and European companies and programs selected for their innovation records (see Appendix A). More striking than the cultural differences among these companies are the similarities between innovative small and large organizations and among innovative organizations in different countries. Effective management of innovation seems much the same, regardless of national boundaries or scale of operations.

There are, of course, many reasons why small companies appear to produce a disproportionate number of innovations. First, innovation occurs in a probabilistic setting. A company never knows whether a particular technical result can be achieved and whether it will succeed in the marketplace. For every new solution that succeeds, tens to hundreds fail. The sheer number of attempts—most by small-scale entrepreneurs—means that some ventures will survive. The 90% to 99% that fail are distributed widely throughout society and receive little notice.

On the other hand, a big company that wishes to move a concept from invention to the marketplace must absorb all potential failure costs itself. This risk may be socially or managerially intolerable, jeopardizing the many other products, projects, jobs, and communities the company supports. Even if its innovation is successful, a big company may face costs that newcomers do not bear, like converting existing operations and customer bases to the new solution.

By contrast, a new enterprise does not risk losing an existing investment base or cannibalizing customer franchises built at great expense. It does not have to change an internal culture that has successfully supported doing things another way or that has developed intellectual depth and belief in the technologies that led to past successes. Organized groups like labor unions, consumer advocates, and government bureaucracies rarely monitor and resist a small company's moves as they might a big company's. Finally, new companies do not face the psychological pain and the economic costs of laying off employees, shutting down plants and even communities, and displacing supplier relationships built with years of mutual commitment and effort. Such barriers to change in large organizations are real, important, and legitimate.

The complex products and systems that society expects large companies to undertake further compound the risks. Only big companies can develop new ships or locomotives; telecommunication networks; or systems for space, defense, air traffic control, hospital care, mass foods delivery, or nationwide computer interactions. These large-scale projects always carry more risk than single-product introductions. A billion-dollar development aircraft, for example, can fail if one inexpensive part in its 100,000 components fails.

Clearly, a single enterprise cannot by itself develop or produce all the parts needed by such large new systems. And communications among the various groups making design and production decisions on components are always incomplete. The probability of error increases exponentially with complexity, while the system innovator's control over decisions decreases significantly—further escalating potential error costs and risks. Such forces inhibit innovation in large organizations. But proper management can lessen these effects.

Of Inventors and Entrepreneurs

A close look at innovative small enterprises reveals much about the successful management of innovation. Of course, not all innovations follow a single pattern. But my research—and other studies in combination—suggest that the following factors are crucial to the success of innovative small companies:

Need orientation. Inventor-entrepreneurs tend to be "need or achievement oriented."[1] They believe that if they "do the job better," rewards will follow. They may at first focus on their own view of market needs. But lacking resources, successful small entrepreneurs soon find that it pays to approach potential customers early, test their solutions in users' hands, learn from these interactions, and adapt designs rapidly. Many studies suggest that effective technological innovation develops hand-in-hand with customer demand.[2]

Experts and fanatics. Company founders tend to be pioneers in their technologies and fanatics when it comes to solving problems. They are often described as "possessed" or "obsessed," working toward their objectives to the exclusion even of family or personal relationships. As both experts and fanatics, they perceive probabilities of success as higher than others do. And their commitment allows them to persevere despite the frustrations, ambiguities, and setbacks that always accompany major innovations.

Long time horizons. Their fanaticism may cause inventor-entrepreneurs to underestimate the obstacles and length of time to success. Time horizons for radical innovations make them essentially "irrational" from a present value viewpoint. In my sample, delays between invention and commercial production ranged from 3 to 25 years.[3] In the late 1930s, for example, industrial chemist Russell Marker was working on steroids called sapogenins when he discovered a technique that would degrade one of these, diosgenin, into the female sex hormone progesterone. By processing some ten tons of Mexican yams in rented and borrowed lab space, Marker finally extracted about four pounds of diosgenin and started a tiny business to produce steroids for the laboratory market. But it was not until 1962, over 23 years later, that Syntex, the company Marker founded, obtained FDA approval for its oral contraceptive.

For both psychological and practical reasons, inventor-entrepreneurs generally avoid early formal plans, proceed step-by-step, and sustain themselves by other income and the momentum of the small advances they achieve as they go along.

Low early costs. Innovators tend to work in homes, basements, warehouses, or low-rent facilities whenever possible. They incur few overhead costs; their limited resources go directly into their projects. They pour nights, weekends, and "sweat capital" into their endeavors. They borrow whatever they can. They invent cheap equipment and prototype processes, often improving on what is available in the marketplace. If one approach fails, few people know; little time or money is lost. All this decreases the costs and risks facing a small operation and improves the present value of its potential success.

Multiple approaches. Technology tends to advance through a series of random—often highly intuitive—insights frequently triggered by gratuitous interactions between the discoverer and the outside world. Only highly committed entrepreneurs can tolerate (and even enjoy) this chaos. They adopt solutions wherever they can be found, unencumbered by formal plans or PERT charts that would limit the range of their imaginations. When the odds of success are low, the participation and interaction of many motivated players increase the chance that one will succeed.

A recent study of initial public offerings made in 1962 shows that only 2% survived and still looked like worthwhile investments 20 years later.[4] Small-scale entrepreneurship looks efficient in part because history only records the survivors.

Flexibility and quickness. Undeterred by committees, board approvals, and other bureaucratic delays, the inventor-entrepreneur can experiment, test, recycle, and try again with little time lost. Because technological progress depends largely on the number of successful experiments accomplished per unit of time, fast-moving small entrepreneurs can gain both timing and performance advantages over clumsier competitors. This responsiveness is often crucial in finding early markets for radical innovations where neither innovators, market researchers, nor users can quite visualize a product's real potential. For example, Edison's lights first appeared on ships and in baseball parks; Astroturf was intended to convert the flat roofs and asphalt playgrounds of city schools into more humane environments; and graphite and boron composites designed for aerospace unexpectedly found their largest markets in sporting goods. Entrepreneurs quickly adjusted their entry strategies to market feedback.

Incentives. Inventor-entrepreneurs can foresee tangible personal rewards if they are successful. Individuals often want to achieve a technical contribution, recognition, power, or sheer independence, as much as money. For the original, driven personalities who create significant innovations, few other paths offer such clear opportunities to fulfill all their economic, psychological, and career goals at once. Consequently, they do not panic or quit when others with solely monetary goals might.

Availability of capital. One of America's great competitive advantages is its rich variety of sources to finance small, low-probability ventures. If entrepreneurs are turned down by one source, other sources can be sought in myriads of creative combinations.

Professionals involved in such financings have developed a characteristic approach to deal with the chaos and uncertainty of innovation. First, they evaluate a proposal's conceptual validity: If the technical problems can be solved, is there a real business there for someone and does it have a large upside potential? Next, they concentrate on people: Is the team thoroughly committed and expert? Is it the best available? Only then do these financiers analyze specific financial estimates in depth. Even then, they recognize that actual outcomes generally depend on subjective factors, not numbers.[5]

Timeliness, aggressiveness, commitment, quality of people, and the flexibility to attack opportunities not at first perceived are crucial. Downside risks are minimized, not by detailed controls, but by spreading risks among multiple projects, keeping early costs low, and gauging the tenacity, flexibility, and capability of the founders.

Bureaucratic Barriers to Innovation

Less innovative companies and, unfortunately, most large corporations operate in a very different fashion. The most notable and common constraints on innovation in larger companies include:

Top management isolation. Many senior executives in big companies have little contact with conditions on the factory floor or with customers who might influence their thinking about technological innovation. Since risk perception is inversely related to familiarity and experience, financially oriented top managers are likely to perceive technological innovations as more problematic than acquisitions that may be just as risky but that will appear more familiar.[6]

Intolerance of fanatics. Big companies often view entrepreneurial fanatics as embarrassments or troublemakers. Many major cities are now ringed by companies founded by these "nonteam" players—often to the regret of their former employers.

Short time horizons. The perceived corporate need to report a continuous stream of quarterly profits conflicts with the long time spans that major innovations normally require. Such pressures often make publicly owned companies favor quick marketing fixes, cost cutting, and acquisition strategies over process, product, or quality innovations that would yield much more in the long run.

Accounting practices. By assessing all its direct, indirect, over-head, overtime, and service costs against a project, large corporations have much higher development expenses compared with entrepreneurs working in garages. A project in a big company can quickly become an exposed political target, its potential net present value may sink unacceptably, and an entry into small markets may not justify its sunk costs. An otherwise viable project may soon founder and disappear.

Excessive rationalism. Managers in big companies often seek orderly advance through early market research studies or PERT planning. Rather than managing the inevitable chaos of innovation productively, these managers soon drive out the very things that lead to innovation in order to prove their announced plans.

Excessive bureaucracy. In the name of efficiency, bureaucratic structures require many approvals and cause delays at every turn. Experiments that a small company can perform in hours may take days or weeks in large organizations. The interactive feedback that fosters innovation is lost, important time windows can be missed, and real costs and risks rise for the corporation.

Inappropriate incentives. Reward and control systems in most big companies are designed to minimize surprises. Yet innovation, by definition, is full of surprises. It often disrupts well-laid plans, accepted power patterns, and entrenched organizational behavior at high costs to many. Few large companies make millionaires of those who create such disruptions, however profitable the innovations may turn out to be. When control systems neither penalize opportunities missed nor reward risks taken, the results are predictable.

How Large Innovative Companies Do It

Yet some big companies are continuously innovative. Although each such enterprise is distinctive, the successful big innovators I studied have developed techniques that emulate or improve on their smaller counterparts' practices. What are the most important patterns?

Atmosphere and vision. Continuous innovation occurs largely because top executives appreciate innovation and manage their company's value system and atmosphere to support it. For example, Sony's founder, Masaru Ibuka, stated in the company's "Purposes of Incorporation" the goal of a "free, dynamic, and pleasant factory . . . where sincerely motivated personnel can exercise their technological skills to the highest level." Ibuka and Sony's chairman, Akio Morita, inculcated the "Sony spirit" through a series of unusual policies: hiring brilliant people with nontraditional skills (like an opera singer) for high management positions, promoting young people over their elders, designing a new type of living accommodation for workers, and providing visible awards for outstanding technical achievements.

Because familiarity can foster understanding and psychological comfort, engineering and scientific leaders are often those who create atmospheres supportive of innovation, especially in a company's early life. Executive vision is more important than a particular management background—as IBM, Genentech, AT&T, Merck, Elf Aquitaine, Pilkington, and others in my sample illustrate. CEOs of these companies value technology and include technical experts in their highest decision circles.

Innovative managements—whether technical or not—project clear long-term visions for their organizations that go beyond simple economic measures. As Intel's chairman, Gordon Moore, says: "We intend to be the outstandingly successful innovative company in this industry. We intend to continue to be a leader in this revolutionary [semiconductor] technology that is changing the way this world is run." Genentech's original plan expresses a similar vision: "We expect to be the first company to commercialize the [rDNA] technology, and we plan to build a major profitable corporation by manufacturing and marketing needed products that benefit mankind. The future uses of genetic engineering are far reaching and many. Any product produced by a living organism is eventually within the company's reach."

Such visions, vigorously supported, are not "management fluff," but have many practical implications. They attract quality people to the company and give focus to their creative and entrepreneurial drives. When combined with sound internal operations, they help channel growth by concentrating attention on the actions that lead to profitability, rather than on profitability itself. Finally, these visions recognize a realistic time frame for innovation and attract the kind of investors who will support it.

Orientation to the market. Innovative companies tie their visions to the practical realities of the marketplace. Although each company uses techniques adapted to its own style and strategy, two elements are always present: a strong market orientation at the very top of the company and mechanisms to ensure interactions between technical and marketing people at lower levels. At Sony, for example, soon after technical people are hired, the company runs them through weeks of retail selling. Sony engineers become sensitive to the ways retail sales practices, product displays, and nonquantifiable customer preferences affect success. Similarly, before AT&T's recent divestiture, Bell Laboratories had an Operating Company Assignment Program to rotate its researchers through AT&T and Western Electric development and production facilities. And it had a rigorous Engineering Complaint System that collected technical problems from operating companies and required Bell Labs to specify within a few weeks how it would resolve or attack each problem.

From top to bench levels in my sample's most innovative companies, managers focus primarily on seeking to anticipate and solve customers' emerging problems.

Small, flat organizations. The most innovative large companies in my sample try to keep the total organization flat and project teams small. Development teams normally include only six or seven key people. This number seems to constitute a critical mass of skills while fostering maximum communication and commitment among members. According to research done by my colleague, Victor McGee, the number of channels of communication increases as $n [2^{(n-1)} - 1]$. Therefore:

For team size	=	1	2	3	4	5	6	7	8	9	10	11
Channels	=	1	2	9	28	75	186	441	1016	2295	5110	11253

Innovative companies also try to keep their operating divisions and total technical units small—below 400 people. Up to this number, only two layers of management are required to maintain a span of control over 7 people. In units much larger than 400, people quickly lose touch with the concept of their product or process, staffs and bureaucracies tend to grow, and projects may go through too many formal screens to survive. Since it takes a chain of yeses and only one no to kill a project, jeopardy multiplies as management layers increase.

Multiple approaches. At first one cannot be sure which of several technical approaches will dominate a field. The history of technology is replete with accidents, mishaps, and chance meetings that allowed one approach or group to emerge rapidly over others. Leo Baekelund was looking for a synthetic shellac when he found Bakelite and started the modern plastics industry. At Syntex, researchers were not looking for an oral contraceptive when they created 19-norprogesterone, the precursor to the active ingredient in half of all contraceptive pills. And the microcomputer was born because Intel's Ted Hoff "happened" to work on a complex calculator just when Digital Equipment Corporation's PDP8 architecture was fresh in his mind.

Such "accidents" are involved in almost all major technological advances. When theory can predict everything, a company has moved to a new stage, from development to production. Murphy's law works because engineers design for what they can foresee; hence what fails is what theory could not predict. And it is rare that the interactions of components and subsystems can be predicted over the lifetime of operations. For example, despite careful theoretical design work, the first high performance jet engine literally tore itself to pieces on its test stand, while others failed in unanticipated operating conditions (like an Iranian sandstorm).

Recognizing the inadequacies of theory, innovative enterprises seem to move faster from paper studies to physical testing than do noninnovative enterprises. When possible, they encourage several prototype programs to proceed in parallel. Sony pursued 10 major options in developing its videotape recorder technology. Each option had two to three subsystem alternatives. Such redundancy helps the company cope with uncertainties in development, motivates people through competition, and improves the amount and quality of information available for making final choices on scale-ups or introductions.

Developmental shoot-outs. Many companies structure shoot-outs among competing approaches only after they reach the prototype stages. They find this practice provides more objective information for making decisions, decreases risk by making choices that best reflect marketplace needs, and helps ensure that the winning option will move ahead with a committed team behind it. Although many managers worry that competing approaches may be inefficient, greater effectiveness in choosing the right solution easily outweighs duplication costs when the market rewards higher performance or when large volumes justify increased sophistication. Under these conditions, parallel development may prove less costly because it both improves the probability of success and reduces development time.

Perhaps the most difficult problem in managing competing projects lies in reintegrating the members of the losing team. If the company is expanding rapidly or if the successful project creates a growth opportunity, losing team members can work on another interesting program or sign on with the winning team as the project moves toward the marketplace. For the shoot-out system to work continuously, however, executives must create a climate that honors high-quality performance whether a project wins or loses, reinvolves people quickly in their technical specialties or in other projects, and accepts and expects rotation among tasks and groups.

At Sony, according to its top R&D manager, the research climate does not penalize the losing team: "We constantly have several alternative projects going. Before the competition is over, before there is a complete loss, we try to smell the potential outcome and begin to prepare for that result as early as possible. Even after we have consensus, we may wait for several months to give the others a chance. Then we begin to give important jobs [on other programs] to members of the losing groups. If your team doesn't win, you may still be evaluated as performing well. Such people have often received my 'crystal award' for outstanding work. We never talk badly about these people. Ibuka's principle is that doing something, even if it fails, is better than doing nothing. A strike-out at Sony is OK, but you must not just stand there. You must swing at the ball as best you can."

Skunkworks. Every highly innovative enterprise in my research sample emulated small company practices by using groups that functioned in a skunkworks style. Small teams of engineers, technicians, designers, and model makers were placed together with no intervening organizational or physical barriers to developing a new product from idea to commercial prototype stages. In innovative Japanese companies, top managers often worked hand-in-hand on projects with young engineers. Surprisingly, *ringi* decision making was not evident in these situations. Soichiro Honda was known for working directly on technical problems and emphasizing his technical points by shouting at his engineers or occasionally even hitting them with wrenches!

The skunkworks approach eliminates bureaucracies, allows fast, unfettered communications, permits rapid turnaround times for experiments, and instills a high level of group identity and loyalty. Interestingly, few successful groups in my research were structured in the classic "venture group" form, with a careful balancing of engineering, production, and marketing talents. Instead they acted on an old truism: introducing a new product or process to the world is like raising a healthy child—it needs one parent (champion) who loves it, one parent (authority figure with resources) to support it, and pediatricians (specialists) to get it through difficult times. It may survive solely in the hands of specialists, but its chances of success are remote.

Interactive learning. Skunkworks are as close as most big companies can come to emulating the highly interactive and motivating learning environment that characterizes successful small ventures. But the best big innovators have gone even farther. Recognizing that the random, chaotic nature of technological change cuts across organizational and even institutional lines, these companies tap into multiple outside sources of technology as well as their customers' capabilities. Enormous external leverages are possible. No company can spend more than a small share of the world's $200 billion devoted to R&D. But like small entrepreneurs, big companies can have much of that total effort cheaply if they try.

In industries such as electronics, customers provide much of the innovation on new products. In other industries, such as textiles, materials or equipment suppliers provide the innovation. In still others, such as biotechnology, universities are dominant, while foreign sources strongly supplement industries such as controlled fusion. Many R&D units have strategies to develop information for trading with outside groups and have teams to cultivate these sources.[7] Large Japanese companies have been notably effective at this. So have U.S. companies as diverse as Du Pont, AT&T, Apple Computer, and Genentech.

An increasing variety of creative relationships exists in which big companies participate—as joint venturers, consortium members, limited partners, guarantors of first markets, major academic funding sources, venture capitalists, spin-off equity holders, and so on. These rival the variety of inventive financing and networking structures that individual entrepreneurs have created.

Indeed, the innovative practices of small and large companies look ever more alike. This resemblance is especially striking in the interactions between companies and customers during development. Many experienced big companies are relying less on early market research and more on interactive development with lead customers. Hewlett-Packard, 3M, Sony, and Raychem frequently introduce radically new products through small teams that work closely with lead customers. These teams learn from their customers' needs and innovations, and rapidly modify designs and entry strategies based on this information.

Formal market analyses continue to be useful for extending product lines, but they are often misleading when applied to radical innovations. Market studies predicted that Haloid would never sell more than 5,000 xerographic machines, that Intel's microprocessor would never sell more than 10% as many units as there were minicomputers, and that Sony's transistor radios and miniature television sets would fail in the marketplace. At the same time, many eventual failures such as Ford's Edsel, IBM's FS system, and the supersonic transport were studied and planned exhaustively on paper, but lost contact with customers' real needs.

A Strategy for Innovation

The flexible management practices needed for major innovations often pose problems for established cultures in big companies. Yet there are reasonable steps managers in these companies can take. Innovation can be bred in a surprising variety of organizations, as many examples show. What are its key elements?

An opportunity orientation. In the 1981–1983 recession, many large companies cut back or closed plants as their "only available solution." Yet I repeatedly found that top managers in these companies took these actions without determining firsthand why their customers were buying from competitors, discerning what niches in their markets were growing, or tapping the innovations their own people had to solve problems. These managers foreclosed innumerable options by defining the issue as cost cutting rather than opportunity seeking. As one frustrated division manager in a manufacturing conglomerate put it: "If management doesn't actively seek or welcome technical opportunities, it sure won't hear about them."

By contrast, Intel met the challenge of the last recession with its "20% solution." The professional staff agreed to work one extra day a week to bring innovations to the marketplace earlier than planned. Despite the difficult times, Intel came out of the recession with several important new products ready to go—and it avoided layoffs.

Entrepreneurial companies recognize that they have almost unlimited access to capital and they structure their practices accordingly. They let it be known that if their people come up with good ideas, they can find the necessary capital—just as private venture capitalists or investment bankers find resources for small entrepreneurs.

Structuring for innovation. Managers need to think carefully about how innovation fits into their strategy and structure their technology, skills, resources, and organizational commitments accordingly. A few examples suggest the variety of strategies and alignments possible:

- Hewlett-Packard and 3M develop product lines around a series of small, discrete, freestanding products. These companies form units that look like entrepreneurial start-ups. Each has a small team, led by a champion, in low-cost facilities. These companies allow many different proposals to come forward and test them as early as possible in the marketplace. They design control systems to spot significant losses on any single entry quickly. They look for high gains on a few winners and blend less successful, smaller entries into prosperous product lines.

- Other companies (like AT&T or the oil majors) have had to make large system investments to last for decades. These companies tend to make long-term needs forecasts. They often start several programs in parallel to be sure of selecting the right technologies. They then extensively test new technologies in use before making systemwide commitments. Often they sacrifice speed of entry for long-term low cost and reliability.

- Intel and Dewey & Almy, suppliers of highly technical specialties to OEMs, develop strong technical sales networks to discover and understand customer needs in depth. These companies try to have technical solutions designed into customers' products. Such companies have flexible applied technology groups working close to the marketplace. They also have quickly expandable plant facilities and a cutting-edge technology (not necessarily basic research) group that allows rapid selection of currently available technologies.

- Dominant producers like IBM or Matsushita are often not the first to introduce new technologies. They do not want to disturb their successful product lines any sooner than necessary. As market demands become clear, these companies establish precise price-performance windows and form overlapping project teams to come up with the best answer for the marketplace. To decrease market risks, they use product shoot-outs as close to the market as possible. They develop extreme depth in production technologies to keep unit costs low from the outset. Finally, depending on the scale of the market entry, they have project teams report as close to the top as necessary to secure needed management attention and resources.

- Merck and Hoffman-LaRoche, basic research companies, maintain laboratories with better facilities, higher pay, and more freedom than most universities can afford. These companies leverage their internal spending through research grants, clinical grants, and research relationships with universities throughout the world. Before they invest $20 million to $50 million to clear a new drug, they must have reasonable assurance that they will be first in the marketplace. They take elaborate precautions to ensure that the new entry is safe and effective, and that it cannot be easily duplicated by others. Their structures are designed to be on the cutting edge of science, but conservative in animal testing, clinical evaluation, and production control.

These examples suggest some ways of linking innovation to strategy. Many other examples, of course, exist. Within a single company, individual divisions may have different strategic needs and hence different structures and practices. No single approach works well for all situations.

Complex portfolio planning. Perhaps the most difficult task for top managers is to balance the needs of existing lines against the needs of potential lines. This problem requires a portfolio strategy much more complex than the popular four-box Boston Consulting Group matrix found in most strategy texts. To allocate resources for innovation strategically, managers need to define the broad, long-term actions within and across divisions necessary to achieve their visions. They should determine which positions to hold at all costs, where to fall back, and where to expand initially and in the more distant future.

A company's strategy may often require investing most resources in current lines. But sufficient resources should also be invested in patterns that ensure intermediate and long-term growth; provide defenses against possible government, labor, competitive, or activist challenges; and generate needed organizational, technical, and external relations flexibilities to handle unforeseen opportunities or threats. Sophisticated portfolio planning within and among divisions can protect both current returns and future prospects—the two critical bases for that most cherished goal, high price-earnings ratios.

An Incrementalist Approach

Such managerial techniques can provide a strategic focus for innovation and help solve many of the timing, coordination, and motivation problems that plague large, bureaucratic organizations. Even more detailed planning techniques may help in guiding the development of the many small innovations that characterize any successful business. My research reveals, however, that few, if any, major innovations result from highly structured planning systems. Within the broad framework I have described, major innovations are best managed as incremental, goal-oriented, interactive learning processes.[8]

Several sophisticated companies have labeled this approach "phased program planning." When they see an important opportunity in the marketplace (or when a laboratory champion presses them), top managers outline some broad, challenging goals for the new programs: "to be the first to prove whether rDNA is commercially feasible for this process," or "to create an economical digital switching system for small country telephone systems." These goals have few key timing, cost, or performance numbers attached. As scientists and engineers (usually from different areas) begin to define technical options, the programs' goals become more specific—though managers still allow much latitude in technical approaches.

As options crystallize, managers try to define the most important technical sequences and critical decision points. They may develop "go, no go" performance criteria for major program phases and communicate these as targets for project teams. In systems innovations, for example, performance specifications must be set to coordinate the interactions of subsystems. Successful companies leave open for as long as possible exactly how these targets can be achieved.

While feeding resources to the most promising options, managers frequently keep other paths open. Many of the best concepts and solutions come from projects partly hidden or "bootlegged" by the organization. Most successful managers try to build some slacks or buffers into their plans to hedge their bets, although they hesitate to announce these actions widely. They permit chaos and replication in early investigations, but insist on much more formal planning and controls as expensive development and scale-up proceed. But even at these later stages, these managers have learned to maintain flexibility and to avoid the tyranny of paper plans. They seek inputs from manufacturing, marketing, and customer groups early. Armed with this information, they are prepared to modify their plans even as they enter the marketplace. A European executive describes this process of directing innovation as "a somewhat orderly tumult that can be managed only in an incremental fashion."

WHY INCREMENTALISM?

The innovative process is inherently incremental. As Thomas Hughes says, "Technological systems evolve through relatively small steps marked by an occasional stubborn obstacle and by constant random breakthroughs interacting across laboratories and borders."[9] A forgotten hypothesis of Einstein's became the laser in Charles Townes's mind as he contemplated azaleas in Franklin Square. The structure of DNA followed a circuitous route through research in biology, organic chemistry, X-ray crystallography, and mathematics toward its Nobel

Prize-winning conception as a spiral staircase of matched base pairs. Such rambling trails are characteristic of virtually all major technological advances.

At the outset of the attack on a technical problem, an innovator often does not know whether his problem is tractable, what approach will prove best, and what concrete characteristics the solution will have if achieved. The logical route, therefore, is to follow several paths—though perhaps with varying degrees of intensity—until more information becomes available. Not knowing precisely where the solution will occur, wise managers establish the widest feasible network for finding and assessing alternative solutions. They keep many options open until one of them seems sure to win. Then they back it heavily.

Managing innovation is like a stud poker game, where one can play several hands. A player has some idea of the likely size of the pot at the beginning, knows the general but not the sure route to winning, buys one card (a project) at a time to gain information about probabilities and the size of the pot, closes hands as they become discouraging, and risks more only late in the hand as knowledge increases.

POLITICAL AND PSYCHOLOGICAL SUPPORT

Incrementalism helps deal with the psychological, political, and motivational factors that are crucial to project success. By keeping goals broad at first, a manager avoids creating undue opposition to a new idea. A few concrete goals may be projected as a challenge. To maintain flexibility, intermediate steps are not developed in detail. Alternate routes can be tried and failures hidden. As early problems are solved, momentum, confidence, and identity build around the new approach. Soon a project develops enough adherents and objective data to withstand its critics' opposition.

As it comes more clearly into competition for resources, its advocates strive to solve problems and maintain its viability. Finally, enough concrete information exists for nontechnical managers to compare the programs fairly with more familiar options. The project now has the legitimacy and political clout to survive—which might never have happened if its totality has been disclosed or planned in detail at the beginning. Many sound technical projects have died because their managers did not deal with the politics of survival.

CHAOS WITHIN GUIDELINES

Effective managers of innovation channel and control its main directions. Like venture capitalists, they administer primarily by setting goals, selecting key people, and establishing a few critical limits and decision points for intervention rather than by implementing elaborate planning or control systems. As technology leads or market needs emerge, these managers set a few—most crucial—performance targets and limits. They allow their technical units to decide how to achieve these, subject to defined constraints and reviews at critical junctures.

Early bench-scale project managers may pursue various options, making little attempt at first to integrate each into a total program. Only after key variables are understood—and perhaps measured and demonstrated in lab models—can more precise planning be meaningful. Even then, many factors may remain unknown; chaos and competition can continue to thrive in the pursuit of the solution. At defined review points, however, only those options that can clear performance milestones may continue.

Choosing which projects to kill is perhaps the hardest decision in the management of innovation. In the end, the decision is often intuitive, resting primarily on a manager's technical knowledge and familiarity with innovation processes. Repeatedly, successful managers told me, "Anyone who thinks he can quantify this decision is either a liar or a fool. . . . There are too many unknowables, variables. . . . Ultimately, one must use intuition, a complex feeling, calibrated by experience. . . . We'd be foolish not to check everything, touch all bases. That's what the models are for. But ultimately it's a judgment about people, commitment, and probabilites. . . . You don't dare use milestones too rigidly."

Even after selecting the approaches to emphasize, innovative managers tend to continue a few others as smaller scale "side bets" or options. In a surprising number of cases, these alternatives prove winners when the planned option fails.

Recognizing the many demands entailed by successful programs, innovative companies find special ways to reward innovators. Sony gives "a small but significant" percentage of a new product's sales to its innovating teams. Pilkington, IBM, and 3M's top executives are often chosen from those who have headed successful new product entries. Intel lets its Magnetic Memory Group operate like a small company, with special performance rewards and simulated stock options. GE, Syntex, and United Technologies help internal innovators establish new companies and take equity positions in "nonrelated" product innovations.

Large companies do not have to make their innovators millionaires, but rewards should be visible and significant. Fortunately, most engineers are happy with the incentives that Tracy Kidder calls "playing pinball"—giving widespread recognition to a job well done and the right to play in the next exciting game.[10] Most innovative companies provide both, but increasingly they are supplementing these with financial rewards to keep their most productive innovators from jumping outside.

Match Management to the Process

Management practices in innovative companies reflect the realities of the innovation process itself. Innovation tends to be individually motivated, opportunistic, customer responsive, tumultuous, nonlinear, and interactive in its development. Managers can plan overall directions and goals, but surprises are likely to abound. Consequently, innovative companies keep their programs flexible for as long as possible and freeze plans only when necessary for strategic purposes such as timing. Even then they keep options open by specifying broad performance goals and allowing different technical approaches to compete for as long as possible.

Executives need to understand and accept the tumultuous realities of innovation, learn from the experiences of other companies, and adapt the most relevant features of these others to their own management practices and cultures. Many features of small company innovators are also applicable in big companies. With top-level understanding, vision, a commitment to customers and solutions, a genuine portfolio strategy, a flexible entrepreneurial atmosphere, and proper incentives for innovative champions, many more large companies can innovate to meet the severe demands of global competition.

Appendix A

The Study

A questionnaire and poll of experts identified several outstanding innovative large companies in Europe, the United States, and Japan for study. These companies had more than $1 billion in sales and programs with at least tens of millions of dollars in initial investment and hundreds of millions of dollars in ultimate annual economic impact. Interviews and secondary sources were used and cross-checked to establish management patterns. Wherever possible, cases on these companies and ventures were written and will be released for public use. Case studies of Sony Corporation, Intel Corporation, Pilkington Brothers, Ltd., and Honda Corporation are already available from the author.

Notes

1. David McClelland, *The Achieving Society* (New York: Halsted Press, 1976); Gene Bylinsky, *The Innovation Millionaires* (New York: Scribner's, 1976).

2. Eric von Hippel, "Get New Products From Customers," *Harvard Business Review,* March–April 1982, p. 117.

3. A study at Battelle found an average of 19.2 years between invention and commercial production. Battelle Memorial Laboratories, "Science, Technology, and Innovation," Report to the National Science Foundation, 1973; R.C. Dean, "The Temporal Mismatch: Innovation's Pace vs. Management's Time Horizon," *Research Management,* May 1974, p. 13.

4. Business Economics Group, W.R. Grace & Co., 1983.

5. Christina C. Pence, *How Venture Capitalists Make Venture Decisions* (Ann Arbor, Mich.: UMI Research Press, 1982).

6. Robert H. Hayes and David A. Garvin, "Managing as if Tomorrow Mattered," *Harvard Business Review,* May–June 1982, p. 70; Robert H. Hayes and William J. Abernathy, "Managing Our Way to Economic Decline," *Harvard Business Review,* July–August 1980, p. 67.

7. In *Managing the Flow of Technology* (Cambridge: MIT Press, 1977), Thomas J. Allen illustrates the enormous leverage provided such technology accessors (called "gatekeepers") in R&D organizations.

8. For a further discussion of incrementalism, see James Brian Quinn, "Managing Strategies Incrementally," *Omega* 10, no. 6 (1982), p. 613; and *Strategies for Change: Logical Incrementalism* (Homewood, Ill.: Dow Jones-Irwin, 1980).

9. Thomas Hughes, "The Inventive Continuum," *Science 84,* November 1984, p. 83.

10. Tracy Kidder, *The Soul of a New Machine* (Boston: Little, Brown, 1981).

7
The Productivity Paradox

Wickham Skinner

American manufacturers' near-heroic efforts to regain a competitive edge through productivity improvements have been disappointing. Worse, the results of these efforts have been paradoxical. The harder these companies pursue productivity, the more elusive it becomes.

In the late 1970s, after facing a severe loss of market share in dozens of industries, U.S. producers aggressively mounted programs to revitalize their manufacturing functions. This effort to restore the productivity gains that had regularly been achieved for over 75 years has been extraordinary. (Productivity is defined by the Bureau of Labor Statistics as the value of goods manufactured divided by the amount of labor input. In this article "productivity" is used in the same sense, that is, as a measure of manufacturing employees' performance.) Few companies have failed to measure and analyze productivity or to set about to raise output/input ratios. But the results overall have been dismal.

From 1978 through 1982 U.S. manufacturing productivity was essentially flat. Although results during the past three years of business upturn have been better, they ran 25% lower than productivity improvements during earlier, postwar upturns.

Consider, for example, the XYZ Corporation, which I visited recently. The company operates a large manufacturing plant, where a well-organized productivity program, marshaling its best manufacturing talent, has been under way for three years. Its objective was to boost productivity so as to remove a 30% competitive cost disadvantage.

The program has included: appointing a corporate productivity manager; establishing departmental productivity committees; raising the number of industrial engineering professionals by 50%; carrying out operation-by-operation analyses to improve efficiency levels, avoid waste, and simplify jobs; retraining employees to work "smarter not harder"; streamlining work flow and materials movement; replacing out-of-date equipment; retooling operations to cut operator time; tightening standards; installing a computerized production control system; training foremen in work simplification; emphasizing good housekeeping and cleanliness; and installing a computer-based, measured-day work plan, which allows for daily performance reports on every operation, worker, and department.

For all this effort—and all the boost it gave to production managers' morale—little good has come of the program. Productivity has crept up by about 7% over three years, but profits remain negligible and market share continues to fall. As one executive said, "It's been great finally getting management support and the resources needed to get this plant cleaned up and efficient. But it is extremely discouraging to have worked so hard and, after three years, to be in worse competitive shape than when we started. I don't know how long we can keep trying harder when it doesn't seem to be getting us anywhere."

Unfortunately, XYZ's frustration with a full-out effort that achieves only insignificant competitive results is typical of what has been going on in much of American industry. Why so little competitive return— even a negative return—on so much effort? Is it the high value of the dollar, which cheapens imports? Is the cost gap just too great for us to overcome? Or are we going at the problems in the wrong way? What is going wrong? Why this apparent paradox?

The Wrong Approach

With these questions in mind, I have visited some 25 manufacturing companies during the last two years. Never have I seen so much energetic attention to productivity starting from the top and ricocheting all the way through organizations. This is American hustle and determination at its best. Productivity committees, productivity czars, productivity seminars, and productivity campaigns abound.

But the harder these companies work to improve productivity, the less they sharpen the competitive edge that *should* be improved by better productivity. Elusive gains and vanishing market share point not to a lack of effort but to a central flaw in how that effort is conceived. The very way managers define productivity improvement and the tools they use to achieve it push their goal further out of reach.

Resolutely chipping away at waste and inefficiency—the heart of most productivity programs—is not enough to restore competitive health. Indeed, a focus on cost reductions (that is, on raising labor output while holding the amount of labor constant or, better, reducing it) is proving harmful.

Let me repeat: not only is the productivity approach to manufacturing management not enough (companies cannot cut costs deeply enough to restore competitive vitality); it actually hurts as much as it helps. It is an instinctive response that absorbs managers' minds and diverts them from more effective manufacturing approaches.

Chipping away at productivity . . .

. . . is mostly concerned with direct labor efficiency, although direct labor costs exceed 10% of sales in only a few industries. Thus even an immense jump in productivity—say 20%—would not reverse the fortunes of import-damaged industries like autos, consumer electronics, textile machinery, shoes, or textiles.

. . . focuses excessively on the efficiency of factory workers. By trying to squeeze out better efficiency from improved attitudes and tighter discipline on a person-by-person and department-by-department basis, the approach detracts attention from the structure of the production system itself.

Production experience regularly observes a "40 40 20" rule. Roughly 40% of any manufacturing-based competitive advantage derives from long-term changes in manufacturing structure (decisions, for example, concerning the number, size, location, and capacity of facilities) and basic approaches in materials and work force management. Another 40% comes from major changes in equipment and process technology. The final 20%—no more—rests on conventional approaches to productivity improvement.

What this rule says is that the least powerful way to bolster competitive advantage is to focus on conventional productivity and cost-cutting approaches. Far more powerful are changes in manufacturing structure and technology. The rule does not, of course, say "Don't try to improve productivity." These well-known tools are easy to use and do help to remove unnecessary fat. But they quickly reach the limits of what they can contribute. Productivity is the wrong tree to bark up.

. . . ignores other ways to compete that use manufacturing as a strategic resource. Quality, reliable delivery, short lead times, customer service, rapid product introduction, flexible capacity, and efficient capital deployment—these, not cost reduction, are the primary operational sources of advantage in today's competitive environment.

. . . fails to provide or support a coherent manufacturing strategy. By assuming that manufacturing's essential task is to make a company the low-cost producer in its industry, this approach rashly rules out other strategies.

Most of the productivity-focused programs I have seen blithely assume that competitive position lost on grounds of higher cost is best recovered by installing cost-reduction programs. This logic is tempting but wrong. These programs cannot succeed. They have the wrong targets and misconstrue the nature of the competitive challenge they are supposed to address. Worse, they incur huge opportunity costs. By tying managers at all levels to short-term considerations, they short-circuit the development of an aggressive manufacturing strategy.

But they also do harm. These programs can, for example, hinder innovation. As William Abernathy's study of auto manufacturers has shown, an industry can easily become the prisoner of its own massive investments in low-cost production and in the organizational systems that support it.[1] When process costs and constraints drive both product and corporate strategy, flexibility gets lost, as does the ability to rapidly introduce product changes or develop new products.

Even more is at stake than getting locked into the wrong equipment. Managers under relentless pressure to maximize productivity resist innovation. Preoccupied as they are with this week's cost performance, they know well that changes in processes or systems will wreak havoc with the results on which they are measured. Consequently, innovations that lead to, say, better service or shorter lead times for product changeovers are certain to suffer.

Innovation is not, however, all that suffers. A full-out concentration on productivity frequently creates an environment that alienates the work force. Pressure for output and efficiency is the staple of factory life as hourly workers experience it. Engineers and supervisors tell them what to do, how to do it, and how long they may take. Theirs is an often unhappy, quota-measured culture—and has been for more than 150 years. In such an environment, even the most reasonable requests are resented.

Recent admirers of the Japanese argue that low cost and high quality can go hand in hand. Indeed, in the right setting managers need not trade one for the other. But in an efficiency-driven operation, this logic can be a trap. When low cost is the goal, quality often gets lost. But when quality is the goal, lower costs do usually follow.

The will to make large investments in radically new process technology gets lost too. The slow adoption of such manufacturing technologies as CAD/CAM, robotics, and flexible machining centers reflects managers' wise assumptions that these investments would initially drive productivity down.

Fears that several years of debugging and learning to use the new gear would hurt productivity have already cost many companies valuable time in mastering these process technologies. Even more troubling, the companies have failed to acquire a strategic resource that could help them restore their competitive position. A productivity focus inevitably forces managers into a short-term, operational mindset. When productivity is driving, experimentation takes a backseat.

The emphasis on direct costs, which attends the productivity focus, leads a company to use management controls that focus on the wrong targets. Inevitably, these controls key on direct labor: overhead is allocated by direct labor; variances from standards are calculated from direct labor. Performance in customer service, delivery, lead times, quality, and asset turns are secondary. The reward system based on such controls drives behavior toward simplistic goals that represent only a small fraction of total costs while the real costs lie in overhead and purchased materials.

Why has this gone on year after year even as the cost mix has steadily moved away from direct labor? By now our accounting and control systems are pathetically old-fashioned and ineffective. But nothing changes. Our continuing obsession with productivity as the be-all measure of factory performance is to blame, not the stubbornness of accountants.

When managers grow up in this atmosphere, their skills and vision never fully develop. They instinctively seize on inefficiencies and waste while missing broad opportunities to compete through manufacturing. The harsh fact is that generations of production managers have been stunted by this efficiency-driven mentality. Theirs is the oldest management function, yet today it is often the most backward. Unable to join finance, marketing, and general management in thinking strategically about their businesses, they are cut off from corporate leadership. As my recent study of 66 "comers" in production management shows, 10 or 15 years' immersion in a productivity-directed organization creates severe limitations of vision.[2] These limitations, in time, form a long-term mind-set that only a few can shake. Today the production function is seldom the place to find managers who can design competitive manufacturing structures.

Indeed, ever since Fredrick Winslow Taylor, our obsession with productivity and efficiency has spoiled the atmosphere of the factory. "Factory" is a bad word. Production managers first came into existence not as architects of competitive systems but as custodians of large, capital-intensive assets. Their job was to control and coordinate all factors of production so as to minimize costs and maximize output. This single dimension of performance is deeply ingrained in the profession and until recently has sufficed as a basis of evaluation.

Not surprisingly, it created a negative, penny-pinching, mechanistic culture in most factories—a culture that has driven out and kept away creative people at all levels. Who among our young today wishes to work in an environment where one is told what to do, how to do it, when to do it, is measured in minutes and sometimes seconds, is supervised closely to prevent any inefficiencies, and is paced by assembly lines or machines to produce at a rapid and relentless pace?

Today's problems in making the factory into a more attractive place to work are not new. They are the direct outcome of the 150-year history of an institution based on productivity. As long as cost and efficiency are the primary measurements of factory success, the manufacturing plant will continue to repel many able, creative people.

Breaking Out

Faced with this paradox—efforts to improve productivity driving competitive success further out of reach—a number of companies have broken out of the bind with extraordinary success. Their experience suggests, however, that breaking loose from so long-established a mind-set is not easy. It requires a change in culture, habits, instincts, and ways of thinking and reasoning. And it means modifying a set of values that current reward systems and day-to-day operational demands reinforce. This is a tall order.

Every company I know that has freed itself from the paradox has done so, in part, by:

Recognizing that its approach to productivity was not working well enough to make the company cost competitive. This recognition allowed managers to seek strategic objectives for manufacturing other than those determined primarily by cost.

About 12 years ago, a key division of American Standard adopted a "become the low-cost producer" strategy. Its productivity-driven focus did little to reduce costs but had an immediate negative effect on quality, delivery, and market share. What Standard needed was a totally new manufacturing strategy—one that allowed different areas of the factory to specialize in different markets and quality levels. When this approach replaced the low-cost strategy, the division regained its strong competitive position within three years.

Accepting the fact that its manufacturing was in trouble and needed to be run differently.

In the mid-1970s officers of the Copeland Corporation, a large producer of refrigeration compressors, decided that their industry was fast becoming mature. An analysis of their nearly obsolete production facilities and equipment made it clear that manufacturing had become a corporate millstone. Without a major change in the number, size, location, and focus of these facilities, long-term survival would be impossible. Copeland made these changes. The results (described later) were remarkable.

Developing and implementing a manufacturing strategy. (See "Manufacturing Strategy.")

When production managers actively seek to understand (and, in some cases, to help develop) the competitive strategy of relevant business units, they are better able to work out the objectives for their own function that will turn it into a competitive weapon. The requirements of such a manufacturing strategy will then determine needed changes in the manufacturing system's structure and infrastructure.

Manufacturing Strategy

A manufacturing strategy describes the competitive leverage required of—and made possible by—the production function. It analyzes the entire manufacturing function relative to its ability to provide such leverage, on which task it then focuses each element of manufacturing structure. It also allows the *structure* to be managed, not just the short-term, operational details of cost, quality, and delivery. And it spells out an internally consistent set of structural decisions designed to forge manufacturing into a strategic weapon. These structural decisions include:

- What to make and what to buy.
- The capacity levels to be provided.
- The number and sizes of plants.

- The location of plants.
- Choices of equipment and process technology.
- The production and inventory control systems.
- The quality control system.
- The cost and other information systems.
- Work force management policies.
- Organizational structure.

At Copeland, this approach led to order-of-magnitude improvements in quality, shortened delivery cycles, lower inventory investments, and much greater flexibility in product and volume changes.

Adopting new process technology. Changes in equipment and process technology are powerful engines of change. Bringing such technology on line helps force adjustments in work flow, key skills, and information systems as well as in systems for inventory control, materials management, and human resource management. There are few more effective means of loosening up old ways of organizing production.

General Electric and Deere & Company have made wholesale process changes at their dishwasher and locomotive (GE) and tractor (Deere) plants—changes that boosted product quality and reliability. Timken and Cooper Industries have each made large investments in radical new technologies that speeded up their ability to deliver new products and customer specials.

Making major changes in the selection, development, assignments, and reward systems for manufacturing managers.

The successful companies I looked at decided they needed a new breed of production leader—managers able to focus on a wider set of objectives than efficiency and cost. It was, however, no simple matter to find or train this new breed.

Some, in fact, turned up in unexpected places: marketing, sales, engineering, research, general management. As a group, they were good team builders and problem solvers and had broad enough experience to hold their own in top corporate councils. Their companies considered them among the most promising, high-potential "comers" for future leadership at the highest levels.

Only when manufacturers were willing to try such novel approaches to the competitive challenges facing them have they broken loose from the productivity paradox and transformed their production function into a strategic weapon. There is hope for manufacturing in America, but it rests on a different way of managing in this oldest of managerial professions.

As we have seen, our pursuit of productivity is paradoxical: the more we pursue it, the more elusive it becomes. An obsession with cost reduction produces a narrowness of vision and an organizational backlash that work against its underlying purpose. To boost productivity in its fullest sense—that is to unleash a powerful team of people supported by the right technology—we must first let go of old-fashioned productivity as a primary goal. In its place we must set a new, simple but powerful objective for manufacturing: to be competitive.

Notes

1. William J. Abernathy and Kenneth Wayne, "Limits of the Learning Curve," *Harvard Business Review,* September–October 1974, p. 109.
2. Wickham Skinner, "The Taming of Lions: How Manufacturing Leadership Evolved, 1780–1984," in *The Uneasy Alliance*, ed. Kim B. Clark, Robert H. Hayes, and Christopher Lorenz (Boston: Harvard Business School Press, 1985), p. 63.

8
From Competitive Advantage to Corporate Strategy

Michael E. Porter

Corporate strategy, the overall plan for a diversified company, is both the darling and the stepchild of contemporary management practice—the darling because CEOs have been obsessed with diversification since the early 1960s, the stepchild because almost no consensus exists about what corporate strategy is, much less about how a company should formulate it.

A diversified company has two levels of strategy: business unit (or competitive) strategy and corporate (or companywide) strategy. Competitive strategy concerns how to create competitive advantage in each of the businesses in which a company competes. Corporate strategy concerns two different questions: what businesses the corporation should be in and how the corporate office should manage the array of business units.

Corporate strategy is what makes the corporate whole add up to more than the sum of its business unit parts.

The track record of corporate strategies has been dismal. I studied the diversification records of 33 large, prestigious U.S. companies over the 1950–1986 period and found that most of them had divested many more acquisitions than they had kept. The corporate strategies of most companies have dissipated instead of created shareholder value.

The need to rethink corporate strategy could hardly be more urgent. By taking over companies and breaking them up, corporate raiders

Author's note: The research for this article was done with the able assistance of my research associate Cheng G. Ong. Malcolm S. Salter, Andrall E. Pearson, A. Michael Keehner, and the Monitor Company also provided helpful comments.

thrive on failed corporate strategy. Fueled by junk bond financing and growing acceptability, raiders can expose any company to takeover, no matter how large or blue chip.

Recognizing past diversification mistakes, some companies have initiated large-scale restructuring programs. Others have done nothing at all. Whatever the response, the strategic questions persist. Those who have restructured must decide what to do next to avoid repeating the past; those who have done nothing must awake to their vulnerability. To survive, companies must understand what good corporate strategy is.

A Sober Picture

While there is disquiet about the success of corporate strategies, none of the available evidence satisfactorily indicates the success or failure of corporate strategy. Most studies have approached the question by measuring the stock market valuation of mergers, captured in the movement of the stock prices of acquiring companies immediately before and after mergers are announced.

These studies show that the market values mergers as neutral or slightly negative, hardly cause for serious concern.[1] Yet the short-term market reaction is a highly imperfect measure of the long-term success of diversification, and no self-respecting executive would judge a corporate strategy this way.

Studying the diversification programs of a company over a long period of time is a much more telling way to determine whether a corporate strategy has succeeded or failed. My study of 33 companies, many of which have reputations for good management, is a unique look at the track record of major corporations. (For an explanation of the research, see Appendix A.) Each company entered an average of 80 new industries and 27 new fields. Just over 70% of the new entries were acquisitions, 22% were start-ups, and 8% were joint ventures. IBM, Exxon, Du Pont, and 3M, for example, focused on start-ups, while ALCO Standard, Beatrice, and Sara Lee diversified almost solely through acquisitions (Exhibit I has a complete rundown).

My data paint a sobering picture of the success ratio of these moves (see Exhibit II). I found that on average corporations divested more than half their acquisitions in new industries and more than 60% of their acquisitions in entirely new fields. Fourteen companies left more than 70% of all the acquisitions they had made in new fields. The track record in unrelated acquisitions is even worse—the average divestment rate is a startling 74% (see Exhibit III). Even a highly respected company like General Electric divested a very high percentage of its acquisitions, particularly those in new fields. Companies near the top of the list in Exhibit II achieved a remarkably low rate of divestment. Some bear witness to the success of well-thought-out corporate strategies. Others, however, enjoy a lower rate simply because they have not faced up to their problem units and divested them.

I calculated total shareholder returns (stock price appreciation plus dividends) over the period of the study for each company so that I could compare them with its divestment rate. While companies near the top of the list have above-average shareholder returns, returns are not a reliable measure of diversification success. Shareholder return often depends heavily on the inherent attractiveness of companies' base industries. Companies like CBS and General Mills had extremely profitable base businesses that subsidized poor diversification track records.

I would like to make one comment on the use of shareholder value to judge performance. Linking shareholder value quantitatively to diversification performance only works if you compare the shareholder value that is with the shareholder value that might have been without diversification. Because such a comparison is virtually impossible to make, my own measure of diversification success—the number of units retained by the company—seems to be as good an indicator as any of the contribution of diversification to corporate performance.

My data give a stark indication of the failure of corporate strategies.[2] Of the 33 companies, 6 had been taken over as my study was being completed (see the note on Exhibit II). Only the lawyers, investment bankers, and original sellers have prospered in most of these acquisitions, not the shareholders.

Premises of Corporate Strategy

Any successful corporate strategy builds on a number of premises. These are facts of life about diversification. They cannot be altered, and when ignored, they explain in part why so many corporate strategies fail.

Competition occurs at the business unit level. Diversified com-

Exhibit I. Diversification profiles of 33 leading U.S. companies

Company	Number total entries	All entries into new industries	Percent acquisitions	Percent joint ventures	Percent start-ups	Entries into new industries that represented entirely new fields	Percent acquisitions	Percent joint ventures	Percent start-ups
ALCO Standard	221	165	99%	0%	1%	56	100%	0%	0%
Allied Corp.	77	49	67	10	22	17	65	6	29
Beatrice	382	204	97	1	2	61	97	0	3
Borden	170	96	77	4	19	32	75	3	22
CBS	148	81	67	16	17	28	65	21	14
Continental Group	75	47	77	6	17	19	79	11	11
Cummins Engine	30	24	54	17	29	13	46	23	31
Du Pont	80	39	33	16	51	19	37	0	63
Exxon	79	56	34	5	61	17	29	6	65
General Electric	160	108	47	20	33	29	48	14	38
General Foods	92	53	91	4	6	22	86	5	9
General Mills	110	102	84	7	9	27	74	7	19
W.R.Grace	275	202	83	7	10	66	74	5	21
Gulf & Western	178	140	91	4	6	48	88	2	10
IBM	46	38	18	18	63	16	19	0	81
IC Industries	67	41	85	3	12	17	88	6	6

ITT	246	178	89	2	9	50	92	0	8
Johnson & Johnson	88	77	77	0	23	18	56	0	44
Mobil	41	32	53	16	31	15	60	7	33
Procter & Gamble	28	23	61	0	39	14	79	0	21
Raytheon	70	58	86	9	5	16	81	19	6
RCA	53	46	35	15	50	19	37	21	42
Rockwell	101	75	73	24	3	27	74	22	4
Sara Lee	197	141	96	1	4	41	95	2	2
Scovill	52	36	97	0	3	12	92	0	8
Signal	53	45	67	4	29	20	75	0	25
Tenneco	85	62	81	6	13	26	73	8	19
3M	144	125	54	2	45	34	71	3	56
TRW	119	82	77	10	13	28	64	11	25
United Technologies	62	49	57	18	24	17	23	17	39
Westinghouse	129	73	63	11	26	36	61	3	36
Wickes	71	47	83	0	17	22	68	0	32
Xerox	59	50	66	6	28	18	50	11	39
Total	**3,788**	**2,644**				906			
Average	**114.8**	**80.1**	**70.3%**	**7.9%**	**21.8%**	**27.4**	**67.9%**	**7.0%**	**25.9%**

Notes: Beatrice, Continental Group, General Foods, RCA, Scovill, and Signal were taken over as the study was being completed. Their data cover the period up through takeover but not subsequent divestments.

The percentage averages may not add up to 100% because of rounding off.

Exhibit II. Acquisition track records of leading U.S. diversifiers ranked by percent divested

Company	All acquisitions in new industries	Percent made by 1980 and then divested	Percent made by 1975 and then divested	Acquisitions in new industries that represented entirely new fields	Percent made by 1980 and then divested	Percent made by 1975 and then divested
Johnson & Johnson	59	17%	12%	10	33%	14%
Procter & Gamble	14	17	17	11	17	17
Raytheon	50	17	26	13	25	33
United Technologies	28	25	13	10	17	0
3M	67	26	27	24	42	45
TRW	63	27	31	18	40	38
IBM	7	33	0*	3	33	0*
Du Pont	13	38	43	7	60	75
Mobil	17	38	57	9	50	50
Borden	74	39	40	24	45	50
IC Industries	35	42	50	15	46	44
Tenneco	50	43	47	19	27	33
Beatrice	198	46	45	59	52	51
ITT	159	52	52	46	61	61
Rockwell	55	56	57	20	71	71
Allied Corp.	33	57	45	11	80	67
Exxon	19	62	20*	5	80	50*

Company						
Sara Lee	135	62	65	39	80	76
General Foods	48	63	62	19	93	93
Scovill	35	64	77	11	64	70
Signal	30	65	63	15	70	67
ALCO Standard	164	65	70	56	72	76
W.R. Grace	167	65	70	49	71	70
General Electric	51	65	78	14	100	100
Wickes	38	67	72	15	73	70
Westinghouse	46	68	69	22	61	59
Xerox	33	71	79	9	100	100
Continental Group	36	71	72	15	60	60
General Mills	86	75	73	20	65	60
Gulf & Western	127	79	78	42	75	72
Cummins Engine	13	80	80	6	83	83
RCA	16	80	92	7	86	100
CBS	54	87	89	18	88	88
Total	2,021			661		
Average per company†	**61.2**	**53.4%**	**56.5%**	**20.0**	**61.2%**	**61.1%**

*Companies with three or fewer acquisitions by the cutoff year.
†Companies with three or fewer acquisitions by the cutoff year are excluded from the average to minimize statistical distortions.
Note: Beatrice, Continental Group, General Foods, RCA, Scovill, and Signal were taken over as the study was being completed. Their data cover the period up through takeover but not subsequent divestments.

Exhibit III. Diversification performance in joint ventures, start-ups, and unrelated acquisitions (Companies in same order as in Exhibit II)

Company	Joint ventures as a percent of new entries	Percent made by 1980 and then divested	Percent made by 1975 and then divested	Start-ups as a percent of new entries	Percent made by 1980 and then divested	Percent made by 1975 and then divested	Acquisitions in unrelated new fields as a percent of total acquisitions in new fields	Percent made by 1980 and then divested	Percent made by 1975 and then divested
Johnson & Johnson	0%	†	†	23%	14%	20%	0%	†	†
Procter & Gamble	0	†	†	39	0	0	9	†	†
Raytheon	9	60%	60%	5	50	50	46	40%	40%
United Technologies	18	50	50	24	11	20	40	0*	0*
3M	2	100*	100*	45	2	3	33	75	86
TRW	10	20	25	13	63	71	39	71	71
IBM	18	100*	†	63	20	22	33	100*	100*
Du Pont	16	100*	†	51	61	61	43	0*	0*
Mobil	16	33	33	31	50	56	67	60	100
Borden	4	33	33	19	17	13	21	80	80
IC Industries	3	100*	100*	13	80	30	33	50	50
Tenneco	6	67	67	13	67	80	42	33	40
Beatrice	1	†	†	2	0	0	63	59	53
ITT	2	0*	†	8	38	57	61	67	64
Rockwell	24	38	42	3	0	0	35	100	100
Allied Corp.	10	100	75	22	38	29	45	50	0

Exxon	5	0	0	61	27	19	100	80	50*
Sara Lee	1	†	†	4	75	100*	41	73	73
General Foods	4	†	†	6	67	50	42	86	83
Scovill	0	†	†	3	100	100*	45	80	100
Signal	4	†	†	29	20	11	67	50	50
ALCO Standard	0	†	†	1	†	†	63	79	81
W.R. Grace	7	33	38	10	71	71	39	65	65
General Electric	20	20	33	33	33	44	36	100	100
Wickes	0	†	†	17	63	57	60	80	75
Westinghouse	11	0*	0*	26	44	44	36	57	67
Xerox	6	100*	100*	28	50	56	22	100	100
Continental Group	6	67	67	17	14	0	40	83	100
General Mills	7	71	71	9	89	80	65	77	67
Gulf & Western	4	75	50	6	100	100	74	77	74
Cummins Engine	17	50	50	29	0	0	67	100	100
RCA	15	67	67	50	99	55	36	100	100
CBS	16	71	71	17	86	80	39	100	100
Average per company‡	**7.9%**	**50.3%**	**48.9%**	**21.8%**	**44.0%**	**40.9%**	**46.1%**	**74.0%**	**74.4%**

*Companies with two or fewer entries.

†No entries in this category.

‡Average excludes companies with two or fewer entries to minimize statistical distortions.

Note: Beatrice, Continental Group, General Foods, RCA, Scovill, and Signal were taken over as the study was being completed. Their data cover the period up through takeover but not subsequent divestments.

panies do not compete; only their business units do. Unless a corporate strategy places primary attention on nurturing the success of each unit, the strategy will fail, no matter how elegantly constructed. Successful corporate strategy must grow out of and reinforce competitive strategy.

Diversification inevitably adds costs and constraints to business units. Obvious costs such as the corporate overhead allocated to a unit may not be as important or subtle as the hidden costs and constraints. A business unit must explain its decisions to top management, spend time complying with planning and other corporate systems, live with parent company guidelines and personnel policies, and forgo the opportunity to motivate employees with direct equity ownership. These costs and constraints can be reduced but not entirely eliminated.

Shareholders can readily diversify themselves. Shareholders can diversify their own portfolios of stocks by selecting those that best match their preferences and risk profiles.[3] Shareholders can often diversify more cheaply than a corporation because they can buy shares at the market price and avoid hefty acquisition premiums.

These premises mean that corporate strategy cannot succeed unless it truly adds value—to business units by providing tangible benefits that offset the inherent costs of lost independence and to shareholders by diversifying in a way they could not replicate.

Passing the Essential Tests

To understand how to formulate corporate strategy, it is necessary to specify the conditions under which diversification will truly create shareholder value. These conditions can be summarized in three essential tests:

1. **The attractiveness test.** The industries chosen for diversification must be structurally attractive or capable of being made attractive.
2. **The cost-of-entry test.** The cost of entry must not capitalize all the future profits.
3. **The better-off test.** Either the new unit must gain competitive advantage from its link with the corporation or vice versa.

Of course, most companies will make certain that their proposed strategies pass some of these tests. But my study clearly shows that when companies ignored one or two of them, the strategic results were disastrous.

HOW ATTRACTIVE IS THE INDUSTRY?

In the long run, the rate of return available from competing in an industry is a function of its underlying structure, which I have described in another *Harvard Business Review* article.[4] An attractive industry with a high average return on investment will be difficult to enter because entry barriers are high, suppliers and buyers have only modest bargaining power, substitute products or services are few, and the rivalry among competitors is stable. An unattractive industry like steel will have structural flaws, including a plethora of substitute materials, powerful and price-sensitive buyers, and excessive rivalry caused by high fixed costs and a large group of competitors, many of whom are state supported.

Diversification cannot create shareholder value unless new industries have favorable structures that support returns exceeding the cost of capital. If the industry doesn't have such returns, the company must be able to restructure the industry or gain a sustainable competitive advantage that leads to returns well above the industry average. An industry need not be attractive before diversification. In fact, a company might benefit from entering before the industry shows its full potential. The diversification can then transform the industry's structure.

In my research, I often found companies had suspended the attractiveness test because they had a vague belief that the industry "fit" very closely with their own businesses. In the hope that the corporate "comfort" they felt would lead to a happy outcome, the companies ignored fundamentally poor industry structures. Unless the close fit allows substantial competitive advantage, however, such comfort will turn into pain when diversification results in poor returns. Royal Dutch Shell and other leading oil companies have had this unhappy experience in a number of chemicals businesses, where poor industry structures overcame the benefits of vertical integration and skills in process technology.

Another common reason for ignoring the attractiveness test is a low entry cost. Sometimes the buyer has an inside track or the owner is anxious to sell. Even if the price is actually low, however, a one-shot gain will not offset a perpetually poor business. Almost always, the company finds it must reinvest in the newly acquired unit, if only to replace fixed assets and fund working capital.

Diversifying companies are also prone to use rapid growth or other simple indicators as a proxy for a target industry's attractiveness. Many that rushed into fast-growing industries (personal computers, video games, and robotics, for example) were burned because they mistook early growth for long-term profit potential. Industries are profitable not because they are sexy or high tech; they are profitable only if their structures are attractive.

WHAT IS THE COST OF ENTRY?

Diversification cannot build shareholder value if the cost of entry into a new business eats up its expected returns. Strong market forces, however, are working to do just that. A company can enter new industries by acquisition or start-up. Acquisitions expose it to an increasingly efficient merger market. An acquirer beats the market if it pays a price not fully reflecting the prospects of the new unit. Yet multiple bidders are commonplace, information flows rapidly, and investment bankers and other intermediaries work aggressively to make the market as efficient as possible. In recent years, new financial instruments such as junk bonds have brought new buyers into the market and made even large companies vulnerable to takeover. Acquisition premiums are high and reflect the acquired company's future prospects—sometimes too well. Philip Morris paid more than four times book value for Seven-Up Company, for example. Simple arithmetic meant that profits had to more than quadruple to sustain the preacquisition ROI. Since there proved to be little Philip Morris could add in marketing prowess to the sophisticated marketing wars in the soft-drink industry, the result was the unsatisfactory financial performance of Seven-Up and ultimately the decision to divest.

In a start-up, the company must overcome entry barriers. It's a real catch-22 situation, however, since attractive industries are attractive because their entry barriers are high. Bearing the full cost of the entry barriers might well dissipate any potential profits. Otherwise, other entrants to the industry would have already eroded its profitability.

In the excitement of finding an appealing new business, companies sometimes forget to apply the cost-of-entry test. The more attractive a new industry, the more expensive it is to get into.

WILL THE BUSINESS BE BETTER OFF?

A corporation must bring some significant competitive advantage to the new unit, or the new unit must offer potential for significant advantage to the corporation. Sometimes, the benefits to the new unit accrue only once, near the time of entry, when the parent instigates a major overhaul of its strategy or installs a first-rate management team. Other diversification yields ongoing competitive advantage if the new unit can market its product through the well-developed distribution system of its sister units, for instance. This is one of the important underpinnings of the merger of Baxter Travenol and American Hospital Supply.

When the benefit to the new unit comes only once, the parent company has no rationale for holding the new unit in its portfolio over the long term. Once the results of the one-time improvement are clear, the diversified company no longer adds value to offset the inevitable costs imposed on the unit. It is best to sell the unit and free up corporate resources.

The better-off test does not imply that diversifying corporate risk creates shareholder value in and of itself. Doing something for shareholders that they can do themselves is not a basis for corporate strategy. (Only in the case of a privately held company, in which the company's and the shareholder's risk are the same, is diversification to reduce risk valuable for its own sake.) Diversification of risk should only be a by-product of corporate strategy, not a prime motivator.

Executives ignore the better-off test most of all or deal with it through arm waving or trumped-up logic rather than hard strategic analysis. One reason is that they confuse company size with shareholder value. In the drive to run a bigger company, they lose sight of their real job. They may justify the suspension of the better-off test by pointing to the way they manage diversity. By cutting corporate staff to the bone and giving business units nearly complete autonomy, they believe they avoid the pitfalls. Such thinking misses the whole point of diversification, which is to create shareholder value rather than to avoid destroying it.

Concepts of Corporate Strategy

The three tests for successful diversification set the standards that any corporate strategy must meet; meeting them is so difficult that most diversification fails. Many companies lack a clear concept of corporate strategy to guide their diversification or pursue a concept that does not address the tests. Others fail because they implement a strategy poorly.

My study has helped me identify four concepts of corporate strategy that have been put into practice—portfolio management, restructuring, transferring skills, and sharing activities. While the concepts are not always mutually exclusive, each rests on a different mechanism by which the corporation creates shareholder value and each requires the diversified company to manage and organize itself in a different way. The first two require no connections among business units; the second two depend on them. (See Exhibit IV.) While all four concepts of strategy have succeeded under the right circumstances, today some make more sense than others. Ignoring any of the concepts is perhaps the quickest road to failure.

PORTFOLIO MANAGEMENT

The concept of corporate strategy most in use is portfolio management, which is based primarily on diversification through acquisition. The corporation acquires sound, attractive companies with competent managers who agree to stay on. While acquired units do not have to be in the same industries as existing units, the best portfolio managers generally limit their range of businesses in some way, in part to limit the specific expertise needed by top management.

The acquired units are autonomous, and the teams that run them are compensated according to unit results. The corporation supplies capital and works with each to infuse it with professional management techniques. At the same time, top management provides objective and dispassionate review of business unit results. Portfolio managers categorize units by potential and regularly transfer resources from units that generate cash to those with high potential and cash needs.

In a portfolio strategy, the corporation seeks to create shareholder value in a number of ways. It uses its expertise and analytical resources to spot attractive acquisition candidates that the individual shareholder could not. The company provides capital on favorable terms that reflect corporatewide fund-raising ability. It introduces professional management skills and discipline. Finally, it provides high-quality review and coaching, unencumbered by conventional wisdom or emotional attachments to the business.

The logic of the portfolio management concept rests on a number of vital assumptions. If a company's diversification plan is to meet the attractiveness and cost-of-entry tests, it must find good but undervalued companies. Acquired companies must be truly undervalued because the parent does little for the new unit once it is acquired. To meet the better-off test, the benefits the corporation provides must yield a significant competitive advantage to acquired units. The style of operating through highly autonomous business units must both develop sound business strategies and motivate managers.

In most countries, the days when portfolio management was a valid concept of corporate strategy are past. In the face of increasingly well-developed capital markets, attractive companies with good managements show up on everyone's computer screen and attract top dollar in terms of acquisition premium. Simply contributing capital isn't contributing much. A sound strategy can easily be funded; small to medium-size companies don't need a munificent parent.

Other benefits have also eroded. Large companies no longer corner the market for professional management skills; in fact, more and more observers believe managers cannot necessarily run anything in the absence of industry-specific knowledge and experience. Another supposed advantage of the portfolio management concept—dispassionate review—rests on similarly shaky ground since the added value of review alone is questionable in a portfolio of sound companies.

The benefit of giving business units complete autonomy is also questionable. Increasingly, a company's business units are interrelated, drawn together by new technology, broadening distribution channels, and changing regulations. Setting strategies of units independently may well undermine unit performance. The companies in my sample that have succeeded in diversification have recognized the value of interrelationships and understood that a strong sense of corporate identity is as important as slavish adherence to parochial business unit financial results.

But it is the sheer complexity of the management task that has ultimately defeated even the best portfolio managers. As the size of the company grows, portfolio managers need to find more and more deals just to maintain growth. Supervising dozens or even hundreds of disparate units and under chain-letter pressures to add more, management begins to make mistakes. At the same time, the inevitable costs of being part of a diversified company take their toll and unit performance slides while the whole company's ROI turns downward. Eventually, a new management team is installed that initiates whole-

Exhibit IV. *Concepts of corporate strategy*

	Portfolio management	Restructuring	Transferring skills	Sharing activities
Strategic prerequisites	Superior insight into identifying and acquiring undervalued companies	Superior insight into identifying restructuring opportunities	Proprietary skills in activities important to competitive advantage in target industries	Activities in existing units that can be shared with new business units to gain competitive advantage
	Willingness to sell off losers quickly or to opportunistically divest good performers when buyers are willing to pay large premiums	Willingness and capability to intervene to transform acquired units	Ability to accomplish the transfer of skills among units on an ongoing basis	Benefits of sharing that outweigh the costs
	Broad guidelines for and constraints on the types of units in the portfolio so that senior management can play the review role effectively	Broad similarities among the units in the portfolio	Acquisitions of beachhead positions in new industries as a base	Both start-ups and acquisitions as entry vehicles
		Willingness to cut losses by selling off units where restructuring proves unfeasible		Ability to overcome organizational resistance to business unit collaboration
	A private company or undeveloped capital markets	Willingness to sell units when restructuring is complete, the results are clear, and market conditions are favorable		
	Ability to shift away from portfolio management as the capital markets get more efficient or the company gets unwieldy			

prerequisites	A very small, low-cost, corporate staff Incentives based largely on business unit results	A corporate organization with the talent and resources to oversee the turnarounds and strategic repositioning of acquired units Incentives based largely on acquired units' results	collaborative business units High-level corporate staff members who see their role primarily as integrators Cross-business-unit committees, task forces, and other forums to serve as focal points for capturing and transferring skills Objectives of line managers that include skills transfer Incentives based in part on corporate results	that are encouraged to share activities An active strategic planning role at group, sector, and corporate levels High-level corporate staff members who see their roles primarily as integrators Incentives based heavily on group and corporate results
Common pitfalls	Pursuing portfolio management in countries with efficient capital marketing and a developed pool of professional management talent Ignoring the fact that industry structure is not attractive	Mistaking rapid growth or a "hot" industry as sufficient evidence of a restructuring opportunity Lacking the resolve or resources to take on troubled situations and to intervene in management Ignoring the fact that industry structure is not attractive Paying lip service to restructuring but actually practicing passive portfolio management	Mistaking similarity or comfort with new businesses as sufficient basis for diversification Providing no practical ways for skills transfer to occur Ignoring the fact that industry structure is not attractive	Sharing for its own sake rather than because it leads to competitive advantage Assuming sharing will occur naturally without senior management playing an active role Ignoring the fact that industry structure is not attractive

sale divestments and pares down the company to its core businesses. The experiences of Gulf & Western, Consolidated Foods (now Sara Lee), and ITT are just a few comparatively recent examples. Reflecting these realities, the U.S. capital markets today reward companies that follow the portfolio management model with a "conglomerate discount"; they value the whole less than the sum of the parts.

In developing countries, where large companies are few, capital markets are undeveloped, and professional management is scarce, portfolio management still works. But it is no longer a valid model for corporate strategy in advanced economies. Nevertheless, the technique is in the limelight today in the United Kingdom, where it is supported so far by a newly energized stock market eager for excitement. But this enthusiasm will wane—as well it should. Portfolio management is no way to conduct corporate strategy.

RESTRUCTURING

Unlike its passive role as a portfolio manager, when it serves as banker and reviewer, a company that bases its strategy on restructuring becomes an active restructurer of business units. The new businesses are not necessarily related to existing units. All that is necessary is unrealized potential.

The restructuring strategy seeks out undeveloped, sick, or threatened organizations or industries on the threshold of significant change. The parent intervenes, frequently changing the unit management team, shifting strategy, or infusing the company with new technology. Then it may make follow-up acquisitions to build a critical mass and sell off unneeded or unconnected parts and thereby reduce the effective acquisition cost. The result is a strengthened company or a transformed industry. As a coda, the parent sells off the stronger unit once results are clear because the parent is no longer adding value and top management decides that its attention should be directed elsewhere. (See "An Uncanny British Restructurer" for an example of restructuring.)

An Uncanny British Restructurer

Hanson Trust, on its way to becoming Britain's largest company, is one of several skillful followers of the restructuring concept. A conglomerate with units in many industries, Hanson might seem on the surface a portfolio manager. In fact, Hanson and one or two other conglomerates have a much more effective corporate strategy. Hanson has acquired companies such as London Brick, Ever Ready Batteries, and SCM, which the city of London rather disdainfully calls "low tech."

Although a mature company suffering from low growth, the typical Hanson target is not just in any industry; it has an attractive structure. Its customer and supplier power is low and rivalry with competitors moderate. The target is a market leader, rich in assets but formerly poor in management. Hanson pays little of the present value of future cash flow out in an acquisition premium and reduces purchase price even further by aggressively selling off businesses that it cannot improve. In this way, it recoups just over a third of the cost of a typical acquisition during the first six months of ownership. Imperial Group's plush properties in London lasted barely two months under Hanson ownership, while Hanson's recent sale of Courage Breweries to Elders recouped £1.4 billion of the original £2.1 billion acquisition price of Imperial Group.

Like the best restructurers, Hanson approaches each unit with a modus operandi that it has perfected through repetition.

Hanson emphasizes low costs and tight financial controls. It has cut an average of 25% of labor costs out of acquired companies, slashed fixed overheads, and tightened capital expenditures. To reinforce its strategy of keeping costs low, Hanson carves out detailed one-year financial budgets with divisional managers and (through generous use of performance-related bonuses and share option schemes) gives them incentive to deliver the goods.

It's too early to tell whether Hanson will adhere to the last tenet of restructuring—selling turned-around units once the results are clear. If it succumbs to the allure of bigness, Hanson may take the course of the failed U.S. conglomerates.

When well implemented, the restructuring concept is sound, for it passes the three tests of successful diversification. The restructurer meets the cost-of-entry test through the types of company it acquires. It limits acquisition premiums by buying companies with problems and lackluster images or by buying into industries with as yet unforeseen potential. Intervention by the corporation clearly meets the better-off test. Provided that the target industries are structurally attractive, the restructuring model can create enormous shareholder value. Some restructuring companies are Loew's, BTR, and General Cinema. Ironically, many of today's restructurers are profiting from yesterday's portfolio management strategies.

To work, the restructuring strategy requires a corporate management team with the insight to spot undervalued companies or positions in industries ripe for transformation. The same insight is necessary to actually turn the units around even though they are in new and unfamiliar businesses.

These requirements expose the restructurer to considerable risk and usually limit the time in which the company can succeed at the strategy. The most skillful proponents understand this problem, recognize their mistakes, and move decisively to dispose of them. The best companies realize they are not just acquiring companies but restructuring an industry. Unless they can integrate the acquisitions to create a whole new strategic position, they are just portfolio managers in disguise. Another important difficulty surfaces if so many other companies join the action that they deplete the pool of suitable candidates and bid their prices up.

Perhaps the greatest pitfall, however, is that companies find it very hard to dispose of business units once they are restructured and performing well. Human nature fights economic rationale. Size supplants shareholder value as the corporate goal. The company does not sell a unit even though the company no longer adds value to the unit. While the transformed units would be better off in another company that had related businesses, the restructuring company instead retains them. Gradually, it becomes a portfolio manager. The parent company's ROI declines as the need for reinvestment in the units and normal business risks eventually offset restructuring's one-shot gain. The perceived need to keep growing intensifies the pace of acquisition; errors result and standards fall. The restructuring company turns into a conglomerate with returns that only equal the average of all industries at best.

TRANSFERRING SKILLS

The purpose of the first two concepts of corporate strategy is to create value through a company's relationship with each autonomous unit. The corporation's role is to be a selector, a banker, and an intervenor.

The last two concepts exploit the interrelationships between businesses. In articulating them, however, one comes face-to-face with the often ill-defined concept of synergy. If you believe the text of the countless corporate annual reports, just about anything is related to just about anything else! But imagined synergy is much more common than real synergy. GM's purchase of Hughes Aircraft simply because cars were going electronic and Hughes was an electronics concern demonstrates the folly of paper synergy. Such corporate relatedness is an ex post facto rationalization of a diversification undertaken for other reasons.

Even synergy that is clearly defined often fails to materialize. Instead of cooperating, business units often compete. A company that can define the synergies it is pursuing still faces significant organizational impediments in achieving them.

But the need to capture the benefits of relationships between businesses has never been more important. Technological and competitive developments already link many businesses and are creating new possibilities for competitive advantage. In such sectors as financial services, computing, office equipment, entertainment, and health care, interrelationships among previously distinct businesses are perhaps the central concern of strategy.

To understand the role of relatedness in corporate strategy, we must give new meaning to this often ill-defined idea. I have identified a good way to start—the value chain.[5] Every business unit is a collection of discrete activities ranging from sales to accounting that allow it to compete. I call them value activities. It is at this level, not in the company as a whole, that the unit achieves competitive advantage.

I group these activities in nine categories. *Primary* activities create the product or service, deliver and market it, and provide after-sale support. The categories of primary activities are inbound logistics, operations, outbound logistics, marketing and sales, and service. *Support* activities provide the input and infrastructure that allow the primary activities to take place. The categories are company infrastructure, human resource management, technology development, and procurement.

The value chain defines the two types of interrelationships that may create synergy. The first is a company's ability to transfer skills or expertise among similar value chains. The second is the ability to share activities. Two business units, for example, can share the same sales force or logistics network.

The value chain helps expose the last two (and most important) concepts of corporate strategy. The transfer of skills among business units in the diversified company is the basis for one concept. While each business unit has a separate value chain, knowledge about how to perform activities is transferred among the units. For example, a toiletries business unit, expert in the marketing of convenience products, transmits ideas on new positioning concepts, promotional techniques, and packaging possibilities to a newly acquired unit that sells cough syrup. Newly entered industries can benefit from the expertise of existing units and vice versa.

These opportunities arise when business units have similar buyers or channels, similar value activities like government relations or procurement, similarities in the broad configuration of the value chain (for example, managing a multisite service organization), or the same strategic concept (for example, low cost). Even though the units operate separately, such similarities allow the sharing of knowledge.

Of course, some similarities are common; one can imagine them at some level between almost any pair of businesses. Countless companies have fallen into the trap of diversifying too readily because of similarities; mere similarity is not enough.

Transferring skills leads to competitive advantage only if the similarities among businesses meet three conditions.

1. The activities involved in the businesses are similar enough that sharing expertise is meaningful. Broad similarities (marketing intensiveness, for example, or a common core process technology such as bending metal) are not a sufficient basis for diversification. The resulting ability to transfer skills is likely to have little impact on competitive advantage.

2. The transfer of skills involves activities important to competitive advantage. Transferring skills in peripheral activities such as government relations or real estate in consumer goods units may be beneficial but is not a basis for diversification.

3. The skills transferred represent a significant source of competitive advantage for the receiving unit. The expertise or skills to be transferred are both advanced and proprietary enough to be beyond the capabilities of competitors.

The transfer of skills is an active process that significantly changes the strategy or operations of the receiving unit. The prospect for change must be specific and identifiable. Almost guaranteeing that no shareholder value will be created, too many companies are satisfied with vague prospects or faint hopes that skills will transfer. The transfer of skills does not happen by accident or by osmosis. The company will have to reassign critical personnel, even on a permanent basis, and the participation and support of high-level management in skills transfer is essential. Many companies have been defeated at skills transfer because they have not provided their business units with any incentives to participate.

Transferring skills meets the tests of diversification if the company truly mobilizes proprietary expertise across units. This makes certain the company can offset the acquisition premium or lower the cost of overcoming entry barriers.

The industries the company chooses for diversification must pass the attractiveness test. Even a close fit that reflects opportunities to transfer skills may not overcome poor industry structure. Opportunities to transfer skills, however, may help the company transform the structures of newly entered industries and send them in favorable directions.

The transfer of skills can be one-time or ongoing. If the company exhausts opportunities to infuse new expertise into a unit after the initial postacquisition period, the unit should ultimately be sold. The corporation is no longer creating shareholder value. Few companies have grasped this point, however, and many gradually suffer mediocre returns. Yet a company diversified into well-chosen businesses can transfer skills eventually in many directions. If corporate management conceives of its role in this way and creates appropriate organizational mechanisms to facilitate cross-unit interchange, the opportunities to share expertise will be meaningful.

By using both acquisitions and internal development, companies can build a transfer-of-skills strategy. The presence of a strong base of skills sometimes creates the possibility for internal entry instead of the acquisition of a going concern. Successful diversifiers that employ the concept of skills transfer may, however, often acquire a company in the target industry as a beachhead and then build on it with their internal expertise. By doing so, they can reduce some of the risks of internal entry and speed up the process. Two companies that have diversified using the transfer-of-skills concept are 3M and Pepsico.

SHARING ACTIVITIES

The fourth concept of corporate strategy is based on sharing activities in the value chains among business units. Procter & Gamble, for example, employs a common physical distribution system and sales force in both paper towels and disposable diapers. McKesson, a leading distribution company, will handle such diverse lines as pharmaceuticals and liquor through superwarehouses.

The ability to share activities is a potent basis for corporate strategy because sharing often enhances competitive advantage by lowering cost or raising differentiation. But not all sharing leads to competitive advantage, and companies can encounter deep organizational resistance to even beneficial sharing possibilities. These hard truths have led many companies to reject synergy prematurely and retreat to the false simplicity of portfolio management.

A cost-benefit analysis of prospective sharing opportunities can determine whether synergy is possible. Sharing can lower costs if it achieves economies of scale, boosts the efficiency of utilization, or helps a company move more rapidly down the learning curve. The costs of General Electric's advertising, sales, and after-sales service activities in major appliances are low because they are spread over a wide range of appliance products. Sharing can also enhance the potential for differentiation. A shared order-processing system, for instance, may allow new features and services that a buyer will value. Sharing can also reduce the cost of differentiation. A shared service network, for example, may make more advanced, remote servicing technology economically feasible. Often, sharing will allow an activity to be wholly reconfigured in ways that can dramatically raise competitive advantage.

Sharing must involve activities that are significant to competitive advantage, not just any activity. P&G's distribution system is such an instance in the diaper and paper towel business, where products are bulky and costly to ship. Conversely, diversification based on the opportunities to share only corporate overhead is rarely, if ever, appropriate.

Sharing activities inevitably involves costs that the benefits must outweigh. One cost is the greater coordination required to manage a shared activity. More important is the need to compromise the design or performance of an activity so that it can be shared. A salesperson handling the products of two business units, for example, must operate in a way that is usually not what either unit would choose were it independent. And if compromise greatly erodes the unit's effectiveness, then sharing may reduce rather than enhance competitive advantage.

Many companies have only superficially identified their potential for sharing. Companies also merge activities without consideration of whether they are sensitive to economies of scale. When they are not, the coordination costs kill the benefits. Companies compound such errors by not identifying costs of sharing in advance, when steps can be taken to minimize them. Costs of compromise can frequently be mitigated by redesigning the activity for sharing. The shared salesperson, for example, can be provided with a remote computer terminal to boost productivity and provide more customer information. Jamming business units together without such thinking exacerbates the costs of sharing.

Despite such pitfalls, opportunities to gain advantage from sharing activities have proliferated because of momentous developments in technology, deregulation, and competition. The infusion of electronics and information systems into many industries creates new opportunities to link businesses. The corporate strategy of sharing can involve both acquisition and internal development. Internal development is often possible because the corporation can bring to bear clear resources in launching a new unit. Start-ups are less difficult to integrate than acquisitions. Companies using the shared-activities concept can also make acquisitions as beachhead landings into a new industry and then integrate the units through sharing with other units. Prime examples of companies that have diversified via using shared activities include P&G, Du Pont, and IBM. The fields into which each has diversified are a cluster of tightly related units. Marriott illustrates both successes and failures in sharing activities over time. (See "Adding Value with Hospitality.")

Adding Value with Hospitality

Marriott began in the restaurant business in Washington, D.C. Because its customers often ordered takeouts on the way to the national airport, Marriott eventually entered airline catering. From there, it jumped into food service management for institutions. Marriott then began broadening its base of family restaurants and entered the hotel industry. More recently, it has moved into restaurants, snack bars, and merchandise shops in airport terminals and into gourmet restaurants. In addition, Marriott has branched out from its hotel business into cruise ships, theme parks, wholesale travel agencies, budget motels, and retirement centers.

Marriott's diversification has exploited well-developed skills in food service and hospitality. Marriott's kitchens prepare food according to more than 6,000 standardized recipe cards; hotel procedures are also standardized and painstakingly documented in elaborate manuals. Marriott shares a number of important activities across units. A shared procurement and distribution system for food serves all Marriott units through nine regional procurement centers. As a result, Marriott earns 50% higher margins on food service than any other hotel company. Marriott also has a fully integrated real estate unit that brings corporatewide power to bear on site acquisitions as well as on the designing and building of all Marriott locations.

Marriott's diversification strategy balances acquisitions and start-ups. Start-ups or small acquisitions are used for initial entry, depending on how close the opportunities for sharing are. To expand its geographic base, Marriott acquires companies and then disposes of the parts that do not fit.

Apart from this success, it is important to note that Marriott has divested 36% of both its acquisitions and its start-ups. While this is an above-average record, Marriott's mistakes are quite illuminating. Marriott has largely failed in diversifying into gourmet restaurants, theme parks, cruise ships, and wholesale travel agencies. In the first three businesses, Marriott discovered it could not transfer skills despite apparent similarities. Standardized menus did not work well in gourmet restaurants. Running cruise ships and theme parks was based more on entertainment and pizzazz than the carefully disciplined management of hotels and mid-price restaurants. The wholesale travel agencies were ill-fated from the start because Marriott had to compete with an important customer for its hotels and had no proprietary skills or opportunities to share with which to add value.

Following the shared-activities model requires an organizational context in which business unit collaboration is encouraged and reinforced. Highly autonomous business units are inimical to such collaboration. The company must put into place a variety of what I call horizontal mechanisms—a strong sense of corporate identity, a clear corporate mission statement that emphasizes the importance of integrating business unit strategies, an incentive system that rewards more than just business unit results, cross-business-unit task forces, and other methods of integrating.

A corporate strategy based on shared activities clearly meets the better-off test because business units gain ongoing tangible advantages from others within the corporation. It also meets the cost-of-entry test by reducing the expense of surmounting the barriers to internal entry. Other bids for acquisitions that do not share opportunities will have lower reservation prices. Even widespread opportunities for sharing activities do not allow a company to suspend the attractiveness test, however. Many diversifiers have made the critical mistake of equating the close fit of a target industry with attractive diversification. Target industries must pass the strict requirement test of having an attractive structure as well as a close fit in opportunities if diversification is to ultimately succeed.

Choosing a Corporate Strategy

Each concept of corporate strategy allows the diversified company to create shareholder value in a different way. Companies can succeed with any of the concepts if they clearly define the corporation's role and objectives, have the skills necessary for meeting the concept's prerequisites, organize themselves to manage diversity in a way that fits the strategy, and find themselves in an appropriate capital market environment. The caveat is that portfolio management is only sensible in limited circumstances.

A company's choice of corporate strategy is partly a legacy of its past. If its business units are in unattractive industries, the company must start from scratch. If the company has few truly proprietary skills or activities it can share in related diversification, then its initial diversification must rely on other concepts. Yet corporate strategy should not be a once-and-for-all choice but a vision that can evolve. A company should choose its long-term preferred concept and then proceed pragmatically toward it from its initial starting point.

Both the strategic logic and the experience of the companies I studied over the last decade suggest that a company will create shareholder value through diversification to a greater and greater extent as its strategy moves from portfolio management toward sharing activities. Because they do not rely on superior insight or other questionable assumptions about the company's capabilities, sharing activities and transferring skills offer the best avenues for value creation.

Each concept of corporate strategy is not mutually exclusive of those that come before, a potent advantage of the third and fourth concepts. A company can employ a restructuring strategy at the same time it transfers skills or shares activities. A strategy based on shared activities becomes more powerful if business units can also exchange skills. As the Marriott case illustrates, a company can often pursue the two strategies together and even incorporate some of the principles of restructuring with them. When it chooses industries in which to transfer skills or share activities, the company can also investigate the possibility of transforming the industry structure. When a company bases its strategy on interrelationships, it has a broader basis on which to create shareholder value than if it rests its entire strategy on transforming companies in unfamiliar industries.

My study supports the soundness of basing a corporate strategy on the transfer of skills or shared activities. The data on the sample companies' diversification programs illustrate some important characteristics of successful diversifiers. They have made a disproportionately low percentage of unrelated acquisitions, *unrelated* being defined as having no clear opportunity to transfer skills or share important activities (see Exhibit III). Even successful diversifiers such as 3M, IBM, and TRW have terrible records when they have strayed into unrelated acquisitions. Successful acquirers diversify into fields, each of which is related to many others. Procter & Gamble and IBM, for example, operate in 18 and 19 interrelated fields respectively and so enjoy numerous opportunities to transfer skills and share activities.

Companies with the best acquisition records tend to make heavier-than-average use of start-ups and joint ventures. Most companies shy away from modes of entry besides acquisition. My results cast doubt on the conventional wisdom regarding start-ups. Exhibit III demonstrates that while joint ventures are about as risky as acquisitions, start-ups are not. Moreover, successful companies often have very good records with start-up units, as 3M, P&G, Johnson & Johnson, IBM, and United Technologies illustrate. When a company has the internal strength to start up a unit, it can be safer and less costly to launch a company than to rely solely on an acquisition and then have to deal with the problem of integration. Japanese diversification histories support the soundness of start-up as an entry alternative.

My data also illustrate that none of the concepts of corporate strategy works when industry structure is poor or implementation is bad, no matter how related the industries are. Xerox acquired companies in related industries, but the businesses had poor structures and its skills were insufficient to provide enough competitive advantage to offset implementation problems.

AN ACTION PROGRAM

To translate the principles of corporate strategy into successful diversification, a company must first take an objective look at its existing businesses and the value added by the corporation. Only through such an assessment can an understanding of good corporate strategy grow. That understanding should guide future diversification as well as the development of skills and activities with which to select further new businesses. The following action program provides a concrete approach to conducting such a review. A company can choose a corporate strategy by:

1. **Identifying the interrelationships among already existing business units.**

   A company should begin to develop a corporate strategy by identifying all the opportunities it has to share activities or transfer skills in its existing portfolio of business units. The company will not only find ways to enhance the competitive advantage of existing units but also come upon several possible diversification avenues. The lack of meaningful interrelationships in the portfolio is an equally important finding, suggesting the need to justify the value added by the corporation or, alternately, a fundamental restructuring.

2. **Selecting the core businesses that will be the foundation of the corporate strategy.**

   Successful diversification starts with an understanding of the core businesses that will serve as the basis for corporate strategy. Core businesses are those that are in an attractive industry, have the potential to achieve sustainable competitive advantage, have important interrelationships with other business units, and provide skills or activities that represent a base from which to diversify.

   The company must first make certain its core businesses are on sound footing by upgrading management, internationalizing strategy, or improving technology. My study shows that geographic extensions of existing units, whether by acquisition, joint venture, or start-up, had a substantially lower divestment rate than diversification.

   The company must then patiently dispose of the units that are not core businesses. Selling them will free resources that could be better deployed elsewhere. In some cases disposal implies immediate liquidation, while in others the company should dress up the units and wait for a propitious market or a particularly eager buyer.

3. **Creating horizontal organizational mechanisms to facilitate interrelationships among the core businesses and lay the groundwork for future related diversification.**

    Top management can facilitate interrelationships by emphasizing cross-unit collaboration, grouping units organizationally and modifying incentives, and taking steps to build a strong sense of corporate identity.

4. **Pursuing diversification opportunities that allow shared activities.**

    This concept of corporate strategy is the most compelling, provided a company's strategy passes all three tests. A company should inventory activities in existing business units that represent the strongest foundation for sharing, such as strong distribution channels or world-class technical facilities. These will in turn lead to potential new business areas. A company can use acquisitions as a beachhead or employ start-ups to exploit internal capabilities and minimize integrating problems.

5. **Pursuing diversification through the transfer of skills if opportunities for sharing activities are limited or exhausted.**

    Companies can pursue this strategy through acquisition, although they may be able to use start-ups if their existing units have important skills they can readily transfer.

    Such diversification is often riskier because of the tough conditions necessary for it to work. Given the uncertainties, a company should avoid diversifying on the basis of skills transfer alone. Rather it should also be viewed as a stepping-stone to subsequent diversification using shared activities. New industries should be chosen that will lead naturally to other businesses. The goal is to build a cluster of related and mutually reinforcing business units. The strategy's logic implies that the company should not set the rate of return standards for the initial foray into a new sector too high.

6. **Pursuing a strategy of restructuring if this fits the skills of management or no good opportunities exist for forging corporate interrelationships.**

    When a company uncovers undermanaged companies and can deploy adequate management talent and resources to the acquired units, then it can use a restructuring strategy. The more developed the capital markets and the more active the market for companies, the more restructuring will require a patient search for that special opportunity rather than a headlong race to acquire as many bad apples as possible. Restructuring can be a permanent strategy, as it is with Loew's, or a way to build a group of businesses that supports a shift to another corporate strategy.

7. **Paying dividends so that the shareholders can be the portfolio managers.**

Paying dividends is better than destroying shareholder value through diversification based on shaky underpinnings. Tax considerations, which some companies cite to avoid dividends, are hardly legitimate reason to diversify if a company cannot demonstrate the capacity to do it profitably.

CREATING A CORPORATE THEME

Defining a corporate theme is a good way to ensure that the corporation will create shareholder value. Having the right theme helps unite the efforts of business units and reinforces the ways they interrelate as well as guides the choice of new businesses to enter. NEC Corporation, with its "C&C" theme, provides a good example. NEC integrates its computer, semiconductor, telecommunications, and consumer electronics businesses by merging computers and communication.

It is all too easy to create a shallow corporate theme. CBS wanted to be an "entertainment company," for example, and built a group of businesses related to leisure time. It entered such industries as toys, crafts, musical instruments, sports teams, and hi-fi retailing. While this corporate theme sounded good, close listening revealed its hollow ring. None of these businesses had any significant opportunity to share activities or transfer skills among themselves or with CBS's traditional broadcasting and record businesses. They were all sold, often at significant losses, except for a few of CBS's publishing-related units. Saddled with the worst acquisition record in my study, CBS has eroded the shareholder value created through its strong performance in broadcasting and records.

Moving from competitive strategy to corporate strategy is the business equivalent of passing through the Bermuda Triangle. The failure of corporate strategy reflects the fact that most diversified companies have failed to think in terms of how they really add value. A corporate strategy that truly enhances the competitive advantage of each business unit is the best defense against the corporate raider. With a sharper focus on the tests of diversification and the explicit choice of a clear concept of corporate strategy, companies' diversification track records from now on can look a lot different.

Appendix

Where the Data Come From

We studied the 1950–1986 diversification histories of 33 large diversified U.S. companies. They were chosen at random from many broad sectors of the economy.

To eliminate distortions caused by World War II, we chose 1950 as the base year and then identified each business the company was in. We tracked every acquisition, joint venture, and start-up made over this period—3,788 in all. We classified each as an entry into an entirely new sector or field (financial services, for example), a new industry within a field the company was already in (insurance, for example), or a geographic extension of an existing product or service. We also classified each new field as related or unrelated to existing units. Then we tracked whether and when each entry was divested or shut down and the number of years each remained part of the corporation.

Our sources included annual reports, 10K forms, the F&S Index, and Moody's, supplemented by our judgment and general knowledge of the industries involved. In a few cases, we asked the companies specific questions.

It is difficult to determine the success of an entry without knowing the full purchase or start-up price, the profit history, the amount and timing of ongoing investments made in the unit, whether any write-offs or write-downs were taken, and the selling price and terms of sale. Instead, we employed a relatively simple way to gauge success: *whether the entry was divested or shut down*. The underlying assumption is that a company will generally not divest or close down a successful business except in a comparatively few special cases. Companies divested many of the entries in our sample within five years, a reflection of disappointment with performance. Of the comparatively few divestments where the company disclosed a loss or a gain, the divestment resulted in a reported loss in more than half the cases.

The data in Exhibit I cover the entire 1950–1986 period. However, the divestment ratios in Exhibit II and Exhibit III do not compare entries and divestments over the entire period because doing so would overstate the success of diversification. Companies usually do not shut down or divest new entries immediately but hold them for some time to give them an opportunity to succeed. Our data show that the average holding period is five to slightly more than ten years, though many divestments occur within five years. To accurately gauge the success of diversification, we calculated the percentage of entries made by 1975 and by 1980 that were divested or closed down as of January 1987. If we had included more recent entries, we would have biased upward our assessment of how successful these entries had been.

As compiled, these data probably understate the rate of failure. Companies tend to announce acquisitions and other forms of new entry with a flourish but divestments and shutdowns with a whimper, if at all. We have done our best to root out every such transaction, but we have undoubtedly missed some. There may also be new entries that we did not uncover, but our best impression is that the number is not large.

Notes

1. The studies also show that sellers of companies capture a large fraction of the gains from merger. See Michael C. Jensen and Richard S. Ruback, "The Market for Corporate Control: The Scientific Evidence," *Journal of Financial Economics*, April 1983, p. 5, and Michael C. Jensen, "Takeovers: Folklore and Science," *Harvard Business Review*, November–December 1984, p. 109.

2. Some recent evidence also supports the conclusion that acquired companies often suffer eroding performance after acquisition. See Frederick M. Scherer, "Mergers, Sell-Offs and Managerial Behavior," in *The Economics of Strategic Planning*, ed. Lacy Glenn Thomas (Lexington, Mass.: Lexington Books, 1986), p. 143, and David A. Ravenscraft and Frederick M. Scherer, "Mergers and Managerial Performance," paper presented at the Conference on Takeovers and Contests for Corporate Control, Columbia Law School, 1985.

3. This observation has been made by a number of authors. See, for example, Malcolm S. Salter and Wolf A. Weinhold, *Diversification Through Acquisition* (New York: Free Press, 1979).

4. See Michael E. Porter, "How Competitive Forces Shape Strategy," *Harvard Business Review*, March–April 1979, p. 86.

5. Michael E. Porter, *Competitive Advantage* (New York: Free Press, 1985).

9

Time—The Next Source of Competitive Advantage

George Stalk, Jr.

Like competition itself, competitive advantage is a constantly moving target. For any company in any industry, the key is not to get stuck with a single simple notion of its source of advantage. The best competitors, the most successful ones, know how to keep moving and always stay on the cutting edge.

Today, *time* is on the cutting edge. The ways leading companies manage time—in production, in new product development and introduction, in sales and distribution—represent the most powerful new sources of competitive advantage. Though certain Western companies are pursuing these advantages, Japanese experience and practice provide the most instructive examples—not because they are necessarily unique but because they best illustrate the evolutionary stages through which leading companies have advanced.

In the period immediately following World War II, Japanese companies used their low labor costs to gain entry to various industries. As wage rates rose and technology became more significant, the Japanese shifted first to scale-based strategies and then to focused factories to achieve advantage. The advent of just-in-time production brought with it a move to flexible factories, as leading Japanese companies sought both low cost and great variety in the market. Cutting-edge Japanese companies today are capitalizing on time as a critical source of competitive advantage: shortening the planning loop in the product development cycle and trimming process time in the factory—managing time the way most companies manage costs, quality, or inventory.

In fact, as a strategic weapon, time is the equivalent of money, productivity, quality, even innovation. Managing time has enabled top

Japanese companies not only to reduce their costs but also to offer broad product lines, cover more market segments, and upgrade the technological sophistication of their products. These companies are time-based competitors.

From Low Wages to Variety Wars

Since 1945, Japanese competitors have shifted their strategic focus at least four times. These early adaptations were straightforward; the shift to time-based competitive advantage is not nearly so obvious. It does, however, represent a logical evolution from the earlier stages.

In the immediate aftermath of World War II, with their economy devastated and the world around them in a shambles, the Japanese concentrated on achieving competitive advantage through low labor costs. Since Japan's workers were still productive and the yen was devalued by 98.8% against the dollar, its labor costs were extraordinarily competitive with those of the West's developed economies.

Hungry for foreign exchange, the Japanese government encouraged companies to make the most of their one edge by targeting industries with high labor content: textiles, shipbuilding, and steel—businesses where the low labor rates more than offset low productivity rates. As a result, Japanese companies took market share from their Western competition.

But this situation did not last long. Rising wages, caused by high inflation, combined with fixed exchange rates to erode the advantage. In many industries, manufacturers could not improve their productivity fast enough to offset escalating labor costs. By the early 1960s, for instance, the textile companies—comprising Japan's largest industry—were hard-pressed. Having lost their competitive edge in world markets, they spiraled downward, first losing share, then volume, then profits, and finally position and prestige. While the problem was most severe for the textile business, the rest of Japanese industry suffered as well.

The only course was adaptation: in the early 1960s, the Japanese shifted their strategy, using capital investment to boost work-force productivity. They inaugurated the era of scale-based strategies, achieving high productivity and low costs by building the largest and most capital-intensive facilities that were technologically feasible. Japanese shipbuilders, for example, revolutionized the industry in their effort to raise labor productivity. Adapting fabrication techniques from mass production processes and using automatic and semi-automatic equipment, they constructed vessels in modules. The approach produced two advantages for the Japanese. It drove up their own productivity and simultaneously erected a high capital-investment barrier to others looking to compete in the business.

The search for ways to achieve even higher productivity and lower costs continued, however. And in the mid-1960s, it led top Japanese companies to a new source of competitive advantage—the focused factory. Focused competitors manufactured products either made nowhere else in the world or located in the high-volume segment of a market, often in the heart of their Western competitors' product lines. Focusing of production allowed the Japanese to remain smaller than established broad-line producers, while still achieving higher productivity and lower costs—giving them great competitive power.

Factory costs are very sensitive to the variety of goods a plant produces. Reduction of the product-line variety by half, for example, raises productivity by 30%, cuts costs 17%, and substantially lowers the break-even point. Cutting the product line in half again boosts productivity by 75%, slashes costs 30%, and diminishes the break-even point to below 50%. (See Exhibit I.)

In industries like bearings, where competition was fierce in the late 1960s, the Japanese fielded product lines with one-half to one-quarter the variety of their Western competitors. Targeting the high-volume segments of the bearing business—bearings for automobile applications was one—the Japanese used the low costs of their highly productive focused factories to undercut the prices of Western competitors.

SKF was one victim. With factories scattered throughout Europe, each geared to a broad product line for the local market, the Swedish company was a big target for the Japanese. SKF reacted by trying to avoid direct competition with the Japanese: it added higher margin products to serve specialized applications. But SKF did not simultaneously drop any low-margin products, thereby complicating its plant operations and adding to production costs. In effect, SKF provided a cost umbrella for the Japanese. As long as they operated beneath it, the Japanese could expand their product line and move into more varied applications.

Avoiding price competition by moving into higher margin products is called margin retreat—a common response to stepped-up competition that eventually leads to corporate suicide. As a company retreats, its costs rise as do its prices, thus "subsidizing" an aggressive competi-

Exhibit I. The benefits of focus

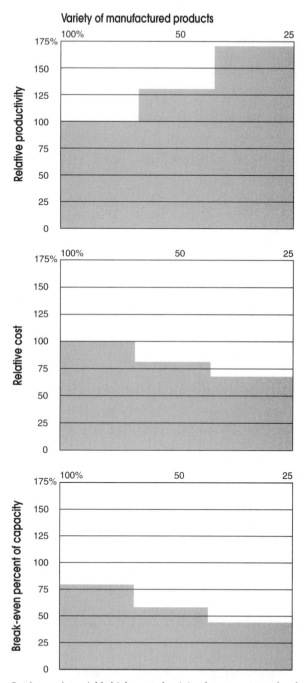

Cutting variety yields higher productivity, lower costs, and reduced break-even points.

tor's expansion into the vacated position. The retreating company's revenue base stops growing and may eventually shrink to the point where it can no longer support the fixed cost of the operation. Retrenchment, restructuring, and further shrinkage follow in a cycle that leads to inevitable extinction.

SKF avoided this fate by adopting the Japanese strategy. After a review of its factories, the company focused each on those products it was best suited to manufacture. If a product did not fit a particular factory, it was either placed in another, more suitable plant or dropped altogether. This strategy not only halted SKF's retreat but also beat back the Japanese advance.

At the same time, however, leading Japanese manufacturers began to move toward a new source of competitive advantage—the flexible factory. Two developments drove this move. First, as they expanded and penetrated more markets, their narrow product lines began to pinch, limiting their ability to grow. Second, with growth limited, the economics of the focus strategy presented them with an unattractive choice: either reduce variety further or accept the higher costs of broader product lines.

In manufacturing, costs fall into two categories: those that respond to volume or scale and those that are driven by variety. Scale-related costs decline as volume increases, usually falling 15% to 25% per unit each time volume doubles. Variety-related costs, on the other hand, reflect the costs of complexity in manufacturing: setup, materials handling, inventory, and many of the overhead costs of a factory. In most cases, as variety increases, costs increase, usually at a rate of 20% to 35% per unit each time variety doubles.

The sum of the scale- and variety-related costs represents the total cost of manufacturing. With effort, managers can determine the optimum cost point for their factories—the point where the combination of volume and variety yields the lowest total manufacturing cost for a particular plant. When markets are good, companies tend to edge toward increased variety in search of higher volumes, even though this will mean increased costs. When times are tough, companies pare their product lines, cutting variety to reduce costs.

In a flexible factory system, variety-driven costs start lower and increase more slowly as variety grows. Scale costs remain unchanged. Thus the optimum cost point for a flexible factory occurs at a higher volume and with greater variety than for a traditional factory. A gap emerges between the costs of the flexible and the traditional factory—a cost/variety gap that represents the competitive advantage of flexible

Exhibit II. The advantage of flexible marketing

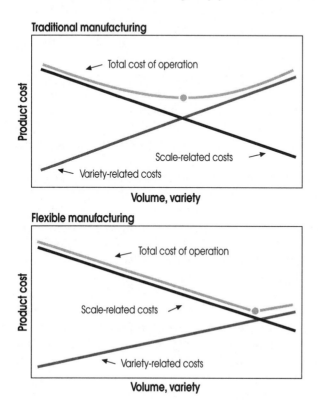

For flexible factories, the optimum cost points occur at a higher volume and with higher variety than for traditional factories.

production. Very simply, a flexible factory enjoys more variety with lower total costs than traditional factories, which are still forced to make the trade-off between scale and variety. (See Exhibit II.)

Yanmar Diesel illustrates how this process works. In 1973, with the Japanese economy in recession, Yanmar Diesel was mired in red ink. Worse, there was no promise that once the recession had passed, the existing strategy and program would guarantee real improvement in the company's condition.

As a Toyota supplier, Yanmar was familiar with the automaker's flexible manufacturing system. Moreover, Yanmar was impressed with the automaker's ability to weather the recession without losing money. Yanmar decided to install the Toyota procedure in its own two factories. The changeover took less than five years and produced dramatic results: manufacturing costs declined 40% to 60%, depending on the product; factory break-even points dropped 80% to 50%; total manufacturing labor productivity improved by more than 100%.

But it was Yanmar's newfound capability in product variety that signaled the arrival of a unique strategic edge: during the restructuring Yanmar more than quadrupled its product line. With focused factories, Yanmar could have doubled productivity in such a short time only by reducing the breadth of the product line by 75%. The Toyota system made Yanmar's factories more flexible, reducing costs and producing a greater variety of products.

As its inventor, Taiichi Ohno, said, the Toyota production system was "born of the need to make many types of automobiles, in small quantities with the same manufacturing process." With its emphasis on just-in-time production, total quality control, employee decision making on the factory floor, and close supplier relations, the Toyota system gave the many Japanese manufacturers who adopted it in the mid-1970s a distinct competitive advantage.

A comparison of a U.S. company with a Japanese competitor in the manufacture of a particular automotive suspension component illustrates the nature and extent of the Japanese advantage. The U.S. company bases its strategy on scale and focus: it produces 10 million units per year—making it the world's largest producer—and offers only 11 types of finished parts. The Japanese company's strategy, on the other hand, is to exploit flexibility. It is both smaller and less focused: it manufactures only 3.5 million units per year but has 38 types of finished parts.

With one-third the scale and more than three times the product variety, the Japanese company also boasts total labor productivity that is half again that of its American competitor. Moreover, the unit cost of the Japanese manufacturer is less than half that of the U.S. company. But interestingly, the productivity of the Japanese direct laborers is not as high as that of the U.S. workers, a reflection of the difference in scale. The Japanese advantage comes from the productivity of the overhead employees: with one-third the volume and three times the variety, the Japanese company has only one-eighteenth the overhead employees. (See Exhibit III.)

In the late 1970s, Japanese companies exploited flexible manufacturing to the point that a new competitive thrust emerged—the variety war. A classic example of a variety war was the battle that erupted between Honda and Yamaha for supremacy in the motorcycle market,

Exhibit III.   Flexible manufacturing's productivity edge (automobile suspension component)

	U.S. competitor	Japanese competitor
Annual volume	10M	3.5M
Employees		
Direct	107	50
Indirect	135	7
Total	242	57
Annual units/employee	43,100	61,400
Types of finished parts	11	38
Unit cost for comparable part (index)	$100	$49

(1987 figures)

a struggle popularly known in Japanese business circles as the H-Y War. Yamaha ignited the H-Y War in 1981 when it announced the opening of a new factory which would make it the world's largest motorcycle manufacturer, a prestigious position held by Honda. But Honda had been concentrating its corporate resources on the automobile business and away from its motorcycle operation. Now, faced with Yamaha's overt and public challenge, Honda chose to counterattack.

Honda launched its response with the war cry, "Yamaha wo tsubusu!" ("We will crush, squash, slaughter Yamaha!") In the no-holds-barred battle that ensued, Honda cut prices, flooded distribution channels, and boosted advertising expenditures. Most important—and most impressive to consumers—Honda also rapidly increased the rate of change in its product line, using variety to bury Yamaha. At the start of the war, Honda had 60 models of motorcycles. Over the next 18 months, Honda introduced or replaced 113 models, effectively turning over its entire product line twice. Yamaha also began the war with 60 models; it was able to manage only 37 changes in its product line during those 18 months.

Honda's new product introductions devastated Yamaha. First, Honda succeeded in making motorcycle design a matter of fashion, where newness and freshness were important attributes for consumers. Second, Honda raised the technological sophistication of its products, introducing four-valve engines, composites, direct drive, and other new features. Next to a Honda, Yamaha products looked old, unattractive, and out of date. Demand for Yamaha products dried up; in a desperate effort to move them, dealers were forced to price them below cost. But even that didn't work. At the most intense point in the H-Y War, Yamaha had more than 12 months of inventory in its dealers' showrooms. Finally Yamaha surrendered. In a public statement, Yamaha President Hideto Eguchi announced, "We want to end the H-Y War. It is our fault. Of course there will be competition in the future but it will be based on a mutual recognition of our respective positions."

Honda didn't go unscathed either. The company's sales and service network was severely disrupted, requiring additional investment before it returned to a stable footing. However, so decisive was its victory that Honda effectively had as much time as it wanted to recover. It had emphatically defended its title as the world's largest motorcycle producer and done so in a way that warned Suzuki and Kawasaki not to challenge that leadership. Variety had won the war.

Time-Based Competitive Advantage

The strength of variety as a competitive weapon raises an interesting question. How could Japanese companies accommodate such rapid rates of change? In Honda's case, there could be only three possible answers. The company did one of the following:

1. Began the development of more than 100 new models 10 to 15 years before the attack.
2. Authorized a sudden, massive spending surge to develop and manufacture products on a crash basis.
3. Used structurally different methods to develop, manufacture, and introduce new products.

In fact, what Honda and other variety-driven competitors pioneered was time-based competitiveness. They managed structural changes that enabled their operations to execute their processes much faster. As a consequence, time became their new source of competitive advantage.

While time is a basic business performance variable, management seldom monitors its consumption explicitly—almost never with the same precision accorded sales and costs. Yet time is a more critical competitive yardstick than traditional financial measurements.

Today's new-generation companies compete with flexible manufacturing and rapid-response systems, expanding variety and increasing innovation. A company that builds its strategy on this cycle is a more powerful competitor than one with a traditional strategy based on low wages, scale, or focus. These older, cost-based strategies require managers to do whatever is necessary to drive down costs: move production to or source from a low-wage country; build new facilities or consolidate old plants to gain economies of scale; or focus operations down to the most economic subset of activities. These tactics reduce costs but at the expense of responsiveness.

In contrast, strategies based on the cycle of flexible manufacturing, rapid response, expanding variety, and increasing innovation are time based. Factories are close to the customers they serve. Organization structures enable fast responses rather than low costs and control. Companies concentrate on reducing if not eliminating delays and using their response advantages to attract the most profitable customers.

Many—but certainly not all—of today's time-based competitors are Japanese. Some of them are Sony, Matsushita, Sharp, Toyota, Hitachi, NEC, Toshiba, Honda, and Hino; time-based Western companies include Benetton, The Limited, Federal Express, Domino's Pizza, Wilson Art, and McDonald's. For these leading competitors, time has become the overarching measurement of performance. By reducing the consumption of time in every aspect of the business, these companies also reduce costs, improve quality, and stay close to their customers.

Breaking the Planning Loop

Companies are systems; time connects all the parts. The most powerful competitors understand this axiom and are breaking the debilitating loop that strangles much of traditional manufacturing planning.

Traditional manufacturing requires long lead times to resolve conflicts between various jobs or activities that require the same resources. The long lead times, in turn, require sales forecasts to guide planning. But sales forecasts are inevitably wrong; by definition they are guesses, however informed. Naturally, as lead times lengthen, the accuracy of sales forecasts declines. With more forecasting errors, inventories balloon and the need for safety stocks at all levels increases. Errors in forecasting also mean more unscheduled jobs that have to be expedited, thereby crowding out scheduled jobs. The need for longer lead times grows even greater and the planning loop expands even more, driving up costs, increasing delays, and creating system inefficiencies.

Managers who find themselves trapped in the planning loop often respond by asking for better forecasts and longer lead times. In other words, they treat the symptoms and worsen the problem. The only way to break the planning loop is to reduce the consumption of time throughout the system; that will, in turn, cut the need for lead time, for estimates, for safety stocks, and all the rest. After all, if a company could ever drive its lead time all the way to zero, it would have to forecast only the next day's sales. While that idea of course is unrealistic, successful time-based competitors in Japan and in the West have kept their lead times from growing and some have even reduced them, thereby diminishing the planning loop's damaging effects.

Thirty years ago, Jay W. Forrester of MIT published a pioneering article in *Harvard Business Review*, "Industrial Dynamics: A Major Breakthrough for Decision Makers" (July–August 1958), which established a model of time's impact on an organization's performance. Using "industrial dynamics"—a concept originally developed for shipboard fire control systems—Forrester tracked the effects of time delays and decision rates within a simple business system consisting of a factory, a factory warehouse, a distributors' inventory, and retailers' inventories. The numbers in Exhibit IV are the delays in the flow of information or product, measured in weeks. In this example, the orders accumulate at the retailer for three weeks, are in the mail for half a week, are delayed at the distributor for two weeks, go back into the mail for another half a week, and need eight weeks for processing at the factory and its warehouse. Then the finished product begins its journey back to the retailer. The cycle takes 19 weeks.

The system in this example is very stable—as long as retail demand is stable or as long as forecasts are accurate 19 weeks into the future. But if unexpected changes occur, the system must respond. Exhibit V, also taken from the Forrester article, shows what happens to this system when a simple change takes place: demand goes up 10%, then flattens. Acting on new forecasts and seeking to cut delivery delays, the factory first responds by ramping up production 40%. When management realizes—too late—that it has overshot the mark, it cuts production 30%. Too late again it learns that it has overcorrected. This ramping up and cutting back continue until finally the system stabilizes, more than a year after the initial 10% increase.

What distorts the system so badly is time: the lengthy delay between

Exhibit IV. Time in the planning loop (in weeks)

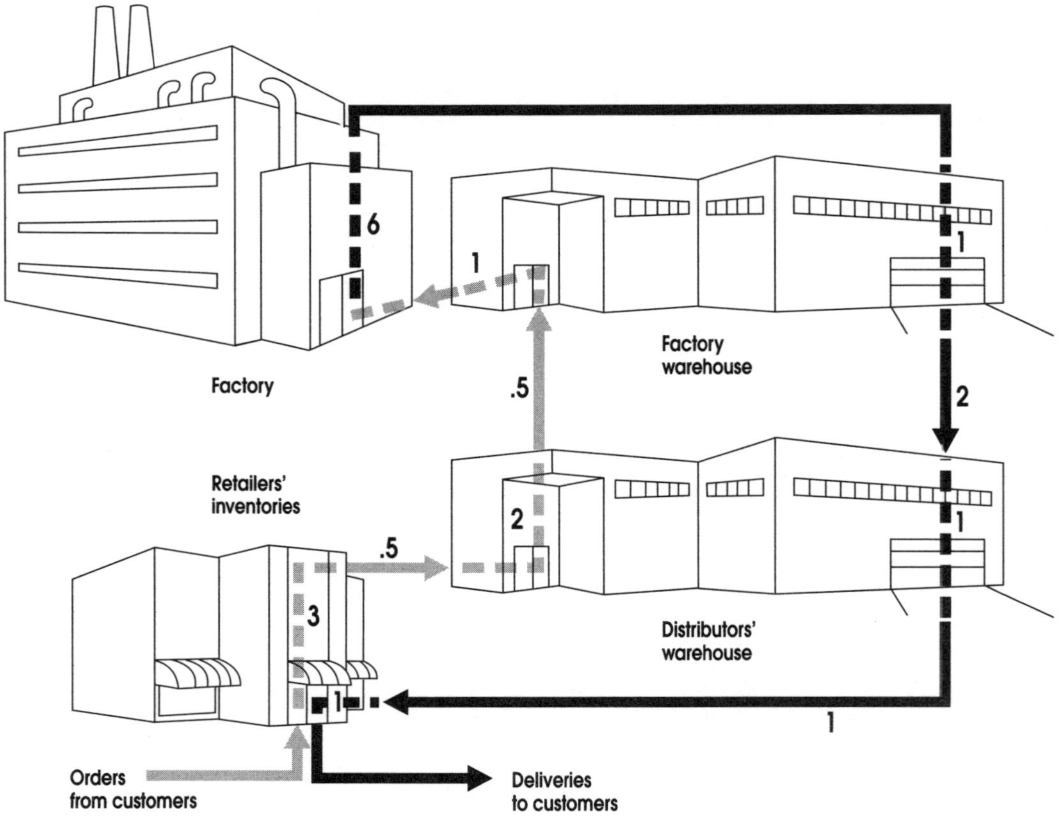
6
1
.5
1
2
Factory
Factory warehouse
Retailers' inventories
2
.5
1
3
1
Distributors' warehouse
1
Orders from customers
Deliveries to customers

Exhibit V.   Unexpected change distorts the system

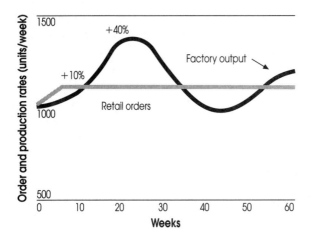

the event that creates the new demand and the time when the factory finally receives the information. The longer that delay, the more distorted is the view of the market. Those distortions reverberate throughout the system, producing disruption, waste, and inefficiency.

These distortions plague business today. To escape them, companies have a choice: they can produce to forecast or they can reduce the time delays in the flow of information and product through the system. The traditional solution is to produce to forecast. The new approach is to reduce time consumption.

Because time flows throughout the system, focusing on time-based competitive performance results in improvements across the board. Companies generally become time-based competitors by first correcting their manufacturing techniques, then fixing sales and distribution, and finally adjusting their approach to innovation. Ultimately, it becomes the basis for a company's overall strategy.

Time-Based Manufacturing

In general, time-based manufacturing policies and practices differ from those of traditional manufacturers along three key dimensions: length of production runs, organization of process components, and complexity of scheduling procedures.

When it comes to lot size, for instance, traditional factories attempt to maximize production runs while time-based manufacturers try to shorten their production runs as much as possible. In fact, many Japanese companies aim for run lengths of a single unit. The thinking behind this is as simple as it is fundamental to competitive success: reduced run lengths mean more frequent production of the complete mix of products and faster response to customers' demands.

Factory layout also contributes to time-based competitive advantage. Traditional factories are usually organized by process technology centers. For example, metal goods manufacturers organize their factories into shearing, punching, and braking departments; electronic assemblers have stuffing, wave soldering, assembly, testing, and packing departments. Parts move from one process technology center to the next. Each step consumes valuable time: parts sit, waiting to move; then move; then wait to be used in the next step. In a traditional manufacturing system, products usually receive value for only .05% to 2.5% of the time that they are in the factory. The rest of the time products sit waiting for something to happen.

Time-based factories, however, are organized by product. To minimize handling and moving of parts, the manufacturing functions for a component or a product are as close together as possible. Parts move from one activity to the next with little or no delay. Because the production process eliminates the need to pile and repile parts, they flow quickly and efficiently through the factory.

In traditional factories, scheduling is also a source of delay and waste. Most traditional factories use central scheduling that requires sophisticated materials resource planning and shop-floor control systems. Even though these systems are advanced, they still waste time: work orders usually flow to the factory floor on a monthly or weekly basis. In the meantime, parts can sit idle.

In time-based factories, local scheduling enables employees to make more production control decisions on the factory floor, without the time-consuming loop back to management for approval. Moreover, the combination of the product-oriented layout of the factory and local scheduling makes the total production process run more smoothly. Once a part starts through the production run, many of the requirements between manufacturing steps are purely automatic and require no intermediate scheduling.

These differences between traditional and time-based factories add up. Flexible factories enjoy big advantages in both productivity and time: labor productivity in time-based factories can be as much as

200% higher than in conventional plants; time-based factories can respond eight to ten times faster than traditional factories. Flexible production means significant improvements in labor and net-asset productivity. These, in turn, yield reductions of up to 20% in overall costs and increases in growth for much less investment.

Toyota offers a dramatic example of the kinds of improvements that leading time-based competitors are making. Dissatisfied with the response time of a supplier, Toyota went to work. It took the supplier 15 days to turn out a component after arrival of the raw materials at its factory. The first step was to cut lot sizes, reducing response time to 6 days. Next Toyota streamlined the factory layout, reducing the number of inventory holding points. The response time fell to 3 days. Finally Toyota eliminated all work-in-progress inventories at the supplier's plant. New response time: 1 day.

Toyota, of course, is not alone in improving manufacturing response times. Matsushita cut the time needed to make washing machines from 360 hours to just 2; Honda slashed its motorcycle fabricating time by 80%; in North America, companies making motor controllers and electrical components for unit air conditioners have improved their manufacturing response times by 90%.

Time-Based Sales and Distribution

A manufacturer's next challenge is to avoid dissipation of factory performance improvements in other parts of the organization. In Jay Forrester's example of the planning loop, the factory and its warehouse accounted for roughly one-half of the system's time. In actuality today, the factory accounts for one-third to one-half of the total time— often the most "visible" portion of time. But other parts of the system are just as important, if less apparent. For example, in the Forrester system, sales and distribution consume as much or more time than manufacturing.

What Forrester modeled, the Japanese experienced. By the late 1970s, leading Japanese companies were finding that inefficient sales and distribution operations undercut the benefits of their flexible manufacturing systems. Toyota, which at that time was divided into two separate companies, Toyota Motor Manufacturing and Toyota Motor Sales, again makes this point. Toyota Motor Manufacturing could manufacture a car in less than 2 days. But Toyota Motor Sales needed from 15 to 26 days to close the sale, transmit the order to the factory, get the order scheduled, and deliver the car to the customer. By the late 1970s, the cost-conscious, competition-minded engineers at Toyota Manufacturing were angry at their counterparts at Toyota Motor Sales, who were frittering away the advantage gained in the production process. The sales and distribution function was generating 20% to 30% of a car's cost to the customer—more than it cost Toyota to manufacture the car!

Finally, in 1982 Toyota moved decisively to remedy the problem. The company merged Toyota Motor Manufacturing and Toyota Motor Sales. The company announced that it wanted to become "more marketing driven." While Toyota assured the public that the reorganization only returned it to its configuration in the 1950s, within 18 months all the Toyota Motor Sales directors retired. Their jobs were left vacant or filled by executives from Toyota Motor Manufacturing.

The company wasted no time in implementing a plan to cut delays in sales and distribution, reduce costs, and improve customer service. The old system, Toyota found, had handled customer orders in batches. Orders and other crucial information would accumulate at one step of the sales and distribution process before dispatch to the next level, which wasted time and generated extra costs.

To speed the flow of information, Toyota had to reduce the size of the information batches. The solution came from a company-developed computer system that tied its salespeople directly to the factory scheduling operation. This link bypassed several levels of the sales and distribution function and enabled the modified system to operate with very small batches of orders.

Toyota expected this new approach to cut the sales and distribution cycle time in half—from four to six weeks to just two to three weeks across Japan. (For the Tokyo and Osaka regions, which account for roughly two-thirds of Japan's population, the goal was to reduce cycle time to just two days.) But by 1987 Toyota had reduced system responsiveness to eight days, including the time required to make the car. In the Forrester example, this achievement is equivalent to cutting the 19-week cycle to 6 weeks. The results were predictable: shorter sales forecasts, lower costs, happier customers.

Time-Based Innovation

A company that can bring out new products three times faster than its competitors enjoys a huge advantage. Today, in one industry after another, Japanese manufacturers are doing just that to their Western competition:

- In projection television, Japanese producers can develop a new television in one-third the time required by U.S. manufacturers.
- In custom plastic injection molds, Japanese companies can develop the molds in one-third the time of U.S. competitors and at one-third the cost.
- In autos, Japanese companies can develop new products in half the time—and with half as many people—as the U.S. and German competition.

To accomplish their fast-paced innovations, leading Japanese manufacturers have introduced a series of organizational techniques that precisely parallel their approach to flexible manufacturing:

- In manufacturing, the Japanese stress short production runs and small lot sizes. In innovation, they favor smaller increments of improvement in new products, but introduce them more often—versus the Western approach of more significant improvements made less often.
- In the organization of product development work, the Japanese use factory cells that are cross-functional teams. Most Western new product development activity is carried out by functional centers.
- In the scheduling of work, Japanese factories stress local responsibility, just as product development scheduling is decentralized. The Western approach to both requires plodding centralized scheduling, plotting, and tracking.

The effects of this time-based advantage are devastating; quite simply, American companies are losing leadership of technology and innovation—supposedly this country's source of long-term advantage.

Unless U.S. companies reduce their new product development and introduction cycles from 36–48 months to 12–18 months, Japanese manufacturers will easily out-innovate and outperform them. Taking the initiative in innovation will require even faster cycle times.

Residential air conditioners illustrate the Japanese ability to introduce more technological innovation in smaller increments—and how in just a few years these improvements add up to remarkably superior products. The Japanese introduce innovations in air conditioners four times faster than their American competitors; in technological sophistication the Japanese products are seven to ten years ahead of U.S. products.

Look at the changes in Mitsubishi Electric's three-horsepower heat pump between 1975 and 1985. From 1975 to 1979, the company did nothing to the product except change the sheet metal work, partly to improve efficiency but mostly to reduce materials costs. In 1979, the technological sophistication of the product was roughly equal to that of the U.S. competition. From this point on, the Japanese first established, and then widened the lead.

In 1980, Mitsubishi introduced its first major improvement: a new product that used integrated circuits to control the air-conditioning cycle. One year later, the company replaced the integrated circuits with microprocessors and added two important innovations to increase consumer demand. The first was "quick connect" freon lines. On the old product (and on the U.S. product), freon lines were made from copper tubing and cut to length, bent, soldered together, purged, and filled with freon—an operation requiring great skill to produce a reliable air conditioner. The Japanese substituted quick-connect freon lines—precharged hoses that simply clicked together. The second innovation was simplified wiring. On the old product (and still today on the U.S. product) the unit had six color-coded wires to connect. The advent of microprocessors made possible a two-wire connection with neutral polarity.

These two changes did not improve the energy-efficiency ratio of the product; nor were they intended to. Rather, the point was to fabricate a unit that would be simpler to install and more reliable, thereby broadening distribution and increasing demand. Because of these innovations, white-goods outlets could sell the new product, and local contractors could easily install it.

In 1982, Mitsubishi introduced a new version of the air conditioner featuring technological advances related to performance. A high efficiency rotary compressor replaced the outdated reciprocating compressor. The condensing unit had louvered fins and inner fin tubes for better heat transfer. Because the balance of the system changed, all the electronics had to change. As a result, the energy-efficiency ratio improved markedly.

In 1983, Mitsubishi added sensors to the unit and more computing power, expanding the electronic control of the cycle and again improving the energy-efficiency ratio.

In 1984, Mitsubishi came out with another version of the product, this time with an inverter that made possible an even higher energy-efficiency ratio. The inverter, which requires additional electronics for the unit, allows unparalleled control over the speed of the electric motor, dramatically boosting the appliance's efficiency.

Using time-based innovation, Mitsubishi transformed its air conditioner. The changes came incrementally and steadily. Overall they gave Mitsubishi—and other Japanese companies on the same track—the position of technological leadership in the global residential air-conditioning industry.

In 1985, a U.S. air-conditioner manufacturer was just debating whether to use integrated circuits in its residential heat pump. In view of its four- to five-year product development cycle, it could not have introduced the innovation until 1989 or 1990—putting the American company ten years behind the Japanese. Faced with this situation, the U.S. air-conditioner company followed the example of many U.S. manufacturers that have lost the lead in technology and innovation: it decided to source its air conditioners and components from its Japanese competition.

Time-Based Strategy

The possibility of establishing a response time advantage opens new avenues for constructing winning competitive strategies. At most companies, strategic choices are limited to three options:

1. Seeking coexistence with competitors. This choice is seldom stable, since competitors refuse to cooperate and stay put.
2. Retreating in the face of competitors. Many companies choose this course; the business press fills its pages with accounts of companies retreating by consolidating plants, focusing their operations, outsourcing, divesting businesses, pulling out of markets, or moving upscale.
3. Attacking, either directly or indirectly. The direct attack involves the classic confrontation—cut price and add capacity, creating head-on competition. Indirect attack requires surprise. Competitors either do not understand the strategies being used against them or they do understand but cannot respond—sometimes because of the speed of the attack, sometimes because of their inability to mount a response.

Of the three options, only an attack creates the opportunity for real growth. Direct attack demands superior resources; it is always expensive and potentially disastrous. Indirect attack promises the most gain for the least cost. Time-based strategy offers a powerful new approach for successful indirect attacks against larger, established competitors.

Consider the remarkable example of Atlas Door, a ten-year-old U.S. company. It has grown at an average annual rate of 15% in an industry with an overall annual growth rate of less than 5%. In recent years, its pretax earnings were 20% of sales, about five times the industry average. Atlas is debt free. In its tenth year the company achieved the number one competitive position in its industry.

The company's product: industrial doors. It is a product with almost infinite variety, involving limitless choices of width and height and material. Because of the importance of variety, inventory is almost useless in meeting customer orders; most doors can be manufactured only after the order has been placed.

Historically, the industry had needed almost four months to respond to an order for a door that was out of stock or customized. Atlas's strategic advantage was time: it could respond in weeks to any order. It had structured its order-entry, engineering, manufacturing, and logistics systems to move information and products quickly and reliably.

First, Atlas built just-in-time factories. These are fairly simple in concept. They require extra tooling and machinery to reduce change-over times and a fabrication process organized by product and scheduled to start and complete all of the parts at the same time. But even the performance of the factory—critical to the company's overall responsiveness—still only accounted for 2 1/2 weeks of the completed product delivery cycle.

Second, Atlas compressed time at the front end of the system, where the order first entered and was processed. Traditionally, when customers, distributors, or salespeople called a door manufacturer with a request for price and delivery, they would have to wait more than one week for a response. If the desired door was not in stock, not in the schedule, or not engineered, the supplier's organization would waste even more time, pushing the search for an answer around the system.

Recognizing the opportunity to cut deeply into the time expenditure in this part of the system, Atlas first streamlined, then automated its entire order-entry, engineering, pricing, and scheduling processes. Today Atlas can price and schedule 95% of its incoming orders while the callers are still on the telephone. It can quickly engineer new special orders because it has preserved on computer the design and production data of all previous special orders—which drastically reduces the amount of re-engineering necessary.

Third, Atlas tightly controlled logistics so that it always shipped only fully complete orders to construction sites. Orders require many components. Gathering all of them at the factory and making sure that they are with the correct order can be a time-consuming task. It is even more time-consuming, however, to get the correct parts to the job site *after* they have missed the initial shipment. Atlas developed a system to track the parts in production and the purchased parts for each order, ensuring arrival of all necessary parts at the shipping dock in time—a just-in-time logistics operation.

When Atlas started operations, distributors were uninterested in its product. The established distributors already carried the door line of a larger competitor; they saw no reason to switch suppliers except, perhaps, for a major price concession. But as a start-up, Atlas was too small to compete on price alone. Instead, it positioned itself as the door supplier of last resort, the company people came to if the established supplier could not deliver or missed a key date.

Of course, with industry lead times of almost four months, some calls inevitably came to Atlas. And when it did get a call, Atlas commanded a higher price because of its faster delivery. Atlas not only got a higher price but its time-based processes also yielded lower costs: it thus enjoyed the best of both worlds.

In ten short years, the company replaced the leading door suppliers in 80% of the distributors in the country. With its strategic advantage the company could be selective, becoming the house supplier for only the strongest distributors.

In the wake of this indirect attack, the established competitors have not responded effectively. The conventional view is that Atlas is a "garage shop operator" that cannot sustain its growth: competitors expect the company's performance to degrade to the industry average as it grows larger. But this response—or nonresponse—only reflects a fundamental lack of understanding of time as the source of competitive advantage. The extra delay in responding only adds to the insurmountable lead the indirect time-based attack has created. While the traditional companies track costs and size, the new competitor derives advantage from time, staying on the cutting edge, leaving its rivals behind.

10
Strategic Intent

Gary Hamel and C.K. Prahalad

Today managers in many industries are working hard to match the competitive advantages of their new global rivals. They are moving manufacturing offshore in search of lower labor costs, rationalizing product lines to capture global scale economies, instituting quality circles and just-in-time production, and adopting Japanese human resource practices. When competitiveness still seems out of reach, they form strategic alliances—often with the very companies that upset the competitive balance in the first place.

Important as these initiatives are, few of them go beyond mere imitation. Too many companies are expending enormous energy simply to reproduce the cost and quality advantages their global competitors already enjoy. Imitation may be the sincerest form of flattery, but it will not lead to competitive revitalization. Strategies based on imitation are transparent to competitors who have already mastered them. Moreover, successful competitors rarely stand still. So it is not surprising that many executives feel trapped in a seemingly endless game of catch-up—regularly surprised by the new accomplishments of their rivals.

For these executives and their companies, regaining competitiveness will mean rethinking many of the basic concepts of strategy.[1] As "strategy" has blossomed, the competitiveness of Western companies has withered. This may be coincidence, but we think not. We believe that the application of concepts such as "strategic fit" (between resources and opportunities), "generic strategies" (low cost vs. differentiation vs. focus), and the "strategy hierarchy" (goals, strategies, and tactics) have often abetted the process of competitive decline. The new global competitors approach strategy from a perspective that is fundamentally different from that which underpins Western management thought. Against such competitors, marginal adjustments to current orthodoxies are no more likely to produce competitive revitalization than are marginal improvements in operating efficiency. ("Remaking Strategy" describes our research and summarizes the two contrasting approaches to strategy we see in large, multinational companies.)

Remaking Strategy

Over the last 10 years, our research on global competition, international alliances, and multinational management has brought us into close contact with senior managers in America, Europe, and Japan. As we tried to unravel the reasons for success and surrender in global markets, we became more and more suspicious that executives in Western and Far Eastern companies often operated with very different conceptions of competitive strategy. Understanding these differences, we thought, might help explain the conduct and outcome of competitive battles as well as supplement traditional explanations for Japan's ascendance and the West's decline.

We began by mapping the implicit strategy models of managers who had participated in our research. Then we built detailed histories of selected competitive battles. We searched for evidence of divergent views of strategy, competitive advantage, and the role of top management.

Two contrasting models of strategy emerged. One, which most Western managers will recognize, centers on the problem of maintaining strategic fit. The other centers on the problem of leveraging resources. The two are not mutually exclusive, but they represent a significant difference in emphasis—an emphasis that deeply affects how competitive battles get played out over time.

Both models recognize the problem of competing in a hostile environment with limited resources. But while the emphasis in the first is on trimming ambitions to match available resources, the emphasis in the second is on leveraging resources to reach seemingly unattainable goals.

Both models recognize that relative competitive advantage determines relative profitability. The first emphasizes the search for advantages that are inherently sustainable, the second emphasizes the need to accelerate organizational learning to outpace competitors in building new advantages.

Both models recognize the difficulty of competing against larger competitors. But while the first leads to a search for niches (or simply dissuades the company from challenging an entrenched competitor), the second produces a quest for new rules that can devalue the incumbent's advantages.

Both models recognize that balance in the scope of an organization's activities reduces risk. The first seeks to reduce financial risk by building a balanced portfolio of cash-generating and cash-consuming businesses. The second seeks to reduce competitive risk by ensuring a well-balanced and sufficiently broad portfolio of advantages.

Both models recognize the need to disaggregate the organization in a way that allows top management to differentiate among the investment needs of various planning units. In the first model, resources are allocated to product-market units in which relatedness is defined by common products, channels, and customers. Each business is assumed to own all the critical skills it needs to execute its strategy successfully. In the second, investments are made in core competences (microprocessor controls or electronic imaging, for example) as well as in product-market units. By tracking these investments across businesses, top management works to assure that the plans of individual strategic units don't undermine future developments by default.

Both models recognize the need for consistency in action across organizational levels. In the first, consistency between corporate and business levels is largely a matter of conforming to financial objectives. Consistency between business and functional levels comes by tightly restricting the means the business uses to achieve its strategy—establishing standard operating procedures, defining the served market, adhering to accepted industry practices. In the second model, business-corporate consistency comes from allegiance to a particular strategic intent. Business-functional consistency comes from allegiance to intermediate-term goals, or challenges, with lower level employees encouraged to invent how those goals will be achieved.

Few Western companies have an enviable track record anticipating the moves of new global competitors. Why? The explanation begins with the way most companies have approached competitor analysis. Typically, competitor analysis focuses on the existing resources (human, technical, and financial) of present competitors. The only companies seen as a threat are those with the resources to erode margins and market share in the next planning period. Resourcefulness, the pace at which new competitive advantages are being built, rarely enters in.

In this respect, traditional competitor analysis is like a snapshot of a moving car. By itself, the photograph yields little information about the car's speed or direction—whether the driver is out for a quiet Sunday drive or warming up for the Grand Prix. Yet many managers have learned through painful experience that a business's initial resource endowment (whether bountiful or meager) is an unreliable predictor of future global success.

Think back. In 1970, few Japanese companies possessed the resource base, manufacturing volume, or technical prowess of U.S. and European industry leaders. Komatsu was less than 35% as large as Caterpillar (measured by sales), was scarcely represented outside Japan, and relied on just one product line—small bulldozers—for most of its revenue. Honda was smaller than American Motors and had not yet begun to export cars to the United States. Canon's first halting steps in the reprographics business looked pitifully small compared with the $4 billion Xerox powerhouse.

If Western managers had extended their competitor analysis to include these companies, it would merely have underlined how dramatic the resource discrepancies between them were. Yet by 1985, Komatsu was a $2.8 billion company with a product scope encompassing a broad range of earth-moving equipment, industrial robots, and semiconductors. Honda manufactured almost as many cars worldwide in 1987 as Chrysler. Canon had matched Xerox's global unit market share.

The lesson is clear: assessing the current tactical advantages of known competitors will not help you understand the resolution, stamina, and inventiveness of potential competitors. Sun-tzu, a Chinese military strategist, made the point 3,000 years ago: "All men can see the tactics whereby I conquer," he wrote, "but what none can see is the strategy out of which great victory is evolved."

Companies that have risen to global leadership over the past 20 years invariably began with ambitions that were out of all proportion to their resources and capabilities. But they created an obsession with winning at all levels of the organization and then sustained that obsession over the 10- to 20-year quest for global leadership. We term this obsession "strategic intent."

On the one hand, strategic intent envisions a desired leadership position and establishes the criterion the organization will use to chart its progress. Komatsu set out to "Encircle Caterpillar." Canon sought to "Beat Xerox." Honda strove to become a second Ford—an automotive pioneer. All are expressions of strategic intent.

At the same time, strategic intent is more than simply unfettered ambition. (Many companies possess an ambitious strategic intent yet fall short of their goals.) The concept also encompasses an active management process that includes: focusing the organization's attention on the essence of winning; motivating people by communicating the value of the target; leaving room for individual and team contributions; sustaining enthusiasm by providing new operational definitions as circumstances change; and using intent consistently to guide resource allocations.

Strategic intent captures the essence of winning. The Apollo program—landing a man on the moon ahead of the Soviets—was as competitively focused as Komatsu's drive against Caterpillar. The space program became the scorecard for America's technology race with the USSR. In the turbulent information technology industry, it was hard to pick a single competitor as a target, so NEC's strategic intent, set in the early 1970s, was to acquire the technologies that would put it in the best position to exploit the convergence of computing and telecommunications. Other industry observers foresaw this convergence, but only NEC made convergence the guiding theme for subsequent strategic decisions by adopting "computing and communications" as its intent. For Coca-Cola, strategic intent has been to put a Coke within "arm's reach" of every consumer in the world.

Strategic intent is stable over time. In battles for global leadership, one of the most critical tasks is to lengthen the organization's attention span. Strategic intent provides consistency to short-term action, while leaving room for reinterpretation as new opportunities emerge. At Komatsu, encircling Caterpillar encompassed a succession of medium-term programs aimed at exploiting specific weaknesses in Caterpillar or building particular competitive advantages. When Caterpillar threatened Komatsu in Japan, for example, Komatsu responded by first improving quality, then driving down costs, then cultivating export markets, and then underwriting new product development.

Strategic intent sets a target that deserves personal effort and commitment. Ask the chairmen of many American corporations how they measure their contributions to their companies' success and you're likely to get an answer expressed in terms of shareholder wealth. In a company that possesses a strategic intent, top management is more likely to talk in terms of global market leadership. Market share leadership typically yields shareholder wealth, to be sure. But the two goals do not have the same motivational impact. It is hard to imagine middle managers, let alone blue-collar employees, waking up each day with the sole thought of creating more shareholder wealth. But mightn't they feel different given the challenge to "Beat Benz"—the rallying cry at one Japanese auto producer? Strategic intent gives employees the only goal that is worthy of commitment: to unseat the best or remain the best, worldwide.

Many companies are more familiar with strategic planning than they are with strategic intent. The planning process typically acts as a "feasibility sieve." Strategies are accepted or rejected on the basis of whether managers can be precise about the "how" as well as the "what" of their plans. Are the milestones clear? Do we have the necessary skills and resources? How will competitors react? Has the market been thoroughly researched? In one form or another, the admonition "Be realistic!" is given to line managers at almost every turn.

But can you *plan* for global leadership? Did Komatsu, Canon, and Honda have detailed, 20-year "strategies" for attacking Western markets? Are Japanese and Korean managers better planners than their Western counterparts? No. As valuable as strategic planning is, global leadership is an objective that lies outside the range of planning. We know of few companies with highly developed planning systems that have managed to set a strategic intent. As tests of strategic fit become more stringent, goals that cannot be planned for fall by the wayside. Yet companies that are afraid to commit to goals that lie outside the range of planning are unlikely to become global leaders.

Although strategic planning is billed as a way of becoming more future oriented, most managers, when pressed, will admit that their strategic plans reveal more about today's problems than tomorrow's opportunities. With a fresh set of problems confronting managers at the beginning of every planning cycle, focus often shifts dramatically from year to year. And with the pace of change accelerating in most industries, the predictive horizon is becoming shorter and shorter. So plans do little more than project the present forward incrementally. The goal of strategic intent is to fold the future back into the present. The important question is not "How will next year be different from this year?" but "What must we do differently next year to get closer to our strategic intent?" Only with a carefully articulated and adhered to strategic intent will a succession of year-on-year plans sum up to global leadership.

Just as you cannot plan a 10- to 20-year quest for global leadership, the chance of falling into a leadership position by accident is also remote. We don't believe that global leadership comes from an undirected process of intrapreneurship. Nor is it the product of a skunkworks or other techniques for internal venturing. Behind such programs lies a nihilistic assumption: the organization is so hidebound, so orthodox ridden that the only way to innovate is to put a few bright people in a dark room, pour in some money, and hope that something wonderful will happen. In this "Silicon Valley" approach to innovation, the only role for top managers is to retrofit their corporate strategy to the entrepreneurial successes that emerge from below. Here the value added of top management is low indeed.

Sadly, this view of innovation may be consistent with the reality in many large companies.[2] On the one hand, top management lacks any particular point of view about desirable ends beyond satisfying shareholders and keeping raiders at bay. On the other, the planning format, reward criteria, definition of served market, and belief in accepted industry practice all work together to tightly constrain the range of available means. As a result, innovation is necessarily an isolated activity. Growth depends more on the inventive capacity of individuals and small teams than on the ability of top management to aggregate the efforts of multiple teams towards an ambitious strategic intent.

In companies that overcame resource constraints to build leadership positions, we see a different relationship between means and ends. While strategic intent is clear about ends, it is flexible as to means—it leaves room for improvisation. Achieving strategic intent requires enormous creativity with respect to means: witness Fujitsu's use of strategic alliances in Europe to attack IBM. But this creativity comes in the service of a clearly prescribed end. Creativity is unbridled, but not uncorralled, because top management establishes the criterion against which employees can pretest the logic of their initiatives. Middle managers must do more than deliver on promised financial targets; they must also deliver on the broad direction implicit in their organization's strategic intent.

Strategic intent implies a sizable stretch for an organization. Current capabilities and resources will not suffice. This forces the organization to be more inventive, to make the most of limited resources. Whereas the traditional view of strategy focuses on the degree of fit between existing resources and current opportunities, strategic intent creates an extreme misfit between resources and ambitions. Top management then challenges the organization to close the gap by systematically building new advantages. For Canon this meant first understanding Xerox's patents, then licensing technology to create a product that would yield early market experience, then gearing up internal R&D efforts, then licensing its own technology to other manufacturers to fund further R&D, then entering market segments in Japan and Europe where Xerox was weak, and so on.

In this respect, strategic intent is like a marathon run in 400-meter sprints. No one knows what the terrain will look like at mile 26, so the role of top management is to focus the organization's attention on the ground to be covered in the next 400 meters. In several companies, management did this by presenting the organization with a series of corporate challenges, each specifying the next hill in the race to achieve strategic intent. One year the challenge might be quality, the next total customer care, the next entry into new markets, the next a rejuvenated product line. As this example indicates, corporate challenges are a way to stage the acquisition of new competitive advantages, a way to identify the focal point for employees' efforts in the near to medium term. As with strategic intent, top management is specific about the ends (reducing product development times by 75%, for example) but less prescriptive about the means.

Like strategic intent, challenges stretch the organization. To preempt Xerox in the personal copier business, Canon set its engineers a target price of $1,000 for a home copier. At the time, Canon's least expensive copier sold for several thousand dollars. Trying to reduce the cost of existing models would not have given Canon the radical price-performance improvement it needed to delay or deter Xerox's entry into personal copiers. Instead, Canon engineers were challenged to reinvent the copier—a challenge they met by substituting a disposable cartridge for the complex image-transfer mechanism used in other copiers.

Corporate challenges come from analyzing competitors as well as from the foreseeable pattern of industry evolution. Together these reveal potential competitive openings and identify the new skills the organization will need to take the initiative away from better positioned players. Exhibit I illustrates the way challenges helped that company achieve its intent.

Exhibit 1. Building competitive advantage at Komatsu

Corporate challenge	Protect Komatsu's home market against Caterpillar	Reduce costs while maintaining quality	Make Komatsu an international enterprise and build export markets	Respond to external shocks that threaten markets	Create new products and markets
Programs	**early 1960s** Licensing deals with Cummins Engine, International Harvester, and Bucyrus-Erie to acquire technology and establish benchmarks	**1965** C D (Cost Down) program	**early 1960s** Develop Eastern bloc countries	**1975** V-10 program to reduce costs by 10% while maintaining quality; reduce parts by 20%; rationalize manufacturing system	**late 1970s** Accelerate product development to expand line
	1961 Project A (for Ace) to advance the product quality of Komatsu's small- and medium-sized bulldozers above Caterpillar's	**1966** Total C D program	**1967** Komatsu Europe marketing subsidiary established	**1977** ¥180 program to budget companywide for 180 yen to the dollar when exchange rate was 240	**1979** Future and Frontiers program to identify new businesses based on society's needs and company's know-how
	1962 Quality Circles companywide to provide training for all employees		**1970** Komatsu America established	**1979** Project E to establish teams to redouble cost and quality efforts in response to oil crisis	**1981** EPOCHS program to reconcile greater product variety with improved production efficiencies
			1972 Project B to improve the durability and reliability and to reduce costs of large bulldozers		
			1972 Project C to improve payloaders		
			1972 Project D to improve hydraulic excavators		
			1974 Establish presales and service department to assist newly industrializing countries in construction projects		

For a challenge to be effective, individuals and teams throughout the organization must understand it and see its implications for their own jobs. Companies that set corporate challenges to create new competitive advantages (as Ford and IBM did with quality improvement) quickly discover that engaging the entire organization requires top management to:

Create a sense of urgency, or quasi crisis, by amplifying weak signals in the environment that point up the need to improve, instead of allowing inaction to precipitate a real crisis. (Komatsu, for example, budgeted on the basis of worst case exchange rates that overvalued the yen.)

Develop a competitor focus at every level through widespread use of competitive intelligence. Every employee should be able to benchmark his or her efforts against best-in-class competitors so that the challenge becomes personal. (For example, Ford showed production-line workers videotapes of operations at Mazda's most efficient plant.)

Provide employees with the skills they need to work effectively—training in statistical tools, problem solving, value engineering, and team building, for example.

Give the organization time to digest one challenge before launching another. When competing initiatives overload the organization, middle managers often try to protect their people from the whipsaw of shifting priorities. But this "wait and see if they're serious this time" attitude ultimately destroys the credibility of corporate challenges.

Establish clear milestones and review mechanisms to track progress and ensure that internal recognition and rewards reinforce desired behavior. The goal is to make the challenge inescapable for everyone in the company.

It is important to distinguish between the process of managing corporate challenges and the advantages that the process creates. Whatever the actual challenge may be—quality, cost, value engineering, or something else—there is the same need to engage employees intellectually and emotionally in the development of new skills. In each case, the challenge will take root only if senior executives and lower level employees feel a reciprocal responsibility for competitiveness.

We believe workers in many companies have been asked to take a disproportionate share of the blame for competitive failure. In one U.S. company, for example, management had sought a 40% wage-package concession from hourly employees to bring labor costs into line with Far Eastern competitors. The result was a long strike and, ultimately, a 10% wage concession from employees on the line. However, direct labor costs in manufacturing accounted for less than 15% of total value added. The company thus succeeded in demoralizing its entire blue-collar work force for the sake of a 1.5% reduction in total costs. Ironically, further analysis showed that their competitors' most significant cost savings came not from lower hourly wages but from better work methods invented by employees. You can imagine how eager the U.S. workers were to make similar contributions after the strike and concessions. Contrast this situation with what happened at Nissan when the yen strengthened: top management took a big pay cut and then asked middle managers and line employees to sacrifice relatively less.

Reciprocal responsibility means shared gain and shared pain. In too many companies, the pain of revitalization falls almost exclusively on the employees least responsible for the enterprise's decline. Too often, workers are asked to commit to corporate goals without any matching commitment from top management—be it employment security, gain sharing, or an ability to influence the direction of the business. This one-sided approach to regaining competitiveness keeps many companies from harnessing the intellectual horsepower of their employees.

Creating a sense of reciprocal responsibility is crucial because competitiveness ultimately depends on the pace at which a company embeds new advantages deep within its organization, not on its stock of advantages at any given time. Thus we need to expand the concept of competitive advantage beyond the scorecard many managers now use: Are my costs lower? Will my product command a price premium?

Few competitive advantages are long lasting. Uncovering a new competitive advantage is a bit like getting a hot tip on a stock: the first person to act on the insight makes more money than the last. When the experience curve was young, a company that built capacity ahead of competitors, dropped prices to fill plants, and reduced costs as volume rose went to the bank. The first mover traded on the fact that competitors undervalued market share—they didn't price to capture additional share because they didn't understand how market share leadership could be translated into lower costs and better margins. But there is no more undervalued market share when each of 20 semiconductor companies builds enough capacity to serve 10% of the world market.

Keeping score of existing advantages is not the same as building new advantages. The essence of strategy lies in creating tomorrow's competitive advantages faster than competitors mimic the ones you possess today. In the 1960s, Japanese producers relied on labor and capital cost advantages. As Western manufacturers began to move production offshore, Japanese companies accelerated their investment in process technology and created scale and quality advantages. Then as their U.S. and European competitors rationalized manufacturing, they added another string to their bow by accelerating the rate of product development. Then they built global brands. Then they deskilled competitors through alliances and outsourcing deals. The moral? An organization's capacity to improve existing skills and learn new ones is the most defensible competitive advantage of all.

To achieve a strategic intent, a company must usually take on larger, better financed competitors. That means carefully managing competitive engagements so that scarce resources are conserved. Managers cannot do that simply by playing the same game better—making marginal improvements to competitors' technology and business practices. Instead, they must fundamentally change the game in ways that disadvantage incumbents—devising novel approaches to market entry, advantage building, and competitive warfare. For smart competitors, the goal is not competitive imitation but competitive innovation, the art of containing competitive risks within manageable proportions.

Four approaches to competitive innovation are evident in the global expansion of Japanese companies. These are: building layers of advantage, searching for loose bricks, changing the terms of engagement, and competing through collaboration.

The wider a company's portfolio of advantages, the less risk it faces in competitive battles. New global competitors have built such portfolios by steadily expanding their arsenals of competitive weapons. They have moved inexorably from less defensible advantages such as low wage costs to more defensible advantages like global brands. The Japanese color television industry illustrates this layering process.

By 1967, Japan had become the largest producer of black-and-white television sets. By 1970, it was closing the gap in color televisions. Japanese manufacturers used their competitive advantage—at that time, primarily, low labor costs—to build a base in the private-label business, then moved quickly to establish world-scale plants. This investment gave them additional layers of advantage—quality and reliability—as well as further cost reductions from process improvements. At the same time, they recognized that these cost-based advantages were vulnerable to changes in labor costs, process and product technology, exchange rates, and trade policy. So throughout the

1970s, they also invested heavily in building channels and brands, thus creating another layer of advantage, a global franchise. In the late 1970s, they enlarged the scope of their products and businesses to amortize these grand investments, and by 1980 all the major players— Matsushita, Sharp, Toshiba, Hitachi, Sanyo—had established related sets of businesses that could support global marketing investments. More recently, they have been investing in regional manufacturing and design centers to tailor their products more closely to national markets.

These manufacturers thought of the various sources of competitive advantage as mutually desirable layers, not mutually exclusive choices. What some call competitive suicide—pursuing both cost and differentiation—is exactly what many competitors strive for.[3] Using flexible manufacturing technologies and better marketing intelligence, they are moving away from standardized "world products" to products like Mazda's mini-van, developed in California expressly for the U.S. market.

Another approach to competitive innovation—searching for loose bricks—exploits the benefits of surprise, which is just as useful in business battles as it is in war. Particularly in the early stages of a war for global markets, successful new competitors work to stay below the response threshold of their larger, more powerful rivals. Staking out underdefended territory is one way to do this.

To find loose bricks, managers must have few orthodoxies about how to break into a market or challenge a competitor. For example, in one large U.S. multinational, we asked several country managers to describe what a Japanese competitor was doing in the local market. The first executive said, "They're coming at us in the low end. Japanese companies always come in at the bottom." The second speaker found the comment interesting but disagreed: "They don't offer any low-end products in my market, but they have some exciting stuff at the top end. We really should reverse engineer that thing." Another colleague told still another story. "They haven't taken any business away from me," he said, "but they've just made me a great offer to supply components." In each country, their Japanese competitor had found a different loose brick.

The search for loose bricks begins with a careful analysis of the competitor's conventional wisdom: How does the company define its "served market"? What activities are most profitable? Which geographic markets are too troublesome to enter? The objective is not to find a corner of the industry (or niche) where larger competitors seldom tread but to build a base of attack just outside the market territory that industry leaders currently occupy. The goal is an uncontested profit sanctuary, which could be a particular product segment (the "low end" in motorcycles), a slice of the value chain (components in the computer industry), or a particular geographic market (Eastern Europe).

When Honda took on leaders in the motorcycle industry, for example, it began with products that were just outside the conventional definition of the leaders' product-market domains. As a result, it could build a base of operations in underdefended territory and then use that base to launch an expanded attack. What many competitors failed to see was Honda's strategic intent and its growing competence in engines and power trains. Yet even as Honda was selling 50cc motorcycles in the United States, it was already racing larger bikes in Europe—assembling the design skills and technology it would need for a systematic expansion across the entire spectrum of motor-related businesses.

Honda's progress in creating a core competence in engines should have warned competitors that it might enter a series of seemingly unrelated industries—automobiles, lawn mowers, marine engines, generators. But with each company fixated on its own market, the threat of Honda's horizontal diversification went unnoticed. Today companies like Matsushita and Toshiba are similarly poised to move in unexpected ways across industry boundaries. In protecting loose bricks, companies must extend their peripheral vision by tracking and anticipating the migration of global competitors across product segments, businesses, national markets, value-added stages, and distribution channels.

Changing the terms of engagement—refusing to accept the front-runner's definition of industry and segment boundaries—represents still another form of competitive innovation. Canon's entry into the copier business illustrates this approach.

During the 1970s, both Kodak and IBM tried to match Xerox's business system in terms of segmentation, products, distribution, service, and pricing. As a result, Xerox had no trouble decoding the new entrants' intentions and developing countermoves. IBM eventually withdrew from the copier business, while Kodak remains a distant second in the large copier market that Xerox still dominates.

Canon, on the other hand, changed the terms of competitive engagement. While Xerox built a wide range of copiers, Canon standardized machines and components to reduce costs. Canon chose to distribute through office-product dealers rather than try to match Xerox's huge direct sales force. It also avoided the need to create a national service network by designing reliability and serviceability into its product and then delegating service responsibility to the dealers. Canon copiers were sold rather than leased, freeing Canon from the burden of financing the lease base. Finally, instead of selling to the heads of corporate duplicating departments, Canon appealed to secretaries and department managers who wanted distributed copying. At each stage, Canon neatly sidestepped a potential barrier to entry.

Canon's experience suggests that there is an important distinction between barriers to entry and barriers to imitation. Competitors that tried to match Xerox's business system had to pay the same entry costs—the barriers to imitation were high. But Canon dramatically reduced the barriers to entry by changing the rules of the game.

Changing the rules also short-circuited Xerox's ability to retaliate quickly against its new rival. Confronted with the need to rethink its business strategy and organization, Xerox was paralyzed for a time. Xerox managers realized that the faster they downsized the product line, developed new channels, and improved reliability, the faster they would erode the company's traditional profit base. What might have been seen as critical success factors—Xerox's national sales force and service network, its large installed base of leased machines, and its reliance on service revenues—instead became barriers to retaliation. In this sense, competitive innovation is like judo: the goal is to use a larger competitor's weight against it. And that happens not by matching the leader's capabilities but by developing contrasting capabilities of one's own.

Competitive innovation works on the premise that a successful competitor is likely to be wedded to a "recipe" for success. That's why the most effective weapon new competitors possess is probably a clean sheet of paper. And why an incumbent's greatest vulnerability is its belief in accepted practice.

Through licensing, outsourcing agreements, and joint ventures, it is sometimes possible to win without fighting. For example, Fujitsu's alliances in Europe with Siemens and STC (Britain's largest computer maker) and in the United States with Amdahl yield manufacturing volume and access to Western markets. In the early 1980s, Matsushita established a joint venture with Thorn (in the United Kingdom), Telefunken (in Germany), and Thomson (in France), which allowed it to quickly multiply the forces arrayed against Philips in the battle for leadership in the European VCR business. In fighting larger global rivals by proxy, Japanese companies have adopted a maxim as old as human conflict itself: my enemy's enemy is my friend.

Hijacking the development efforts of potential rivals is another goal of competitive collaboration. In the consumer electronics war, Japanese competitors attacked traditional businesses like TVs and hi-fis while volunteering to manufacture "next generation" products like VCRs, camcorders, and compact disc players for Western rivals. They hoped their rivals would ratchet down development spending, and in most cases that is precisely what happened. But companies that abandoned their own development efforts seldom reemerged as serious competitors in subsequent new product battles.

Collaboration can also be used to calibrate competitors' strengths and weaknesses. Toyota's joint venture with GM, and Mazda's with Ford, give these automakers an invaluable vantage point for assessing the progress their U.S. rivals have made in cost reduction, quality, and technology. They can also learn how GM and Ford compete—when they will fight and when they won't. Of course, the reverse is also true: Ford and GM have an equal opportunity to learn from their partner-competitors.

The route to competitive revitalization we have been mapping implies a new view of strategy. Strategic intent assures consistency in resource allocation over the long term. Clearly articulated corporate challenges focus the efforts of individuals in the medium term. Finally, competitive innovation helps reduce competitive risk in the short term. This consistency in the long term, focus in the medium term, and inventiveness and involvement in the short term provide the key to leveraging limited resources in pursuit of ambitious goals. But just as there is a process of winning, so there is a process of surrender. Revitalization requires understanding that process too.

Given their technological leadership and access to large regional markets, how did U.S. and European companies lose their apparent birthright to dominate global industries? There is no simple answer. Few companies recognize the value of documenting failure. Fewer still search their own managerial orthodoxies for the seeds for competitive surrender. But we believe there is a pathology of surrender (summarized in "The Process of Surrender") that gives some important clues.

The Process of Surrender

In the battles for global leadership that have taken place during the last two decades, we have seen a pattern of competitive attack and retrenchment that was remarkably similar across industries. We call this the process of surrender.

The process started with unseen intent. Not possessing long-term, competitor-focused goals themselves, Western companies did not ascribe such intentions to their rivals. They also calculated the threat posed by potential competitors in terms of their existing resources rather than their resourcefulness. This led to systematic underestimation of smaller rivals who were fast gaining technology through licensing arrangements, acquiring market understanding from downstream OEM partners, and improving product quality and manufacturing productivity through companywide employee involvement programs. Oblivious of the strategic intent and intangible advantages of their rivals, American and European businesses were caught off guard.

Adding to the competitive surprise was the fact that the new entrants typically attacked the periphery of a market (Honda in small motorcycles, Yamaha in grand pianos, Toshiba in small black-and-white televisions) before going head-to-head with incumbents. Incumbents often misread these attacks seeing them as part of a niche strategy and not as a search for "loose bricks." Unconventional market entry strategies (minority holdings in less developed countries, use of nontraditional channels, extensive corporate advertising) were ignored or dismissed as quirky. For example, managers we spoke with said Japanese companies' position in the European computer industry was nonexistent. In terms of brand share that's nearly true, but the Japanese control as much as one-third of the manufacturing value added in the hardware sales of European-based computer businesses. Similarly, German auto producers claimed to feel unconcerned over the proclivity of Japanese producers to move upmarket. But with its low-end models under tremendous pressure from Japanese producers, Porsche has now announced that it will no longer make "entry level" cars.

Western managers often misinterpreted their rivals' tactics. They believed that Japanese and Korean companies were competing solely on the basis of cost and quality. This typically produced a partial response to those competitors' initiatives: moving manufacturing offshore, outsourcing, or instituting a quality program. Seldom was the full extent of the competitive threat appreciated—the multiple layers of advantage, the expansion across related product segments, the development of global brand positions. Imitating the currently visible tactics of rivals put Western businesses into a perpetual catch-up trap. One by one, companies lost battles and came to see surrender as inevitable. Surrender was not inevitable, of course, but the attack was staged in a way that disguised ultimate intentions and sidestepped direct confrontation.

It is not very comforting to think that the essence of Western strategic thought can be reduced to eight rules for excellence, seven S's, five competitive forces, four product life-cycle stages, three generic strategies, and innumerable two-by-two matrices.[4] Yet for the past 20 years, "advances" in strategy have taken the form of ever more typologies, heuristics, and laundry lists, often with dubious empirical bases. Moreover, even reasonable concepts like the product life cycle, experience curve, product portfolios, and generic strategies often have toxic side effects: They reduce the number of strategic options management is willing to consider. They create a preference for selling businesses rather than defending them. They yield predictable strategies that rivals easily decode.

Strategy "recipes" limit opportunities for competitive innovation. A company may have 40 businesses and only four strategies—invest, hold, harvest, or divest. Too often strategy is seen as a positioning exercise in which options are tested by how they fit the existing industry structure. But current industry structure reflects the strengths of the industry leader; and playing by the leader's rules is usually competitive suicide.

Armed with concepts like segmentation, the value chain, competitor benchmarking, strategic groups, and mobility barriers, many managers have become better and better at drawing industry maps. But while they have been busy map making, their competitors have been moving entire continents. The strategist's goal is not to find a niche within the existing industry space but to create new space that is uniquely suited to the company's own strengths, space that is off the map.

This is particularly true now that industry boundaries are becoming more and more unstable. In industries such as financial services and communications, rapidly changing technology, deregulation, and globalization have undermined the value of traditional industry analysis. Map-making skills are worth little in the epicenter of an earthquake. But an industry in upheaval presents opportunities for ambitious companies to redraw the map in their favor, so long as they can think outside traditional industry boundaries.

Concepts like "mature" and "declining" are largely definitional. What most executives mean when they label a business mature is that sales growth has stagnated in their current geographic markets for existing products sold through existing channels. In such cases, it's not the industry that is mature, but the executives' conception of the industry. Asked if the piano business was mature, a senior executive in Yamaha replied, "Only if we can't take any market share from anybody anywhere in the world and still make money. And anyway, we're not in the 'piano' business, we're in the 'keyboard' business." Year after year, Sony has revitalized its radio and tape recorder businesses, despite the fact that other manufacturers long ago abandoned these businesses as mature.

A narrow concept of maturity can foreclose a company from a broad stream of future opportunities. In the 1970s, several U.S. companies thought that consumer electronics had become a mature industry. What could possibly top the color TV? they asked themselves. RCA and GE, distracted by opportunities in more "attractive" industries like mainframe computers, left Japanese producers with a virtual monopoly in VCRs, camcorders, and compact disc players. Ironically, the TV business, once thought mature, is on the verge of a dramatic renaissance. A $20 billion-a-year business will be created when high-definition television is launched in the United States. But the pioneers of television may capture only a small part of this bonanza.

Most of the tools of strategic analysis are focused domestically. Few force managers to consider global opportunities and threats. For example, portfolio planning portrays top management's investment options as an array of businesses rather than as an array of geographic markets. The result is predictable: as businesses come under attack from foreign competitors, the company attempts to abandon them and enter others in which the forces of global competition are not yet so strong. In the short term, this may be an appropriate response to waning competitiveness, but there are fewer and fewer businesses in which a domestic-oriented company can find refuge. We seldom hear such companies asking: Can we move into emerging markets overseas ahead of our global rivals and prolong the profitability of this business? Can we counterattack in our global competitors' home markets and slow the pace of their expansion? A senior executive in one successful global company made a telling comment: "We're glad to find a competitor managing by the portfolio concept—we can almost predict how much share we'll have to take away to put the business on the CEO's 'sell list.'"

Companies can also be overcommitted to organizational recipes, such as strategic business units and the decentralization an SBU structure implies. Decentralization is seductive because it places the responsibility for success or failure squarely on the shoulders of line managers. Each business is assumed to have all the resources it needs to execute its strategies successfully, and in this no-excuses environment, it is hard for top management to fail. But desirable as clear lines of responsibility and accountability are, competitive revitalization requires positive value added from top management.

Few companies with a strong SBU orientation have built successful global distribution and brand positions. Investments in a global brand franchise typically transcend the resources and risk propensity of a single business. While some Western companies have had global brand positions for 30 or 40 years or more (Heinz, Siemens, IBM, Ford, and Kodak, for example), it is hard to identify any American or European company that has created a new global brand franchise in the last 10 to 15 years. Yet Japanese companies have created a score or more— NEC, Fujitsu, Panasonic (Matsushita), Toshiba, Sony, Seiko, Epson, Canon, Minolta, and Honda, among them.

General Electric's situation is typical. In many of its businesses, this American giant has been almost unknown in Europe and Asia. GE made no coordinated effort to build a global corporate franchise. Any GE business with international ambitions had to bear the burden of establishing its credibility and credentials in the new market alone. Not surprisingly, some once-strong GE businesses opted out of the difficult task of building a global brand position. In contrast, smaller Korean companies like Samsung, Daewoo, and Lucky Gold Star are busy building global-brand umbrellas that will ease market entry for a whole range of businesses. The underlying principle is simple: economies of scope may be as important as economies of scale in entering global markets. But capturing economies of scope demands interbusiness coordination that only top management can provide.

We believe that inflexible SBU-type organizations have also contributed to the deskilling of some companies. For a single SBU, incapable of sustaining investment in a core competence such as semiconductors, optical media, or combustion engines, the only way to remain competitive is to purchase key components from potential (often Japanese or Korean) competitors. For an SBU defined in product-market terms, competitiveness means offering an end product that is competitive in price and performance. But that gives an SBU manager little incentive to distinguish between external sourcing that achieves "product embodied" competitiveness and internal development that yields deeply embedded organizational competences that can be exploited across multiple businesses. Where upstream component manufacturing activities are seen as cost centers with cost-plus transfer pricing, additional investment in the core activity may seem a less profitable use of capital than investment in downstream activities. To make matters worse, internal accounting data may not reflect the competitive value of retaining control over core competence.

Together a shared global corporate brand franchise and shared core competence act as mortar in many Japanese companies. Lacking this mortar, a company's businesses are truly loose bricks—easily knocked out by global competitors that steadily invest in core competences. Such competitors can co-opt domestically oriented companies into long-term sourcing dependence and capture the economies of scope of global brand investment through interbusiness coordination.

Last in decentralization's list of dangers is the standard of managerial performance typically used in SBU organizations. In many companies, business unit managers are rewarded solely on the basis of their performance against return on investment targets. Unfortunately, that often leads to denominator management because executives soon discover that reductions in investment and head count—the denominator—"improve" the financial ratios by which they are measured more easily than growth in the numerator—revenues. It also fosters a hair-trigger sensitivity to industry downturns that can be very costly. Managers who are quick to reduce investment and dismiss workers find it takes much longer to regain lost skills and catch up on investment when the industry turns upward again. As a result, they lose market share in every business cycle. Particularly in industries where there is fierce competition for the best people and where competitors invest relentlessly, denominator management creates a retrenchment ratchet.

The concept of the general manager as a movable peg reinforces the problem of denominator management. Business schools are guilty here because they have perpetuated the notion that a manager with net present value calculations in one hand and portfolio planning in the other can manage any business anywhere.

In many diversified companies, top management evaluates line managers on numbers alone because no other basis for dialogue exists. Managers move so many times as part of their "career development" that they often do not understand the nuances of the businesses they are managing. At GE, for example, one fast-track manager heading an important new venture had moved across five businesses in five years. His series of quick successes finally came to an end when he confronted a Japanese competitor whose managers had been plodding along in the same business for more than a decade.

Regardless of ability and effort, fast-track managers are unlikely to develop the deep business knowledge they need to discuss technology options, competitors' strategies, and global opportunities substantively. Invariably, therefore, discussions gravitate to "the numbers," while the value added of managers is limited to the financial and planning savvy they carry from job to job. Knowledge of the company's internal planning and accounting systems substitutes for substantive knowledge of the business, making competitive innovation unlikely.

When managers know that their assignments have a two- to three-year time frame, they feel great pressure to create a good track record fast. This pressure often takes one of two forms. Either the manager does not commit to goals whose time line extends beyond his or her expected tenure. Or ambitious goals are adopted and squeezed into an unrealistically short time frame. Aiming to be number one in a business is the essence of strategic intent; but imposing a three- to four-year horizon on the effort simply invites disaster. Acquisitions are made with little attention to the problems of integration. The organization becomes overloaded with initiatives. Collaborative ventures are formed without adequate attention to competitive consequences.

Almost every strategic management theory and nearly every corporate planning system is premised on a strategy hierarchy in which corporate goals guide business unit strategies and business unit strategies guide functional tactics.[5] In this hierarchy, senior management makes strategy and lower levels execute it. The dichotomy between formulation and implementation is familiar and widely accepted. But the strategy hierarchy undermines competitiveness by fostering an elitist view of management that tends to disenfranchise most of the organization. Employees fail to identify with corporate goals or involve themselves deeply in the work of becoming more competitive.

The strategy hierarchy isn't the only explanation for an elitist view of management, of course. The myths that grow up around successful top managers—"Lee Iacocca saved Chrysler," "Carlo De Benedetti rescued Olivetti," "John Sculley turned Apple around"—perpetuate it. So does the turbulent business environment. Middle managers buffeted by circumstances that seem to be beyond their control desperately want to believe that top management has all the answers. And top management, in turn, hesitates to admit it does not for fear of demoralizing lower level employees.

The result of all this is often a code of silence in which the full extent of a company's competitiveness problem is not widely shared. We interviewed business unit managers in one company, for example, who were extremely anxious because top management wasn't talking openly about the competitive challenges the company faced. They assumed the lack of communication indicated a lack of awareness on their senior managers' part. But when asked whether they were open with their own employees, these same managers replied that while they could face up to the problems, the people below them could not. Indeed, the only time the work force heard about the company's competitiveness problems was during wage negotiations when problems were used to extract concessions.

Unfortunately, a threat that everyone perceives but no one talks about creates more anxiety than a threat that has been clearly identified and made the focal point for the problem-solving efforts of the entire company. That is one reason honesty and humility on the part of top management may be the first prerequisite of revitalization. Another reason is the need to make participation more than a buzzword.

Programs such as quality circles and total customer service often fall short of expectations because management does not recognize that successful implementation requires more than administrative structures. Difficulties in embedding new capabilities are typically put down to "communication" problems, with the unstated assumption that if only downward communication were more effective—"if only middle management would get the message straight"—the new program would quickly take root. The need for upward communication is often ignored, or assumed to mean nothing more than feedback. In contrast, Japanese companies win, not because they have smarter managers, but because they have developed ways to harness the "wisdom of the anthill." They realize that top managers are a bit like the astronauts who circle the earth in the space shuttle. It may be the astronauts who get all the glory, but everyone knows that the real intelligence behind the mission is located firmly on the ground.

Where strategy formulation is an elitist activity it is also difficult to produce truly creative strategies. For one thing, there are not enough heads and points of view in divisional or corporate planning departments to challenge conventional wisdom. For another, creative strategies seldom emerge from the annual planning ritual. The starting point for next year's strategy is almost always this year's strategy. Improvements are incremental. The company sticks to the segments and territories it knows, even though the real opportunities may be elsewhere. The impetus for Canon's pioneering entry into the personal copier business came from an overseas sales subsidiary—not from planners in Japan.

The goal of the strategy hierarchy remains valid—to ensure consistency up and down the organization. But this consistency is better derived from a clearly articulated strategic intent than from inflexibly applied top-down plans. In the 1990s, the challenge will be to enfranchise employees to invent the means to accomplish ambitious ends.

We seldom found cautious administrators among the top managements of companies that came from behind to challenge incumbents for global leadership. But in studying organizations that had surrendered, we invariably found senior managers who, for whatever reason, lacked the courage to commit their companies to heroic goals—goals that lay beyond the reach of planning and existing resources. The conservative goals they set failed to generate pressure and enthusiasm for competitive innovation or give the organization much useful guidance. Financial targets and vague mission statements just cannot provide the consistent direction that is a prerequisite for winning a global competitive war.

This kind of conservatism is usually blamed on the financial markets. But we believe that in most cases investors' so-called short-term orientation simply reflects their lack of confidence in the ability of senior managers to conceive and deliver stretch goals. The chairman of one company complained bitterly that even after improving return on capital employed to over 40% (by ruthlessly divesting lackluster businesses and downsizing others), the stock market held the company to an 8:1 price/earnings ratio. Of course the market's message was clear: "We don't trust you. You've shown no ability to achieve profitable growth. Just cut out the slack, manage the denominators, and perhaps you'll be taken over by a company that can use your resources more creatively." Very little in the track record of most large Western companies warrants the confidence of the stock market. Investors aren't hopelessly short-term, they're justifiably skeptical.

We believe that top management's caution reflects a lack of confidence in its own ability to involve the entire organization in revitalization—as opposed to simply raising financial targets. Developing faith in the organization's ability to deliver on tough goals, motivating it to do so, focusing its attention long enough to internalize new capabilities—this is the real challenge for top management. Only by rising to this challenge will senior managers gain the courage they need to commit themselves and their companies to global leadership.

Notes

1. Among the first to apply the concept of strategy to management were H. Igor Ansoff in *Corporate Strategy: An Analytic Approach to Business Policy for Growth and Expansion* (New York: McGraw-Hill, 1965) and Kenneth R. Andrews in *The Concept of Corporate Strategy* (Homewood, Ill.: Dow Jones-Irwin, 1971).

2. Robert A. Burgelman, "A Process Model of Internal Corporate Venturing in the Diversified Major Firm," *Administrative Science Quarterly*, June 1983.

3. For example, see Michael E. Porter, *Competitive Strategy* (New York: Free Press, 1980).

4. Strategic frameworks for resource allocation in diversified companies are summarized in Charles W. Hofer and Dan E. Schendel, *Strategy Formulation: Analytical Concepts* (St. Paul, Minn.: West Publishing, 1978).

5. For example, see Peter Lorange and Richard F. Vancil, *Strategic Planning Systems* (Englewood Cliffs, N.J.: Prentice-Hall, 1977).

11

Motorola U: When Training Becomes an Education

William Wiggenhorn

At Motorola we require three things of our manufacturing employees. They must have communication and computation skills at the seventh grade level, soon going up to eighth and ninth. They must be able to do basic problem solving—not only as individuals but also as members of a team. And they must accept our definition of work and the workweek: the time it takes to ship perfect product to the customer who's ordered it. That can mean a workweek of 50 or even 60 hours, but we need people willing to work against quality and output instead of a time clock.

These requirements are relatively new. Ten years ago, we hired people to perform set tasks and didn't ask them to do a lot of thinking. If a machine went down, workers raised their hands, and a troubleshooter came to fix it. Ten years ago, we saw quality control as a screening process, catching defects before they got out the door. Ten years ago, most workers and some managers learned their jobs by observation, experience, and trial and error. When we did train people, we simply taught them new techniques on top of the basic math and communication skills we supposed they brought with them from school or college.

Then all the rules of manufacturing and competition changed, and in our drive to change with them, we found we had to rewrite the rules of corporate training and education. We learned that line workers had to actually understand their work and their equipment, that senior management had to exemplify and reinforce new methods and skills if they were going to stick, that change had to be continuous and participative, and that education—not just instruction—was the only way to make all this occur.

Finally, just as we began to capitalize on the change we thought we were achieving, we discovered to our utter astonishment that much of our work force was illiterate. They couldn't read. They couldn't do simple arithmetic like percentages and fractions. At one plant, a supplier changed its packaging, and we found in the nick of time that our people were working by the color of the package, not by what it said. In Illinois, we found a foreign-born employee who didn't know the difference between the present tense and the past. He was never sure if we were talking about what *was* happening or what *had* happened.

These discoveries led us into areas of education we had never meant to enter and into budgetary realms we would have found unthinkable 10 years earlier. From the kind of skill instruction we envisioned at the outset, we moved out in both directions: down, toward grade school basics as fundamental as the three Rs; up, toward new concepts of work, quality, community, learning, and leadership. From a contemplated total budget of $35 million over a five-year period, a sum many thought excessive, we came to spend $60 million annually—plus another $60 million in lost work time—and everyone thought it was money well invested.

Today we expect workers to know their equipment and begin any troubleshooting process themselves. If they do need an expert, they must be able to describe the malfunction in detail. In other words, they have to be able to analyze problems and then communicate them.

Today we see quality as a process that prevents defects from occurring, a common corporate language that pervades the company and applies to security guards and secretaries as well as manufacturing staff. (For more about this, see "The Language of Quality.")

The Language of Quality

The mathematics of quality are difficult. Even the vocabulary—bell curves, probability functions, standard deviations expressed in multiples of the Greek letter Σ—can be formidable. At Motorola, we have nevertheless tried to teach at least a basic version of this math to every employee and to extend the concepts and terminology of industrial quality into every corner of the business—training, public relations, finance, security, even cooking. In 1983, we thought three days of training on quality would be enough. Today we have 28 days of material—quality tools, quality strategy, quality techniques, quality feedback mechanisms—and over the course of several years, we expect our engineers and manufacturing middle managers to have all 28.

The corporate goal is to achieve a quality standard by 1992 equivalent to what the statisticians and industrial engineers call Six Sigma, which means six standard deviations from a statistical performance average. In plain English, Six Sigma translates into 3.4 defects per million opportunities, or production that is 99.99966% defect free. (By contrast, and according to formulas not worth explaining here, 5Σ is 233 defects per million, and 4Σ is 6,210. Airlines achieve 6.5Σ in safety—counting fatalities as defects—but only 3.5 to 4Σ in baggage handling. Doctors and pharmacists achieve an accuracy of just under 5Σ in writing and filling prescriptions.)

Motorola has not yet reached Six Sigma in manufacturing or in any other function. But we have achieved our initial goal of creating a common vocabulary that lets every person in the company speak the same quality language. Everyone pursues his or her own job version of Six Sigma, and everyone shares a sense of what it means, objectively and subjectively, to take part in the process of getting from where we are to where we want to be. The idea of 3.4 defects per million opportunities may sound ridiculous for a course instructor or a chef, but there is always some way to apply the standard and strive for the goal. In effect, the Six Sigma process means changing the way people do things so that nothing can go wrong.

Applied to the chef, the process of reaching Six Sigma by 1992 means he can burn five muffins this year, two muffins next year, and eventually none at all. Of course, Six Sigma applied to muffins is in one sense a fiction, and if we presented it to the chef as an ultimatum, it would also be insulting. The real point is that importing that quality language from manufacturing to the rest of the company stimulates a kind of discussion we might not otherwise have had. It also tells people they're important, since the time-cycle and quality standards so vital to manufacturing and product design now also apply to the chef, the security guard, and the clerical support people.

What we actually said to the chef was that he made a consistently Six Sigma chocolate chip cookie—in my opinion it ranks with the best in the world—and we wanted him to do the same with muffins. We asked him what changes we needed to make so he could accomplish that. He said, "The reason I can't make better muffins is that you don't trust me with the key to the freezer. I have to make the batter the night before because when I get here in the morning the makings are still locked up. When batter sits for 12 hours, it's never as good as batter you make fresh and pop directly in the oven." He was right, of course. The language of quality can also be used to talk about trust.

Security guards are another good example. Every morning they have to get 12,000 employees and about 400 visitors through the gates in half an hour. What's their assignment—to keep people out, bring people in, protect property? As we now define it, their job is to make sure the right people get in quickly and, if there are problems, to handle them politely and professionally. Quality is measured accordingly—a "customer" complaint is a defect, and a customer is anyone who comes to the gate.

Today Motorola has one of the most comprehensive and effective corporate training and education programs in the world and, in a recent leap of ambition, our own corporate university.

Why in the world, you ask, should any corporation have its own university? My answer is the story of how we came to have ours. In part, it is a kind of odyssey, a 10-year expedition full of well-meaning mistakes, heroic misapprehensions, and shocking discoveries. In part, it is a slowly unfolding definition of education and change that shows why successful companies in today's business climate must not only train workers but build educational systems.

An MBA in Four Weeks

In 1979, Bob Galvin, then Motorola's CEO and now chairman of the executive committee, asked the human resource department to put together a five-year training plan. He believed that all employees needed upgrading in their skills if the company was going to survive.

Galvin had made two earlier attempts at companywide education. The first focused on new tools, new technology, and teamwork, but it didn't produce the results he wanted. Plant managers brought in new equipment but wouldn't change the support systems and their own work patterns.

So he set up the Motorola Executive Institute, an intensive, one-time course for 400 executives that tried to give them an MBA in four weeks. The participants learned a great deal, but again, the ultimate results were disappointing.

Galvin, who understood that change had to force its way through a company from the top down, had been driving home the point that those who lead often lose their power—or their right to lead—because they're unwilling to change. He now realized that the top probably wasn't going to lead the attack until all employees wanted change to take place. Motorola had to educate everyone and make people see the need for change.

To carry out this training program, we set up an education service department—MTEC, the Motorola Training and Education Center—with its own board of directors consisting of Galvin himself, two of his top executives, and senior managers from each of Motorola's operating units. MTEC had two principal goals: to expand the participative management process and to help improve product quality tenfold in five years.

Our charter was not so much to educate people as to be an agent of change, with an emphasis on retraining workers and redefining jobs. Our first order of business was to analyze the jobs that existed then, in 1980, and try to anticipate what they'd look like in the future. The first thing we learned was not to look too far ahead. If we made a two-year projection and trained people for that, then change didn't arrive quickly enough for people to make the shift. We had to anticipate, plan curricula, then train separately for each incremental change. We had thought progress would be made in leaps, but it took place one step at a time.

To meet the quality target, we developed a five-part curriculum. First came statistical process control, which consisted of instruction in seven quality tools. Basic industrial problem solving was second. Third was a course on how to present conceptual material, a tricky assignment for an hourly worker presenting a technical solution to an engineer. Fourth was a course on effective meetings that emphasized the role of participant as well as that of chairperson. Finally we had a program on goal setting that taught people how to define objectives, how to describe them in writing, and how to measure progress.

So far so good. In the early 1980s, at a typical plant with 2,500 workers, MTEC was using 50,000 hours of employee time—a lot of time away from the job for what some people considered a pretty esoteric program. We thought it was worth the investment. Putting quality tools in the hands of every employee was the only way to overcome the old emphasis on shipment goals, even when meeting those goals meant shipping defective products.

Yet the skeptics were right. We were wasting everyone's time. We designed and taught courses, and people took them and went back to their jobs, and nothing changed. We had made a series of false assumptions.

Getting People to Want to Learn

Our first mistake was to assume that once we described the courses, the people who needed them most would sign up to take them. They didn't. We also assumed that the courses would be popular, but enrollment was never in danger of swamping our capacities.

The old approach had been to learn by watching others. When technology changed once in five years, on-the-job training made some sense, but people can't handle constant innovation by watching one another. Yet somehow the culture told them they didn't learn things any other way. Since people resisted formal classes, we developed self-help material so they could pick up a package and take it home. That failed too. People just didn't see homework as real training, which left us in a bind: our employees didn't seem to believe the training was necessary, but if it was necessary, then it had to take place in a formal classroom, not at home. So we dropped the learn-at-home program. Not because people couldn't learn that way but because we couldn't get people to *want* to learn that way.

Training, it appeared, was not something we could deliver like milk and expect people to consume spontaneously. It was not simply a matter of instructing or giving people a chance to instruct themselves. We had to motivate people to want to learn, and that meant overcoming complacency.

When Motorola hired people in the old days, we hired them for life. People grew up in their jobs, acquired competencies and titles, moved from work force to management. All employees became members of our Service Club at the end of 10 years, which meant we wouldn't terminate them except for poor performance or dishonesty. We never gave anyone an absolute right to lifelong employment, but we did provide an unmistakable opportunity to stay.

This was the employment model that built the corporation and made it successful, and we believed the loyalty it inspired gave us added value. We hadn't yet realized in the early 1980s that there was going to be a skill shortage, but we clearly needed to upgrade our training. A lot of our competitors, especially in the semiconductor business, hired people, used their skills, terminated them when their skills were out of date, then hired new people with new skills. But we had plants where 60% to 70% of the workers were Service Club members.

We didn't want to break a model that had worked for 50 years, but we had some people who thought that if they made that 10-year mark they could mentally retire, and that was an attitude we had to fix. In the end, we had to let people know that "poor performance" included an unwillingness to change. We had to abandon paternalism for shared responsibility.

A second major misconception was that senior managers needed only a briefing to understand the new quality systems. Conceptually, in fact, they grasped them very quickly and believed in their importance. But their behavior patterns didn't change, and that made life very difficult for middle managers.

Operations review is a good example. If a production team had mastered the new techniques and was eager to apply them, and if senior management paid lip service to quality but still placed its highest priority on shipping goals, middle managers got caught in the squeeze. Workers expected them to emphasize quality even if that made some deliveries late. Top management expected them to improve quality but not at the expense of schedule.

Workers began to wonder why they'd taken the training. They'd learned how to keep a Pareto chart and make an Ishikawa diagram, but no one ever appeared on the floor and asked to see one. On the contrary, some of their immediate managers wanted product shipped even if it wasn't perfect. Top managers, on the other hand, began to wonder why it was that people took the courses so carefully designed for them and then went back to their jobs and did nothing different. Shipping goals were being met, but quality was not improving.

At about this point in our frustration, we asked two universities to evaluate our return on investment. They identified three groups.

- In those few plants where the work force absorbed the whole curriculum of quality tools and process skills and where senior managers reinforced the training by means of new questions appropriate to the new methods, we were getting a $33 return for every dollar spent, including the cost of wages paid while people sat in class.

- Plants that made use of either the quality tools or the process skills but not both, and then reinforced what they taught, broke even.

- Finally, plants that taught all or part of the curriculum but failed to reinforce with follow-up meetings and a new, genuine emphasis on quality had a negative return on investment.

We were learning our first lesson all over again, that change is not just driven from the top—change must *begin* at the top. We had also begun to understand that one secret of manufacturing success was a language common to every employee, in this case a common language of quality. But if quality was to be the new language, every top manager had better learn to speak it like a native. Since Bob Galvin believed quality training was useless unless top managers gave quality even more attention than they gave quarterly results, he dramatized the point at operations review meetings. He insisted that quality reports come first, not last, on the agenda, and then he left before the financial results were discussed.

Thin Ice

By 1984, we were admittedly a little disappointed by what we had achieved so far, but we believed we could address the problem with a new, double-edged initiative. First, by hiring and training more carefully, we would bring our manufacturing talent up to the standard in product design, and second, having now learned our lesson about top executive involvement, we would offer the training to upper management as well as line workers.

There was no question that manufacturing was a second-class citizen. Our recruiting strategy had always been to find the best engineers, and the best engineers went into product design. We had never deliberately looked for the best manufacturing or materials-management people. We now consciously upgraded the status, rewards, and recruiting for Motorola manufacturing.

We also put together a two-week program of courses that tried to project what our kind of manufacturing would look like in 10 years and to think about the changes we would have to make to stay competitive. We wanted all the decision makers in manufacturing to take part.

We began, as so often before and since, by repeating a past mistake. We assumed the proper people at the top would sign up without prompting. What we found was that many simply delegated the program to subordinates. Our advisory board—Galvin and 11 senior managers—soon saw what was happening and changed the policy. From then on, the board "invited" people to take the training, and board members began by inviting themselves, then everyone else at the top.

The curriculum centered on manufacturing technologies—computer-aided design, new quality measurements, computer-integrated manufacturing, just-in-time—as well as on what we called "unity of purpose," our name for the empowered work force. We also began to focus on time. We used to take three to seven years to design a new product; now we were shooting for 18 months. Finally, we started talking about a contract book where marketing, product design, and manufacturing would meet, argue, and reach genuine agreement about the needs of the market, the right new product, and the schedules and responsibilities of each group in producing it.

Historically, such agreements had often been made but never kept. The three departments would meet and agree, product design would go home and invent something quite different but wonderfully state-of-the-art, manufacturing would do a complete redesign to permit actual production in the real world, and finally marketing would find itself with a product bearing little resemblance to what it had asked for and been promised.

We wanted to use the training to send a message to the company about achieving quality through the integration of efforts across functions, a message not just about quality of product but about quality of people, quality of service, quality of the total organization.

In 1985, we also started an annual training and education event for senior management. Each year, the CEO picks a topic of critical concern and brings his top executives together to thrash it out with the help of some carefully chosen experts.

That first year the topic was competition, especially Asian competition. There were Asian companies—whole Asian countries—going after every market segment we were in. Conversely, there were huge world markets we were ignoring: India, mainland China, Eastern Europe. The goal was to scare the wits out of all the participants and wake them up to the perils and opportunities of our position. We had people calling themselves worldwide product or marketing managers who didn't even have a passport.

From 1985 to 1987, our top 200 people spent 17 days each in the classroom. Ten days on manufacturing, five days on global competition, and two more days on cycle-time management. We then drove that training down through the organization via the major components of the curriculum. What was 10 days for a vice president might have been eight hours for a production worker, but eventually they were all speaking the same language. Or so we believed.

In 1985, we decided, after considerable fact finding and lengthy deliberation, to open our new cellular manufacturing facility in the United States rather than take it offshore. Top management had just gone through its workshop on foreign competition, and there was a general feeling that, with our manufacturing expertise, we should be able to compete with anyone in the world. We acknowledged the fact that it wasn't only low-cost labor we'd been going offshore to get but brains—first-rate manufacturing know-how. In our naive self-satisfaction over the success of our training programs, we figured we now had across-the-board know-how in Illinois.

Our work force in Arlington Heights, outside Chicago, knew radio technology, and given the similarities, we believed these workers could make the bridge to cellular. In addition, they had improved quality tenfold in the first five years of training and were well on their way to doing it again. Nevertheless, we were making what was fundamentally an emotional commitment, not a hard-nosed business decision. However much quality had improved, it had probably not improved enough to compete in new technologies when our labor was going to cost us more than it cost our Asian competitors. However thoroughly the Arlington Heights workers understood radios, we were about to empower them to do much more than they had done in the past—not just one or two assembly functions but quality control, flexible manufacturing, and mentoring for the several thousand new hires we'd eventually have to add.

Maybe we sensed the thin ice we were on. In any case, we did a quick math assessment to see exactly where we stood with regard to further training. The scores were a shock. Only 40% passed a test containing some questions as simple as "Ten is what percent of 100?"

The Work Force That Couldn't Read

Let me dwell for a moment on the full drama of those results. The Arlington Heights work force was going to lead the company into global competition in a new technology, and 60% seemed to have trouble with simple arithmetic. We needed a work force capable of operating and maintaining sophisticated new equipment and facilities to a zero-defect standard, and most of them could not calculate decimals, fractions, and percents.

It took us several months and a number of math classes to discover that the real cause of much of this poor math performance was an inability to read or, in the case of many immigrants, to comprehend English as a second language. Those who'd missed the simple percentage question had been unable to read the words. In a sense, this was good news: it meant their math might not be as bad as we'd feared. But the news was bad enough even with the silver lining. For years, we'd been moving computers into the work line to let everyone interface with a keyboard and a screen; since 1980, the number of computer terminals at Motorola had gone from 5,000 to 55,000. At the new plant, workers would need to feed data into these terminals and extract information from them. Now we had reason to wonder if they'd be able to use their computers effectively.

And yet these people were superior employees who had improved quality tenfold and more. How had they done that if they couldn't read? It was a mystery—and a great problem.

The mystery was easily solved. In the early 1980s, we had had several layers of middle managers who acted as translators. They took the directions on the screens and put them into spoken English or, in many cases, Polish or Spanish, and the workers—dedicated, motivated people—carried them out.

The problem, however, remained. In fact, it grew rapidly more serious as we began to set up the new plant. We had begun to remove layers of middle management in the mid-1980s, and in setting up the new factory we wanted to leave no more than two or three levels between the plant manager and the greenest entry-level hire. For that to work, we had to have people with basic skills who were quick to learn—and quick to teach. After all, we couldn't staff the whole plant with our current employees, even if they all had the necessary skills. We had to have a cadre of 400 to 500 people who could serve as teachers and role models for others as we brought them in.

In the old days, our selection criteria had been simply, "Are you willing to work? Do you have a good record of showing up for work? Are you motivated to work?" We didn't ask people if they could read. We didn't ask them to do arithmetic. We didn't ask them to demonstrate an ability to solve problems or work on a team or do anything except show up and be productive for so many hours a week.

The obvious, drastic answer would have been to fire that old work force and hire people who could meet our standards, but that was not an acceptable approach for our company and probably not a realistic one given the educational level of the available labor pool. We quickly implemented a standard for new hires based on seventh grade math and reading skills, but as we recruited people from the outside, we found remarkably few who met that seventh grade standard.

We look for many things in our applicants, beyond literacy. For example, they must also be punctual and responsible. But at some installations, the requirements are even higher. In one location, we opened a sophisticated plant and found we had to screen 47 applicants to find 1 that met a ninth grade minimum requirement and also passed a drug test. This was admittedly an extreme situation, and the results were also skewed by the drug test. Still, at 1 applicant in 47, a company soon runs out of potential hires, especially if anyone else is competing for the labor supply.

We quickly saw that a higher set of standards for new hires was not the whole answer to our Illinois problem, particularly since we weren't willing to lay off dedicated people who'd been with us for years. And Arlington Heights was no isolated pocket. Documenting installations one by one, we concluded that about half of our 25,000 manufacturing and support people in the United States failed to meet the seventh grade yardstick in English and math.

At a plant in Florida, we offered English as a second language, thinking maybe 60 people would sign up, and we got 600—one out of three employees. By signing up, they were telling us they couldn't read the memos we sent them, the work order changes, the labels on boxes.

Joining Forces with the Schools

When we started MTEC in 1980, it was on the assumption that our people had the basic skills for the jobs they were doing. For five years, we saw ourselves as an agent of change, a school for the language of quality, a counselor and goad to senior management, a vocational instructor in the new skills and measurement systems that would enable our employees to lead the electronics industry in sophistication and quality control.

Our charter as an educational program was to provide continuous training to every employee. Then suddenly, to meet our business needs, we found we had to add remedial elementary education. We had never wanted to be in the grade school business, and it threw our investment strategy into chaos. An annual budget projected at $35 million to $40 million for the early 1980s had grown to $50 million a year by 1988, and we were going to need $35 million more over a three- to five-year period to correct the literacy problem.

Yet budget was only one of our problems. Morale was an even thornier issue. Remedial education made many people uncomfortable, and some were literally afraid of school, an environment in which they had failed as children. We didn't want to embarrass them; these weren't marginal workers, remember, but valuable, experienced employees. Yet they were also people with serious math and literacy problems, and we had to educate them.

We took the position that remedial math and language instruction was simply another form of skills training. We videotaped older employees within a few years of retirement and had them say to others their own age and younger, "Look, we're not going to get out of here without learning new skills. We need to go to class. Back in 1955, we had another moment of truth when we had to move from tubes to transistors. We did it then; we can do it now."

We also had Bob Galvin respond personally to letters. If a man wrote to ask if he really had to go back to school at 58 and study math, Bob would write back, "Yes, you do. But everyone does. You do your job well, but without more math you won't survive in the work environment another seven years."

We adopted a policy that said everyone had a right to retraining when technology changed. But if people refused the retraining, then we said we'd dismiss them. In fact, we had refusals from 18 employees with long service, and we dismissed all but one. That sent another strong message.

There was also a flip side to the policy. It said that if people took retraining and failed, then it was our job to figure out a way of helping them succeed. After all, nearly one-fifth of the U.S. population has some kind of learning disability. If some of our employees couldn't learn to read and compute in conventional classrooms, we tried to help them learn some other way. If they couldn't learn at all but had met our hiring standards 20 or 30 years ago and worked hard ever since, we found jobs for them at Motorola anyway.

Uncovering widespread math and reading problems was a great shock to the system, but it had the beneficial effect of pushing us into three watershed decisions that shaped the whole future of MTEC and Motorola. First, we realized that remedial elementary education was not something we could do well ourselves, so we turned for help to community colleges and other local institutions. Second, we decided to take a harder look at certain other skills. We had always assumed, for example, that high school and junior college graduates came to us equipped with technical and business skills like accounting, computer operation, statistics, and basic electronics. When we discovered they did not—by this time nothing surprised us—we decided to go back to the community colleges that were already helping us with remedial math and English. We told them what we needed, and they had courses with the corresponding titles, so we sent them our people.

Our next surprise was that the courses weren't quite what the titles implied. The community colleges had fallen behind. Their theories, labs, and techniques were simply not up to modern industrial standards. They hadn't known where we were going, and we hadn't bothered to tell them.

This discovery forced our third major decision—to begin building the educational partnerships and dialogues that eventually led us to Motorola University.

We've deliberately tried to treat our educational suppliers the same way we treat our component and chemical suppliers. To begin with, that means acknowledging that in a certain sense we buy what they produce. To make that work, they have to know what we need, and we have to know what not to duplicate. We exchange faculty, jointly develop curriculum, share lab equipment, and tend our mutual feedback mechanisms. In half our plants, as an experiment, we have vocational training experts—community college staff members whom we pay full-time—to act as the ongoing bridge between the changes going on in our business and the changes necessary in the college curriculum. We're also developing dialogues with engineering schools, as well as elementary and secondary schools, about what we need and how it differs from what they provide.

Dialogue means not a single meeting, or two or three, but regular meetings every few weeks. We get presidents, deans, superintendents, principals, professors, and teachers to sit down with our vice presidents for manufacturing and quality, our CFO, the managers of various plants and functions and talk about our needs and theirs.

Schools and colleges have no self-evident need to collaborate with us to the extent we'd like them to. Some educators and academics believe businesspeople are universally unprincipled, that the reason for our involvement in education is to serve ourselves at the expense, somehow, of the community at large.

Yet in the course of talking and interacting, we've found that the benefits to all parties have emerged quite clearly. Some of our strongest support comes from the people who teach remedial English and math. They know how widespread the problem is beyond Motorola and seem grateful that we're eager to attack illiteracy without assessing blame. The point is not that our concern with education is utterly altruistic but that better and more relevant education helps business, labor, and the schools themselves.

This last point is important. Take the case of a community college. To begin with, we supply them with, say, a thousand students a year, and a thousand tuitions. We also donate equipment. More important than either of these benefits, perhaps, is the fact that we offer an insight into what the globally competitive marketplace demands of students and educators. Most colleges are very resource poor. But the dialogue means that they can come into our plants, talk to us, study state-of-the-art manufacturing, and they can use our facilities to pursue their own staff development. We provide summer internships for their teachers and set aside a certain number of in-house training slots each year for community college faculty. We encourage them to use our labs and equipment to teach not only Motorolans but all their students. We believe—and I think they believe—that the mutual benefits are huge.

We've assigned one of our senior people to be the director of institutional relationships. His job is to understand and try to improve the supply lines that run from elementary schools, high schools, and colleges to Motorola. He's there to diagnose their needs, communicate ours, and fund projects that bridge the gap. Motorola has set up an account—in addition to the $60 million education budget—that we can use to invest in schools that are willing to undertake change and to work with us to address the needs of the populations that supply our work force.

For example, two of our scientists came up with an electronics kit that costs only $10 to produce. Then we discovered that the average high school physics teacher has only $2 per student to spend. So we decided to use the account to donate the kits to schools we draw students from and to teach the teachers how to use them.

We also sponsor a planning institute for superintendents from 52 school districts in 18 states on how to build strategic education plans and work with their business constituencies, of which we are one element. We're also trying to build a volunteer corps of Motorola employees who want to work with schools and teach, plan, or translate particular classes into industry-specific programs.

Open-Ended Education

In 1980, we thought we could provide *x* amount of training, get everybody up to speed, then back off. Now we know it's open-ended. Whenever we reach a certain level of expertise or performance, there's always another one to go for. Now we know it's a continuous investment from both sides—from the individuals who attend classes and apply new skills and from the corporation that designs new training programs and makes the time available to take them. In fact, we now know there is no real distinction between corporate education and every other kind. Education is a strenuous, universal, unending human activity that neither business nor society can live without. That insight was another that led us to Motorola University.

When Bob Galvin first suggested a university in 1979, the company wasn't ready. Galvin started interviewing presidents of real universities for advice and leads, but in the meantime I interviewed 22 senior Motorola executives to get their reactions. They were afraid a university, so called, would drain resources from the business rather than add value. For my own part, I was afraid the name "university" was too pretentious. This wasn't to be a seat of free and open inquiry. This was to be training and education for work force and managers.

Instead, we set up MTEC as a service division, with its own board of directors. That made us the only corporation in the United States with a training advisory board that included the CEO and other senior officers. But it didn't make us a university.

Then in 1989, CEO George Fisher made the suggestion. He believed the word university would give us greater autonomy. He also thought it would create an expectation we'd have to grow into.

A great deal had changed in those nine years. First of all, most of our senior clientele—the 22 executives and their fellow skeptics—had stopped seeing education as a cost and had begun to accept it as an indispensable investment. They'd seen returns. Most other people in the company had seen more than that. They'd seen themselves picking up marketable skills; they'd felt themselves growing in self-esteem and self-confidence.

Another difference was that by 1989 we were working closely with the schools, and when public educators heard the word university, their response was positive, even enthusiastic. They took it to mean that we were serious about education, not just enthralled with our own bottom line.

But what *was* a university? And more to the point, what was a

Motorola University? What kind of model should we work from? There were several that might apply, it seemed to me.

One came from the charter of the City University of New York, which says that one of the university's central missions is to meet the needs of the city's residents. What we had was a training department that focused on the needs of the organization. Becoming a university would mean a shift toward meeting the needs of individuals, the "residents" of the corporation.

Another possible model was the open university of the United Kingdom, which, instead of bringing people to the education, takes the education to the people and puts it in a context they can understand.

A third possibility was the model described by Cardinal Newman in *The Idea of a University*, which, after 150 years, is still the cornerstone of liberal education. Newman's ideal university had no place for vocational training, so in that sense he and we part ways. But in another sense, we're in complete agreement. Newman wanted his university to mold the kind of individual who can "fill any post with credit" and "master any subject with facility"—an excellent description of what we wanted Motorola University to do.

Our evolving vision of the university contains elements of all three models. We try to make our education relevant to the corporation, to the job, and to the individual. We also try to bridge the gap between our company and the institutions that supply us with people. We don't intend to grant degrees, but we do intend to design courses that accrediting boards will certify and that the universities that give degrees will count. (See "Curriculum Development at Motorola U.")

Curriculum Development at Motorola U

Motorola never farms out curriculum design—the road map that shows what we need to learn. But we may contract with an individual, a group, or a college to design a particular course, which we then turn over to our deans of delivery—one for the United States, one for the rest of the world—for distribution. Those deans search out instructors through the colleges or just hire free agents, whom we train. Sometimes, too, courses are packaged as software, as videos, or go out via satellite.

For each functional area we have a course-design team of instructional system designers whom we think of as product engineers in terms of title, pay, status, and job security. Their expertise is knowing how to extract the skill requirements from a job analysis and package them into training for adults.

Of 1,200 people involved in training and education at Motorola—including 110 full-time and 300 part-time staff at Motorola University—23 are product design engineers. They're like department chairs, and the senior product manager is like a dean. The faculty are the actual course writers, audiovisual specialists, and instructors.

We divide each functional curriculum—engineering, manufacturing, sales and marketing—into three parts: relational skills, technical skills, and business skills. M.U. itself is responsible for teaching relational skills—customer satisfaction, effective meetings, effective manufacturing supervision, negotiation, effective presentations. Since 1985, however, we have developed the curriculum for technical and business skills—basic math, electronics, accounting, computer operation, statistical process control—in cooperation with community colleges and technical schools.

As a result of what we've learned over the last decade, the Motorola curriculum has two more critically important elements. The first is culture. Culture in a corporation is partly a question of history and of common language—a form of tribal storytelling. At Motorola, for example, we believe in taking risks. Our history shows it was one of the things that made us great. Telling those stories creates a tradition of risk, invests it with value, and encourages young people to go out and do the same.

But culture is not only inherited, it's also created. Teamwork is an example. Our history is one of individual contributors, not teams. So training has to emphasize team building and downplay the Lone Ranger culture we valued in the 1950s and 1960s.

The second extra element is remedial reading and math, which today means algebra. In most of our factories, we want analyses and experiments requiring algebra done right on the line. As for reading, we've found that the engineering group writes work order changes, product specifications, and product manuals at a fourteenth to seventeenth grade level—to be read by people who read at the fourth to sixth grade level. We're trying to lower the former and raise the latter. When we talk about a literate work force by 1992, we mean seventh grade. But our goal remains ninth grade by 1995.

We are entering a new era of partnership with established universities. We give them feedback on the courses they teach and even on their faculties. Most companies have just blindly reimbursed tuition costs, but we think we have a legitimate interest in the schools that prepare our future employees and in the colleges that provide continuing adult education at our expense.

For example, Motorola and Northwestern jointly designed a quality course for the second year of Northwestern's MBA program. Northwestern also offers courses taught half-term by one of its professors and half-term by one of our experts—first half, theory; second half, application. We work closely with the Illinois Institute of Technology as well, and with Arizona State University. For the first time, we actually evaluate university services, not just assume they must be good.

We avoid collegiate trappings—no professors or basketball teams—but we do make academic appointments of a kind: we name people to staff positions, and for two or three years they leave their jobs and devote themselves to educational activities. (See "Finding and Training Faculty.") We also have a Motorola University Press that prints more than a million pages a month and plans to publish a series of books on design and quality written by one of our employees.

Finding and Training Faculty

I own a videotape of an all-day engineering class whose instructor, in closing the session, thanks the students for their active participation. In fact, except to breathe, not one of them has made a sound. In eight hours of teaching, the instructor never asks a question. He never makes eye contact. He is on top of his subject technically, but the class is boring beyond belief.

The teachers at Motorola University aren't there to implant data. They're there to transfer information and get it applied quickly. We design curricula and train teachers with that end in mind.

Training and certification of all teachers is in four phases of 40 hours each. The first phase is procedural: how to use flip charts, foils, chalkboards; how to manage a classroom; how to ask questions; how to observe, listen, and reinforce.

The second phase deals with the particular kinds of behavior we want to see teachers and students exhibit. We believe in participative management, so instructors must be models of openness and respect for other opinions. We also emphasize teamwork, so teachers must encourage mutual support and try to curb the competitive, who's-best model most people learned in school.

The third 40 hours deals with subject matter. We walk teachers through the course and then we walk them through the research that underlies it. We don't want them to teach *their* version of, say, Effective Meetings; we want them to teach *ours*. Not everyone can deliver on those terms. For example, few academics can do it our way. They're used to interpreting material independently, so after the first page, it tends to take on their own particular slant. It may make a fascinating course, but we can't have 3,000 people learning 35 different versions of Effective Meetings.

Finally, we assign teachers to master instructors who use them as coteachers and then have them teach on their own with feedback before turning them loose.

We have found three groups of people who make especially good teachers. The first is recently retired Motorola employees. We start talking to them six months out and try to get them through certification before retirement. Those who make it are superb. They believe in what they're teaching, they know how to apply it, and they can tell the stories from the past and relate them to the future.

We have one powerful, middle-management course on managing change—specifically, the change that must take place if Motorola is to prosper over the next decade—that is taught by insiders only. Bill Weisz, a former CEO and now a vice chairman of the board, devotes the last seven hours to the topic "I built this bureaucracy, and if I was 25 years old, here's how I'd blow it up and build what we need for the next 10 years."

The second group consists of married women with college degrees whose children have left home. Lack of experience makes it hard for them to find jobs, so we've worked out programs with community colleges to screen them and reorient them to the business world. In courses like Effective Meetings, Interpersonal Skills, and Basic Sales Skills, they're our best performers by far. Most students think they're old business hands, but their actual experience—community politics, selling ideas to children, managing teenagers—is just as rich and certainly just as useful.

The third group represents a kind of talent sharing. Like most other companies, Motorola has a rule against rehiring people who've taken early retirement. Now we trade early retirement talent with other companies. AT&T gives us a list of 100 potential instructors who've just left, and we give them our list. It's been a success. People like translating their experience from AT&T or IBM and making it relevant and effective in our different world. Eventually we hope to change the rules so that people who pass our certification will always have an alternative to early retirement.

As for Newman's grander concept of the university, our commitment is not to buildings or a bureaucracy but to creating an environment for learning, a continuing openness to new ideas. We do teach vocational subjects, but we also teach supervocational subjects—functional skills raised to a higher level. We not only teach people how to respond quickly to new technologies, we try to commit them to the goal of anticipating new technologies. We not only teach people how to lead a department to better performance and higher quality, we try to dedicate them to the idea of continuing, innovative leadership in the workplace and the marketplace. We not only teach skills, we try to breathe the very spirit of creativity and flexibility into manufacturing and management.

Electrifying the Now and Future Employee

The word university is undeniably ambitious, but Motorola management has always tried to use words in ways that force people to rethink their assumptions. The term university will arouse curiosity and, I hope, raise the expectations of our work force and our training and education staff. We could have called it an educational resource facility, but who would that have electrified?

As a first step, we have decided that Motorola University will be a global institution. We are already working on a formal relationship with the Asia Pacific International University, based in Macao. Motorola University is presently open to the employees of our suppliers, of our principal customers, and even of our educational partners, but we envision a time when the university will accept students from outside our immediate community of companies and institutions, people who will not necessarily work for Motorola or any of our suppliers or customers at any time in their lives.

At the same time, one of our goals is to have the best graduates of the best institutions want to work for us. To achieve that, we must attract young people into our classrooms so they'll know how good we are, and, just as important, so they'll know they have to take certain steps in their own development in order to work for us or someone like us as adults.

One of the things we have on the drawing board is a math-and-science summer institute for fifth, sixth, and seventh graders. Another is a simulation using an aircraft from the movie *Top Gun*. We'll stop the plane in mid-takeoff from a carrier and dissect it, showing the geometric and algebraic principles used in its design, then relate that back to the computer to show the same principles used in the design of other things. The goal is not to teach kids design but to show them that algebra is worth suffering through.

The point of a program like that is not to get kids to work for Motorola. We'd like the really inspired ones to want to work for us when that time comes. But if not, well, at least they'll be able to work for someone.

12
The Computerless Computer Company

Andrew S. Rappaport and Shmuel Halevi

By the year 2000, the most successful computer companies will be those that buy computers rather than build them. The leaders will leverage fabulously cheap and powerful hardware to create and deliver new applications, pioneer and control new computing paradigms, and assemble distribution and integration expertise that creates enduring influence with customers. So long as companies have reliable supplies of adequate hardware—and this seldom means the most advanced hardware—there are fewer advantages and a growing number of disadvantages to building it. The future belongs to the computerless computer company.

Within the American high-technology community, the erosion of U.S. market share in global semiconductor and computer production has inspired a sense of dread. Anxious U.S. executives point to Japan's 43% share of the U.S. market for laptop computers, the fastest growing segment of the computer hardware industry. They despair over Japan's dominance of worldwide DRAM production—and over the fact that Taiwanese and Korean manufacturers pose the one modest challenge to Japanese hegemony in semiconductor memories. They anguish over advances by companies such as NEC and Fujitsu in manufacturing supercomputers whose speed approximates that of supercomputers built by Cray Research and Thinking Machines, the U.S. performance leaders in this "strategic" technology.

This competitive erosion is unsettling—but the dread is misplaced. In fact, computer executives should encourage the trend. It is good news for the leading U.S. computer companies—provided they escape the past and redirect their technology, manufacturing, and marketing strategies to embrace the new realities. The strategic goal of U.S. companies should not be to build computers. It should be to create persistent value in computing. Increasingly, computers themselves are marginal to the creation of value in computing. Defining how computers are used, not how they are manufactured, will create real value—and thus market power, employment, and wealth—in the decades ahead.

The computer industry is experiencing a profound strategic inversion driven by the relentless advance of its own technology. For most of its history, the industry has been constrained by the limited capabilities of its hardware. Computers were neither powerful nor affordable enough to deliver effectively the applications envisioned for them. As each new generation of semiconductor technology made possible cheaper, smaller, and more powerful computers, these computers opened up more and more applications. Customers responded by spending more and more money on the industry's products. Between 1980 and 1985, for example, the average end-user price per MIPS (millions of instructions per second), the standard measure of computer performance, declined from about $250,000 to $25,000. Over this same period, annual per capita computer spending in the United States rose from $90 to $180.

Today the situation has changed. All the forces that drove the advance of hardware power—more powerful microprocessors, the integration of more functions onto fewer chips, cheaper and more efficient manufacturing—remain in place. From 1985 through 1990, the average price per MIPS fell at roughly the same rate as during the previous five years, from $25,000 to less than $2,500. Yet these advances no longer directly enable new applications.

Put simply, computers have become *too powerful* for the uses to which they are being put. As a result, customers have limited their spending. Over the last five years, per capita consumption in the United States rose only 4% per year, to roughly $200. Not surprisingly, industry profitability has deteriorated. From 1980 through 1985, after-tax profits for the 14 largest U.S. computer manufacturers averaged 11.5% of revenues. From 1985 through 1990, profits averaged only 6.5% of revenues.

Value derives from scarcity. In the computer industry, scarcity now resides in the gap between power—what computers and their underlying semiconductor technologies are capable of doing—and utility—what human imagination and software engineering are capable of enabling computers to do. And that is the good news. U.S. companies lead the world in most of the technologies that bridge this gap: micro-processor architectures, operating systems, user interfaces, data bases, application software. This lead is neither permanent nor invulnerable, but it does provide the basis for a powerful and productive industry.

Implicit in most discussions of U.S. high technology is the assumption that a true computer company is one that manufactures systems hardware. We disagree. A computer company *is the primary source of computing for its customers.* Thus Microsoft, the world's leading developer of systems software for personal computers, is not a "software" com-pany. Microsoft is a computer company. Indeed, Microsoft's MS-DOS and Windows operating environments may be the world's two leading computer brands—eminently more valuable than brand names like Intel or Compaq. Customers have come to insist on MS-DOS or Win-dows computing. They are largely indifferent to the microprocessor around which the software environment is designed (other than its price/performance characteristics and its ability to run the software) and increasingly indifferent to the nameplate on the hardware that delivers the environment.

Similarly, Mentor Graphics, a $400 million enterprise that is consid-ered the world's leading supplier of software for electronic design automation, is a computer company, not a software company. In fact, it is more of a true computer company than the hardware manufac-turer, Hewlett-Packard, that builds most of the workstations on which Mentor delivers its systems. The more than eight million lines of code that comprise Mentor's Concurrent Design Environment, some of the most sophisticated workstation software ever developed, and Mentor's deep immersion in the needs of its primary customers—designers of integrated circuits, printed circuit boards, and electronic systems—are a more enduring source of utility than the price/performance ratios of Hewlett-Packard hardware. Mentor, not Hewlett-Packard, defines the computing environment of its customers. Thus Mentor, not Hewlett-Packard, has real influence with customers. And it is influence with customers, not vertical integration, that is the true measure of a com-pany's market standing and staying power.

Microsoft, Apple, and Core Competition

Consider the rise of Microsoft, which conventional wisdom correctly describes as the most powerful company in the computer industry. Microsoft generates annual revenues of some $1.5 billion, employs more than 4,500 people, and commands a market value of $13 billion, which is second only to IBM's among U.S. computer companies and is 70% more than the market value of Digital Equipment Corporation, a company 10 times Microsoft's size.

Yet Microsoft neither builds nor distributes computers. Rather, it dictates how computers are designed, built, and applied. Its Windows 3.0 operating system is a distinct computing paradigm. It defines how millions of computer users expect to interact with their software and the coding environment in which thousands of developers write new applications. Microsoft thrives because it bridges the gap between power and utility, and it does so in a way that both maintains its proprietary position and leverages rather than replicates the massive capital investments made by less influential hardware companies. It understands that it is more rewarding to "tax" the path between hardware production and consumption than to build hardware.

Now think about Apple Computer. One of the great computer success stories of the 1980s, Apple also represents one of the great missed opportunities. As a family of personal computers, the Macintosh continues to set the standards by which the industry measures ease of use, graphics power, and software and network integration. But as a company, Apple continues to lose ground to rivals that sell hardware based on the far less elegant Windows and Unix operating systems. Many analysts worry about Apple's long-term survival as a vibrant, independent computer supplier. Indeed, despite generating 1990 revenues of nearly $5.6 billion, Apple's market value is only $8 billion—40% less than Microsoft's value.

The comparison between Apple and Microsoft is a case study in the changing nature of value in the computer industry and the strategic consequences of failing to recognize the change. Apple beat Microsoft by six years, a lifetime in computers, in developing a graphics-oriented operating environment. So why is Microsoft the most powerful company in the computer industry while Apple wages a battle for long-term survival? Because Apple defined its business as building computer hardware (worse yet, proprietary hardware) rather than delivering the utility associated with its pioneering user interface and graphics capabilities. The Macintosh's most important advantage has always been its operating system—a software achievement whose technical virtues dwarf anything delivered by Microsoft. Had Apple embraced the computer industry's strategic inversion and thus focused on leveraging this software advantage, it would be in a very different position today.

Think back to the early 1980s. Apple was certainly correct to develop a proprietary hardware architecture for the Macintosh. Designing its radical new operating system around the IBM personal computer, already the emerging standard, would have involved unacceptable price/performance penalties. The company was also right to build its own computers. The unique advantages of the Macintosh meant that for most early customers price was less an issue than functionality was. By using low-cost components to build high-utility machines, Apple's control of production became a source of fabulous profits and the basis of a remarkable competitive strike against industry leader IBM. The company's manufacturing engine, symbolized by its highly automated assembly plants in California, Ireland, and Singapore, played a meaningful role in value creation.

Within a few years, however, that strategic logic had become obsolete. Product improvement in the vastly larger IBM-compatible market was proceeding at a furious rate, driven by the rise of an intensely competitive "clone" hardware market. Meanwhile, the Macintosh's success spurred Microsoft to invest resources to imitate many of the Macintosh's features—imitations that became possible because of the dramatic price/performance gains in the underlying IBM-compatible hardware. By the late 1980s Apple's main rival was no longer IBM; it was Microsoft.

In this competition, Microsoft had (and still has) a decisive advantage—despite the technical shortcomings of Windows. Microsoft is the only computer company that benefits directly from global R&D spending on computer hardware. Giant manufacturers like IBM, Compaq, and Toshiba devote roughly $5 billion per year (more than three times Microsoft's annual revenues) to investments designed to improve hardware platforms that have little intrinsic utility without Microsoft operating systems. In contrast, the Macintosh operating system benefits only from Apple's R&D spending.

What's more, the Windows environment is available on hardware that covers a seemingly unlimited spectrum in terms of size, features, and price points. There is a Windows product for every niche and a niche for every Windows product. The Macintosh operating environment is available only on the narrow range of computers that Apple has the capacity to develop internally. In short, Apple's proprietary research and manufacturing engine has become a burden rather than an asset.

How might Apple have embraced the new logic of the computer industry and leveraged its core strengths? Consider one alternative scenario. In 1987, the company unveiled its second-generation computers, the Macintosh SE and the Macintosh II. At that time, it should also have made the following announcements. First, it would authorize other companies to build personal computers based on the Macintosh operating system. It would require that the operating system accompany every clone and charge a "tax" of, say, $100 on every unit. Second, it would design and market a version of the Macintosh user interface for the IBM-compatible world, again charging $100 for every copy of the operating system. Third, it would stop manufacturing low-end hardware (leaving competition in these segments, as well as in laptops, to its licensees) and build only high-performance computers.

Together, these announcements would have repositioned Apple as the driver of utility in an intensely competitive worldwide Macintosh industry—a company that defines how computers are *used*, not how they are built. The Macintosh operating system could easily have accounted for one-third of the personal computer market rather than the 10% it has held until quite recently. To match its current hardware revenues, the repositioned Apple would have had to supply only one-third of all Macintosh-compatible computers—and at much higher gross margins. Moreover, by collecting its $100 operating-system tax on every clone, Apple would be capturing additional revenues of $400 million per year with almost no associated expenses—a significant source of profits for a company that earned less than $500 million in 1990.

The new Apple could have tapped these larger profits to advance its position as a driver of computing utility, particularly in applications software. Claris, Apple's applications subsidiary, now generates annual revenues of less than $100 million. It is a shadow of what it could have been had it received the strategic attention and financial and human resources it deserved. Precisely because Apple defined itself as a hardware company, it chose to limit its commitment to developing applications software. Ironically, its chief rival, Microsoft, is now one of the leading suppliers of applications for Apple—hardly a comforting situation.

The missed opportunity was vast. Put simply, Apple could have been Microsoft—a fabulously profitable computer company whose software defines the desktop computing environment. It would still build computers, but only high-performance, high-margin units. Meanwhile, Microsoft would be a less imposing version of the enterprise it is today. No one would be calling it the most powerful company in the computer industry.

The Fabless Semiconductor Company

You can't understand the computer industry without understanding the semiconductor industry. Virtually all major changes in the computer industry trace their origins to semiconductors. The rise of the computerless computer company is no exception. The relentless advance of chip performance is the most important driver of enhanced computer performance and is thus the major factor behind the computer industry's technological overcapacity. What's more, dramatic advances in "silicon integration" (packing more functions onto a single chip) are making it harder to identify where a semiconductor company ends and a computer company begins. As we shall see, this blurring of boundaries represents a serious challenge to computer manufacturers—and increases the pressure to focus on utility rather than on manufacturing.

But the semiconductor industry is important to the computer industry for another reason. It is a window into the future. The wrenching strategic transformation of semiconductor production in the 1980s is a preview of the changes that will sweep the computer industry in the 1990s. As such, it is worth exploring in some detail.

Much of the U.S. semiconductor industry is in crisis. Last year, six of America's eight largest chip manufacturers lost money. Advanced Micro Devices, once an industry giant, has generated profits in only two of the last six years. National Semiconductor, another pioneer, has turned a profit only once in the last six years. For the United States as a whole, it is fair to conclude that investment in semiconductor manufacturing over the last five years has destroyed more economic value than it has created.

Conventional wisdom explains these dire results by looking at Japan's dominance of semiconductor memories and other high-volume chip markets—a convenient but misguided analysis. The reality is that dramatically changing technology and economics have made obsolete the traditional model of semiconductor production—a model built around high-volume wafer fabrication and vertical integration. Most large, established U.S. manufacturers have chosen to ignore or resist this unsettling new reality. They have suffered dearly as a result. But a new breed of companies and a few members of the establishment have embraced the industry's transformation. These companies have succeeded spectacularly in revenue growth, profits, and technology leadership.

For 25 years after the creation of the chip, semi-conductor manufacturing processes—etching small circuits onto silicon chips—were the industry's single greatest source of value. Since the raw power delivered by integrated circuits was limited and expensive, computer companies were eager for cheaper and more powerful chips, which required manufacturing excellence. Semiconductor companies with the best manufacturing processes were able to design and produce chips with ever-smaller electrical components that performed better and cost less than rival chips. At any given time, relatively few suppliers were able to produce such state-of-the-art chips.

In this respect, silicon was the most valuable real estate in the world. Chip designers strove for the smallest possible die sizes. Fabrication processes isolated flaws to the smallest possible areas. Marketing groups searched for the highest volume business opportunities so fabs could ride down the learning curve as fast as possible—thus generating the highest yields and the lowest costs possible. What could be designed was governed by what could be built quickly and economically.

Today that logic has been overturned. The new power of semiconductor process technology has eliminated the role of fabs as the primary source of advantage. It is still possible to develop manufacturing processes that yield marginal improvements over industry standards. But these improvements no longer translate into decisive market advantages for the chips. Silicon integration has become so efficient that successful producers now emphasize larger chips instead of smaller ones. And because production lines can cheaply fabricate more and more complex devices, high volumes are no longer crucial.

Semiconductor value is now a function of specialization. And specialization depends on responsive design, not high-volume, low-cost production. Indeed, under this new logic, "wasteful" production is good, if "wasting" silicon makes it possible to design chips faster, to design faster or more functional chips, or both. With the exception of commodity memory markets, there is no correlation between manufacturing prowess and market share or profits. What can be built is governed by what can be designed.

There's more. As chip density and performance advance, so does the potential output of existing fabs. The semiconductor world is on the brink of astounding excess capacity. Consider some rough calculations. Today a typical 6-inch silicon wafer yields about 5 million transistors. Worldwide logic-chip revenues are on the order of $25 billion, with an average selling price of $1,000 per wafer. That means worldwide logic-chip shipments total some 125 million million transistors. By 1999, the potential capacity of a wafer will be 3.5 billion transistors. If manufacturers process the same number of logic wafers in 1999 as they do today, and the average area of a wafer increases by 15% per year, a likely development, the total number of transistors produced in 1999 would rise to 85 *billion* million—almost 1,000 times the number consumed in 1990. Even if an explosion in new computer applications doubles the demand for transistors every two years, logic demand in 1999 would total only 3.5 billion million transistors—a mere 4% of available capacity. The world could turn 96% of its wafer fabs into warehouses and still have enough capacity to meet demand. Moreover, the small size of these transistors adds further to the silicon performance surplus.

Historically, of course, chip and systems designers have been able to use all the logic transistors at their disposal. But it's doubtful that this trend will continue. Memory chips that grow from one million to four million bits don't change fundamentally; they are bigger, more powerful versions of existing chips. Microprocessors must be reinvented if they are to tap the power of four million as opposed to one million transistors. So while process improvements continually and efficiently accelerate the production of logic transistors, design complexity will increasingly constrain their consumption. For many designs, the most advanced semiconductor processes will yield chip capabilities that are not necessary—or even possible—to exploit.

In other words, semiconductor manufacturing has become so advanced and so much more powerful than the underlying needs of the chips themselves that most companies selling high-performance products do not require access to the most advanced manufacturing facilities. The most successful chip companies of the 1980s recognized this overcapacity and leveraged rather than contributed to it. They demonstrated that 90th-percentile manufacturing technology, of which there is a growing abundance in the world, is more than adequate to produce the world's highest value chips—so long as the chips incorporate world-class design. These companies became fabless chip producers.

Our earlier comparison of Microsoft and Apple underscored the consequences of misperceiving the computer industry's strategic trajectory. There are similar comparisons in the chip world. Consider the struggles of LSI Logic, one of the fastest growing semiconductor companies of the 1980s. LSI was a pioneer in anticipating the demand for low-volume, specialized chips designed quickly and efficiently. Its leadership in application-specific integrated circuits (ASICs) was a function of its close relationship with customers and the elegance and power of its design methodologies and software. Early on, LSI Logic did not manufacture the chips it sold. Toshiba, a leader in the manufacturing processes best suited to ASICs, produced chips on a contract basis.

LSI went public in 1983 and raised $152 million, then the largest IPO in history. At the time, the company's agenda was quite sensible. It used its new financial resources (as well as additional borrowings) to wean itself from Toshiba and vertically integrate its manufacturing. It built three large fabs—one in Silicon Valley, one in Japan (a joint venture with Kawasaki Steel), and one in the United Kingdom. By 1985, LSI was making virtually all the chips it sold.

By some measures, this strategy has paid off. The company's position in the world semiconductor market has climbed impressively. It still holds the leading share of the noncaptive market for CMOS gate arrays, even though Toshiba and Fujitsu are now major players. It designs RISC microprocessors licensed from MIPS Computer Systems and Sun Microsystems as well as PC chip sets and chips for computer graphics, video compression, and digital signal processing. Its marketplace success has been matched by impressive revenue growth—from less than $200 million in 1986 to nearly $700 million in 1990.

Like Apple, though, LSI's undeniable successes have been matched by missed opportunities. The company has never generated annual profits of more than $25 million, and it has lost money (a combined $60 million) over the last two years. Why? Because it has contributed to worldwide manufacturing overcapacity rather than exploited it. LSI's core value added has always been its intellectual capabilities, and it has done a good job defending and enhancing them. But base manufacturing, especially for ASICs, is a pedestrian and undifferentiated activity that adds almost no value.

It is also a costly activity. To illustrate the point, we've done some calculations to "reinvent" LSI Logic under a strategy that leverages the worldwide glut of manufacturing capacity. This is an admittedly unfair exercise, since LSI cannot simply reinvent itself to accommodate a new strategy. But it illuminates the radical transformation of the semiconductor industry as well as the future strategic and investment decisions that chip companies like LSI will have to make to stay competitive.

Our reinvented company is identical to the current LSI except that it has chosen to continue buying wafers from outside vendors and not to build three high-volume fabs. This saves massive annual charges for depreciation and amortization, maintenance, and interest. With the same revenues, the new LSI Logic posts strikingly different earnings results: net income of nearly $47 million in 1990 rather than a loss of $33 million, a pretax return on equity of 22%, combined earnings of nearly $127 million over the last four years rather than a net loss of more than $22 million. Last year, LSI announced it would invest an additional $90 million for a second wafer fab in Japan. The reinvented LSI would not make such an investment. Instead, it would invest in profit-generating activities like design, customer support, and systems-level integration.

Some may protest that our scenario raises the dangerous specter of production "dependence" on Toshiba, one of LSI's chief ASIC competitors. This concern is misplaced. There are fabs—in Japan, Korea, Taiwan, Europe, the United States—willing and able to build the wafers LSI Logic needs. Our reinvented LSI would still own low-volume metalization facilities in which final customization takes place. Indeed, it might have more such facilities since it would not have made its huge fab investments. All told, the new LSI would be one of the semiconductor industry's most glorious financial success stories—even though it could not point to one million square feet of manufacturing space as a measure of its muscle.

There is a company that serves as a model for the new generation of semiconductor suppliers. Its name is XiCirTera & Technotek, our hypothetical bundling of five Silicon Valley companies: Xilinx, Cirrus Logic, Altera, Chips & Technologies, and Weitek. All five design and sell semiconductors but do not manufacture them. Together these companies would be a major industry force. Their combined 1990 revenues of $620 million would rank seventh among U.S. merchant suppliers. Their combined pretax ROE of 26% is a close second to Intel's—a remarkable performance given Intel's near-monopoly position in microprocessors. Their combined market value is nearly $1.4 billion—behind only Intel, Motorola, and Texas Instruments and nearly four times the market value of comparably sized LSI Logic. (See Exhibit I.)

These companies sell different products—high-performance storage chips, field-programmable logic, math coprocessors—but their strategic models share several core principles. Like Microsoft, they do not confuse manufacturing with delivering and controlling value. Rather, they position themselves to benefit directly from worldwide improvements in manufacturing technologies. So they focus on highly differentiated chips for niche markets. They focus on their real sources of advantage and invest accordingly in design tools, systems integra-

Exhibit I.   Profits without production

Company	1990 revenues*	1990 net income	Market value (as of 4/10/91)	1990 pretax return on equity
Altera	$ 78.3	$13.4	$ 324.9	34.0%
Chips & Technologies	268.7	11.8	135.4	13.5
Cirrus Logic	131.2	18.8	306.1	40.9
Xilinx	83.7	13.9	506.9	26.7
Weitek	57.8	7.0	108.8	30.1
	$619.7	$64.9	$1,382.1	26.4%

*All dollars in millions

tion, and customer support. They develop their chips so as to maximize their outsourcing options, which means designing chips that do not require state-of-the-art processes to produce state-of-the-art value.

Here it is worth pausing to consider the case of Intel. On the surface, Intel looks like a striking exception to nearly all of the trends we've discussed. A vertically integrated chip manufacturer, Intel posts fabulous financial results—1990 revenues of nearly $4 billion, net income of $650 million, pretax ROE of 27%. Indeed, Intel has announced plans to invest as much as $1 billion per year in plant and equipment for the next several years—an announcement widely interpreted as a sign of its commitment to manufacturing competitiveness. But Intel is not successful because it manufactures chips. Intel's chips are so successful and its near-monopoly position in microprocessors so powerful that it can afford the luxury of manufacturing them.

Take Intel's high-performance 80486 microprocessor. A fabless semiconductor company can purchase chips of similar size, using the same processes, for less than $100 on the open market. Yet Intel sells the 80486 for $500. The company's well-deserved "knowledge tax" is more than $400—80% of the final selling price. Incremental improvements in the cost and quality of Intel's manufacturing systems can have little impact on the product's margins, which are a function of the chip's proprietary design. Intel has chosen to invest some of its knowledge-based margins in manufacturing facilities. But these facilities are not critical to generating the margins in the first place. Intel is the exception that proves the rule.

Laptop Computers—Japan's Hollow Victory

As we noted earlier, the transformation of the semiconductor industry is more than just a preview of the computer industry's future. The transformation is itself eroding the traditional sources of value in the computer industry and accelerating the rise of the computerless computer company. The key force is silicon integration, which is proceeding so dramatically that it has become difficult to identify where a semiconductor company ends and a computer company begins.

Consider Intel's 80386 SL microprocessor, the central component of many new high-performance notebook computers. The 386 SL (a two-chip set) integrates virtually every chip in a DOS-compatible PC except for some peripheral functions and a memory subsystem. Essentially, it is a computer. So it is only natural for Intel and other semiconductor companies to start building computers themselves. And that's precisely what Intel is doing. Its systems business already generates annual revenues of some $1 billion. The company builds personal computers for AT&T and Unisys and is even building a supercomputer based on parallel architectures.

It is only a modest overstatement to say that Intel and Compaq, one of Intel's most important customers, are in the same business today. Both sell computers that are used as components in a value-added chain involving applications, distribution, integration, and support. The vast majority of Intel's "computers" are shipped in chip form surrounded by plastic or ceramic packaging with lead wires. Compaq's computers, which run the same software, are shipped in box form surrounded by a plastic case with cables and a keyboard. But this is a distinction without powerful strategic significance. Compaq is vulnerable unless it can find new ways to create and deliver distinct computing utility.

This strategic imperative is not unique to Compaq. The entire laptop computer market, in which Compaq is a major player, is a case study in the industry's transformation. Few issues have triggered such intense anxiety among U.S. computer executives as recent trends in the market for laptops. One representative forecast concludes that shipments of desktop computers in the United States peaked at 6 million units in 1990 and will slide to 5 million units by 1993—even as shipments of laptops soar from roughly 800,000 units to 2.5 million units. The source of anxiety is Japan's 43% of the 1990 laptop market as well as its commanding position in supplying key components to U.S. laptop manufacturers.

Indeed, in last year's controversial *Harvard Business Review* article "Computers and the Coming of the U.S. Keiretsu" (July–August 1990), MIT's Charles Ferguson opened up a Compaq LTE laptop to reveal its Japanese-origin display, power-management system, and miniaturization technologies. Ferguson and others consider such "hollowing out" of laptop hardware evidence of strategic vulnerability for Compaq and the rest of the U.S. computer industry.

Such worries, by now an article of faith in the computer industry, again confuse vertical integration and manufacturing competence with value. Laptop computers do represent an important advance in the generation of raw computer power. But without major innovations in user interfaces, operating systems, applications, communications, and integration, these new machines will contribute little additional computing utility. Unlike PCs, whose price/performance ratios represented a qualitative advance over previous hardware categories, laptops do not by themselves create a new computing paradigm. They behave the same way PCs do, run the same software, and are largely applied to the same business problems. Without new applications, they will merely replace PCs rather than expand the computer hardware market.

Consider the relative strengths of Toshiba and Grid Systems, two pioneers in the laptop market. Toshiba's rise to prominence—it is the largest laptop supplier in Europe and Japan and the second largest in the United States—has sent shock waves through the U.S. computer industry. The company invested hundreds of millions of dollars, aggressively pursued hardware innovations in power-management systems and miniaturization, and emerged as a market-share leader. Toshiba plans to invest more than $600 million over the next four years to improve display technology and production, and it expects to introduce a color laptop display later this year. Its highly automated assembly line in Ome, outside Tokyo, already assembles up to 60,000 laptops a week.

Thus has Toshiba won in laptops. Yet what a hollow victory! Already, the company's market position is under siege. A dozen or more established hardware manufacturers—including AT&T, Compaq, IBM, NCR, NEC, Olivetti, Sharp, and Texas Instruments—have or are about to introduce laptops whose price/performance ratios hold their own against Toshiba's models. A host of aggressive new suppliers—from young-but-accomplished companies like AST Research to rank up-starts such as Twinheads and Zeos—market laptops that outperform and underprice most everything Toshiba offers. Moreover, the next generation of laptops will be so powerful, so inexpensive, and so standardized in size and features that opportunities for meaningful hardware differentiation will virtually evaporate.

Like Toshiba, Grid Systems made an early commitment to laptops, introducing its first model in 1982. Grid designs and manufactures the laptops it sells in a production facility in Fremont, California, and has been the source of several important hardware innovations. Its products were the first to incorporate a nonvolatile bubble memory, the first to contain a built-in 1,200-baud modem, the first to use light-emitting electroluminescent displays. Grid's hardware capabilities may no longer be the world's most advanced, but they are on par with those of above-average manufacturers.

Yet Grid does not define its business as manufacturing laptop computers. Its business is analyzing, designing, and implementing computer systems that meet the needs of certain mobile professionals working outside the office. Its target markets are sales representatives, engineers, service technicians, and auditors who require specialized hardware, customized applications software, and extensive communications links to local, regional, and national offices. The hardware Grid manufactures is of marginal importance to the computing utility it delivers. The company has spent years studying and responding to the field automation needs of its target customers. Its sales force and service technicians have unsurpassed knowledge of target industries such as pharmaceuticals, insurance, and apparel. The capabilities and performance of the applications and networking software it develops or resells cannot be easily or quickly duplicated by rivals.

Grid's fiscal 1990 revenues of $190 million do not rank with Toshiba's laptop revenues. But Grid's present strategic positioning is decisively more secure. Toshiba is selling an easily replaceable component, not a system with unique and persistent value. There are no real "Toshiba customers" for laptops. There are laptop customers who, at a given moment, may make certain price/performance calculations and choose a Toshiba over a rival brand. But a month later, if AST Research, NEC, or Kyocera offers a laptop with superior price/performance, those same customers may well defect from Toshiba. In contrast, there are hundreds of loyal Grid Systems customers—companies that have thoroughly embraced Grid's customized applications and superior technical support. Grid's hardware prowess may not compare with Toshiba's. But its market power, as measured by the extent of its influence with customers, is far greater.

As the performance of laptop hardware continues to advance, and as manufacturers in Korea, Taiwan, Eastern Europe, and China master 90th-percentile hardware technology, Grid would be wise to outsource the computers on which it delivers its utility—and to focus its resources on extending its lead in software, service, and support. It might choose to design and build specialized hardware or hardware subsystems that enable its software to deliver even greater performance advantages. It might form partnerships with manufacturers willing to build customized versions of industry-standard equipment. But fundamentally, Grid's evolution into a computerless computer company would dramatically enhance its market power and strategic position.

Laptop computers will be to the 1990s what semiconductor memories were to the 1980s—commodities of the purest sort. Of course, their sheer production volume will give laptops political visibility, much like DRAMs. American computer executives will see millions of laptops shipped each year, shipments that generate billions of dollars of revenue, and ask, "Shouldn't U.S. companies control production for that market?" We hope they will then pose a second question: "Control it to what end?"

Here's how we would answer that question. The massive investments required to keep pace in a hardware technology whose power already vastly outruns its utility cannot be justified on economic or strategic grounds. What matters is not who manufactures laptop computers but who creates utility for users. And utility is a function of whether and how these new computers are deployed for new applications. So long as U.S. computer companies have an adequate supply of the hardware—and the vast proliferation of marginally differentiated hardware producers on several continents guarantees this supply—there are few advantages to building it. Controlling how laptops are used, not how they are manufactured, creates real value. That means an investment focus on software development, systems integration, marketing, and training.

New Rules for Computerless Competition

The rise of the computerless computer company overturns many of the industry's most cherished strategic assumptions. The industry's obsession with MIPS, price/performance ratios, and other benchmarks of hardware power creates a familiar and well-bounded arena for competition. But these measures have lost their value as a source of differentiation. Companies must find new sources of value—which means an external focus on business mission and markets rather than an internal focus on hardware and day-to-day operations.

Successful computer companies will play by a new set of strategic rules. Three are particularly important.

Compete on utility, not power. "Open systems" has become the rallying cry of the U.S. computer industry. Manufacturers race to design and build standardized computers that are (at least in theory) compatible with each other, and they hope against hope that price/performance leads of three or six months will provide competitive differentiation and consistent profits. But adherence to standards is a self-limiting strategy. Beyond a certain point, no computer supplier can be qualitatively more "open" than its rivals. As for differentiation, success requires an endless stream of new products, the development of which is marginally profitable at best because of abruptly short product lives. In fact, a hardware strategy based on adherence to "open systems" is a prescription for corporate suicide. Companies that live by low entry barriers also die by them.

In this era of open systems, the suppliers that survive will be those that *close* their systems as they add new utility. While they might adhere to standards drawn from historical innovation, their forward-looking efforts will identify high-value areas that are not yet standardized and create proprietary concepts and technologies that become candidates for the next wave of standards: pen-based operating systems, natural language interfaces, multimedia data storage and recall, and more. But virtually all of these undeveloped standards represent software challenges, not hardware challenges. They can be created by layering software on top of existing hardware or, in a few cases, layering small hardware subsystems on top of already standardized hardware platforms.

Consider the rise of Sun Microsystems, now a $2.5 billion manufacturer of computer hardware. Conventional wisdom attributes Sun's spectacular growth to its adherence to an open operating system,

Unix, and the dramatic price/performance advantages of its work-station technology—in short, to its superior generation of computer power.

There is some truth to this, of course, but the real lessons are more subtle. Sun workstations do not just deliver raw power; they deliver *utility* to a carefully identified group of target users. From the begin-ning, Sun understood that there were thousands of software develop-ers inside large companies eager to work on Unix rather than on the proprietary Domain operating system sold by Apollo, then the leader in workstations, or on minicomputer systems sold by DEC and others. To these end users, Unix was the essence of the utility Sun delivered. It was not the speed of Sun workstations but their operating platform that was the basis of their differentiation and value. Sun assembled an aggressive direct sales force, targeted these Unix enthusiasts, and built its business. Like Apple, Sun's achievements in software and marketing, not its manufacturing prowess, gave the company its com-petitive edge.

What's more, Sun's Unix is "standardized" more in rhetoric than in reality. In the early 1980s, there were several versions of Unix available, all of which were incompatible or insufficient for many of the software applications Sun's target users wanted to develop. Sun contributed some key new features to the public-domain Unix—vir-tual memory and superior networking were especially important—and thus meaningfully differentiated its operating system. In so doing, Sun positioned itself as the driver of Unix standards.

Monopolize the true sources of added value; create vigorous competition for enabling components. The development of a new computer system brings together a wide range of technologies, only a few of which contribute to ultimate competitive advantage. Successful companies don't compete on (and even give away) the enabling technologies on which their core utility is based. Such "technological promiscuity" has three important benefits. It stimulates cutthroat competition in the markets for enabling components and thus leads to lower overall systems costs. It disrupts the strategies of imitative competitors that compete on the basis of mastering these standardized components. Finally, it liberates companies to focus on their true sources of market power and leverage their lead.

Here again Sun is a model. In 1989, the company moved to abandon the Motorola and Intel microprocessors at the heart of its existing workstations and began to build a new class of workstations around superfast RISC architectures. It was a momentous strategic decision.

Sun replaced the microprocessors with a chip of its own design, the Sparc, and thus exerted more control over its destiny. But Sun wisely chose not to build the chip itself or to outsource its production to a single manufacturer. Rather, it created a hotly competitive market in Sparc microprocessors by licensing the design to such chip manufacturers as Fujitsu, Philips, Texas Instruments, and Toshiba. It also encouraged these and other companies to design and build Sparc "clones" that would compete with Sun's own hardware.

This has been a high-stakes gamble. Sun has directly sown the seeds of its own competition in a way no other hardware manufacturer has ever done. But the benefits are enormous. Microprocessors are the single most important and expensive component of a workstation, and today there are suppliers around the world driving down the cost and pushing up the performance of Sun's Sparc chip. Moreover, no segment of the hardware market will be left unserved by Sparc-compatible products, even if Sun chooses not to build them. ICL, the British manufacturer, has even introduced a Sparc-compatible minicomputer. Toshiba has introduced a Sparc-based portable computer.

The results speak for themselves. In 1990, Sun claimed 38% of the workstation market, well above the market share of Hewlett-Packard, its leading rival. Computers incorporating the Sparc architecture accounted for a staggering 60% of the workstation industry's RISC unit volume. Independent software vendors have developed more than 2,100 applications for Sparc hardware—more than twice the number available for workstations designed by IBM and DEC.

At some point, though, the worldwide market in Sparc-compatible computers will become more efficient at manufacturing computer systems than Sun itself. When this day arrives, and it will arrive within a few years, Sun will face yet another crossroads. Like Intel, it will be in a position where manufacturing does not contribute to margins but instead is a "reward" for doing everything else (customer support, distribution, integration) right. The transition will be unsettling, and it is bound to meet resistance within the company. But the very success of Sun's business model encourages its evolution into a computerless computer company.

Maximize the sophistication of the value you deliver; minimize the sophistication of the technology you consume. Value in the computer industry is a function of differentiation, not standardization. And differentiation has little to do with raw processing power. This market reality has enormous implications for corporate technology choices. Rather than favor the most advanced hardware, the computerless computer company will favor second-tier technologies. For companies whose proprietary systems contribute superior utility, "advanced" base technologies are likely to create strategic vulnerabilities. A company that builds systems around 90th-percentile hardware technologies will have numerous, equally satisfactory sources of supply and thus more easily controllable costs and technology risks.

In the mid-1980s, for example, the start-up Silicon Graphics combined innovative design with unspectacular semiconductor processes to challenge the market position of Evans & Sutherland, the leader in high-performance graphics workstations. Evans & Sutherland responded with a new class of hardware based on advanced semiconductor and packaging technologies in a bid to up the ante on performance. But this risky new technology extended the development cycle well beyond the available market window. Silicon Graphics leveraged its competitive breathing space to establish software support, to drive high-performance graphics into new applications, and to establish a strong brand image.

Today Silicon Graphics is the world's leading supplier of general-purpose, high-performance graphics workstations, with annual revenues exceeding $400 million. Evans & Sutherland eventually abandoned its advanced technology efforts and entered the market with a weakly differentiated system. Its annual sales are $150 million, up only modestly from its revenues when Silicon Graphics entered the market.

Reversal of Fortunes

Few companies in any industry have the strategic foresight or courage to fundamentally transform business models that have led to success. But fundamentally new technological and economic forces demand just such courage. The computer companies that prosper into the next century will be those that focus on inventing new markets rather than on building new products.

And what's good for computer companies is good for the country. The United States cannot regain its place in world competition by investing in lost and backward-looking hardware technologies—no matter their one-time prominence. Reversing America's technology fortunes requires reversing its national technology priorities. A recent report by the Council on Competitiveness, a Washington-based organization supported by established technology companies, took stock

Exhibit II.   U.S. technology . . .

Electronic components

	U.S. Position			
Technology	**Strong**	**Competitive**	**Weak**	**Losing badly or lost**
Microelectronics				
Logic chips		☐		
Memory chips				☐
Microprocessors	☐			
Submicron technology		☐		
Electronic Controls				
Actuators			☐	
Sensors		☐		
Optoelectronic components				
Laser devices			☐	
Photonics			☐	
Electronic packaging and interconnections				
Multichip packaging systems				☐
Printed circuit board technology				☐
Displays				
Electroluminescent				☐
Liquid crystal				☐
Plasma and vacuum fluorescent				☐
Hard-copy technology				
Electrophotography			☐	
Electrostatic			☐	
Information storage				
Magnetic information storage	☐			
Optical information storage				☐

The Council on Competitiveness recently published a bleak assessment of the U.S. position in global technology competition. In fact, these two tables from its report paint a different picture.

Source: Gaining New Ground: Technology Priorities for America's Future.

. . .Strong Where It Matters

Information Technologies

U.S. Position

Technology	Strong	Competitive	Weak	Losing badly or Lost
Software				
Applications software	☐			
Artificial intelligence	☐			
Computer modeling and simulation	☐			
Expert systems	☐			
High-level software languages	☐			
Software engineering	☐			
Computers				
Hardware integration		☐		
Neural networks	☐			
Operating systems	☐			
Processor architecture	☐			
Human Interface and Visualization Technologies				
Animation and full-motion video	☐			
Graphics hardware and software	☐			
Handwriting and speech recognition	☐			
Natural language	☐			
Optical character recognition	☐			
Database Systems				
Data representation	☐			
Retrieval and update	☐			
Semantic modeling and interpretation	☐			
Networks and Communications				
Broadband switching		☐		
Digital infrastructure		☐		
Fiber-optic systems		☐		
Multiplexing		☐		
Portable Telecommunications Equipment and Systems				
Digital signal processing		☐		
Spectrum technologies		☐		
Transmitters and receivers	☐			

of the U.S. competitive position in high technology. With some dismay, it described the United States as "weak" or "losing badly" in such basic technologies as memory chips, semiconductor packaging, and flat-panel displays. But the same study describes as "strong" or "competitive" the U.S. position in applications software, high-level software languages, computer architectures, data base systems, and user interfaces—the very software-based technologies required to invent new markets for the hardware technologies controlled offshore. (See Exhibit II.)

Investing to regain lost strength in hardware technologies is risky and unrewarding. Investing to capitalize on applications strength and to leverage the investments of other countries in enabling technologies is more likely to allow the United States to extend its leadership—and more likely to result in U.S. control of high-technology markets. Companies and countries that control markets hold power, profit, and employment advantages over those that merely control technology. That's the central lesson of companies like Microsoft, the fabless chip producers, and Sun Microsystems. It is a lesson more companies must learn.

13
Balancing Corporate Power: A New Federalist Paper

Charles Handy

One of the world's oldest political philosophies is its newest subject of interest. The European Community, the new Commonwealth of Independent States, Canada, Czechoslovakia, and many more are all reexamining what federalism really means. Businesses and other organizations are beginning to do the same. Everywhere companies are restructuring, creating integrated organizations, global networks, and "leaner, meaner" corporate centers. In so doing, whether they recognize it or not, they are on a path to federalism as the way to govern their increasingly complex organizations.

The prospect of applying political principles to management issues makes a great deal of sense, given that organizations today are more and more seen as minisocieties rather than as impersonal systems. But the concept of federalism is particularly appropriate since it offers a well-recognized way to deal with paradoxes of power and control: the need to make things big by keeping them small; to encourage autonomy but within bounds; to combine variety and shared purpose, individuality and partnership, local and global, tribal region and nation state, or nation state and regional bloc. Change a few of the terms and these political issues can be found on the agendas of senior managers in most of the world's large companies.

It is therefore no accident that Percy Barnevik, the CEO of Asea Brown Boveri, has described his sprawling "multidomestic" enterprise of 1,100 separate companies and 210,000 employees as a federation. Nor is it accidental that John Akers has called IBM's restructuring a move to federalism. Basel-based Ciba-Geigy recently moved from a management pyramid with a matrix designed around businesses, functions, and regions to an organization with 14 separate businesses controlling 94% of all the company's spending—a federal organization.

Although they do not always call it federalism, businesses in every country are moving in the same direction: General Electric, Johnson & Johnson, and Coca-Cola in the United States; Grand Metropolitan and British Petroleum in Great Britain; Accor in France; and Honda in Japan. Older global companies, such as Royal Dutch Shell and Unilever, went federal decades ago, pulled that way by the demand for autonomy from their overseas subsidiaries. But they, too, are always flexing their structures and fine-tuning the balance of power because federalism is not a static system.

Neither, however, is federalism just a classy word for restructuring. The thinking behind it, the belief, for instance, that autonomy releases energy; that people have the right to do things in their own way as long as it is in the common interest; that people need to be well-informed, well-intentioned, and well-educated to interpret that common interest; that individuals prefer being led to being managed: these principles reach into the guts of the organization or, more correctly, into its soul—the way it goes about its business day by day. Federalism properly understood is not so much a political structure or system as it is a way of life.

It is, however, the structure that changes first, as organizations twist and turn in their attempts to cope with the paradoxes of modern business. To understand federalism at work, we first need to examine these paradoxes and the ways in which organizations are evolving to deal with them. Then a look at the five key principles of federalism will show how this particular political theory can illuminate these paradoxes and point the way to some practical action.

Every organization is different, so there will be no common or even constant solution to each dilemma. And a federal organization can be particularly exhausting to govern since it relies as much on influence, trust, and empathy as on formal power and explicit controls. But in today's complex world of interrelationships and constant change, the move to federalism is inevitable. And that which is inevitable it is best to understand so that we may profit from it.

The first paradox is that organizations need to be both big and small at the same time, be they corporations or nations. On the one hand, the economies of scale still apply. The discovery and development of new sources of oil and gas require resources that no small niche player could contemplate. Big is essential as well for pharmaceutical companies if they are to finance the massive research programs on which their future depends. Bigness also makes an organization less dependent on a few crucial people or on outside expertise.

At the same time, businesses and nations need to be small. Everywhere small nation states and regions are flexing their muscles and demanding more autonomy. People want to identify with something closer to them and of human scale. We want villages, even in the midst of our cities. It is no different in organizations. Small may not always be beautiful but it is more comfortable. It is also more flexible and more likely to be innovative.

This paradox, how to be big but small, dominates politics and business today. In politics, federalism has been the traditional answer, although its subtleties are not always well understood even by politicians. In business, federalism is not simple decentralization with the center acting as a banker to the separate businesses like the conglomerates of old. That loses the advantages of scale, of being able to develop lead technologies across a range of separate businesses, of combining to purchase or bid for a major contract that might involve the skills of several businesses.

But neither is federalism a simple divisionalization, the grouping of businesses under sets of umbrellas. That leaves too much power in the hands of those holding the umbrellas and pays too little attention to local needs or to the knowledge and contacts of those out in the marketplace. Nor is it a matter of simply empowering those on the front line or in the separate countries. That ignores the expertise of people farther back or in other groupings.

Federalism responds to all these pressures, balancing power among those in the center of the organization, those in the centers of expertise, and those in the center of the action, the operating businesses. It is worth noting that Barnevik talks about centralized *reporting*, not centralized control, because most of his key people are not located at the center of ABB's matrix of global business strands and national companies.

The true centers of federal organizations are dispersed throughout the operations. They meet frequently and they talk often, but they do not need to live together. Doing so would be a mistake because it would concentrate too much power in one group and in one place, whereas federalism gets its strength and energy from spreading responsibility across many decision points. ABB's situation may seem extreme, but there exists one private company, also nominally based in Switzerland, that employs 80,000 people worldwide but has no one employed in its central company.

That is not completely true. There is one person who infuses the whole organization with his personality—though not with his power—and holds everything together with his vision. The same is, by all accounts, true of Barnevik, who seems to be everywhere at once, leading seminars with his managers, prodding, questioning, inspiring, "being a missionary," as the CEO of another global corporation once put it. Federalist centers are always small to the point of minimalist. They exist to coordinate, not to control.

Business's second paradox lies in its declared preference for free and open markets as the best guarantee of efficiency, even as its managers instinctively organize their own operations for centralized control.

Two hundred years ago, the political philosopher Edmund Burke argued that centralized power would always lead to bureaucratic procedures that ultimately stifle innovation, stamp out individual differences, and therefore inhibit growth. Yet in the interests of efficiency, businesses do their best to build *identikit* operations around the globe. If something works in Milwaukee it ought to work in Manchester, the logic goes, and it certainly makes it more convenient for those in the center if it does. Also, of course, there is management's conviction that only the center can know the whole picture, only the center can take decisions that are in the best interest of all.

That conviction may well be true. But the costs are high, the bureaucracy disabling, the delays and demotivation crippling. That is why in many businesses the breakup value of the operations exceeds the market value of the total enterprise. The center has a negative added value, or, to put it another way, the transaction costs of central planning and control exceed the contribution that they undoubtedly make.

"Think global, act local" may be the fashionable slogan for dealing with this paradox, but it will not work very well as long as all real power resides in what is usually still called the *Head* Office or sometimes, suggestively, the Kremlin. On the other hand, a hollow corporation can soon lack direction, standards, or any sort of cohesion.

One British furniture company had a rule that it would only grow outward, not upward. No business unit would contain more than 100 people. So as the company prospered, it built new factories and mini-businesses, each autonomous, each responsible for generating its own customers and expertise, each remitting its profits to the center and drawing on the center—and the others—only if needed. The system worked well in the days of heady growth. But come the recession and the need to allocate scarce resources, there was no one left with the power, authority, or knowledge to make those strategic decisions. Left to themselves, the locals could not think globally, and on occasion five separate business units would be found competing against each other for the same order. Open markets, on their own, do not necessarily work any better than central planning. A bit of both is needed—the federal compromise.

"What you do not own you cannot command" sums up the next paradox: the desire to run a business as if it were yours when you cannot afford, or may not want, to make it yours. Wholly owned business empires are becoming a thing of the past. In some countries, local representation is a matter of law, as nationalism fights back against the increasing globalization of everything. But in any case, empires are too expensive and too risky. It is cheaper and safer to expand one's scope by a series of alliances and ventures. When Pepsi-Cola and Whitbread jointly formed Pizza Hut, U.K., Pepsi needed Whitbread's knowledge of British leisure and property markets, while Whitbread needed Pepsi's pizza know-how. One without the other could not have done it.

Alliances, however, are notoriously difficult to manage. Part-owned companies do not take kindly to orders from a head office in another country. Neither do alliances. Rather like marriages, each one is unique, to be lived with rather than managed, better built on mutual respect and shared interests than on legal documents and tight controls. In these circumstances, power perforce has to be shared, autonomy granted, and the marriage held together by trust and common goals, two of federalism's chief ingredients.

At the same time that these paradoxes are triggering structural changes in large organizations, another force is pushing companies toward federalism. I call this force *the pull of the professionals,* and it affects the processes of an organization as much as it does the structure.

As organizations everywhere realign themselves around their core activities and competences, they are realizing that their people are truly their chief assets. Often this realization becomes apparent only in a takeover or merger, when the business, if it is any good, is typically valued at four or five times the value of its tangible assets. The difference is the potential added value of its intangible assets, the intellectual property residing in its key people.

These human assets are far from fixed. They could walk out the door next Monday. They are the new professionals, high achievers for the most part, who see themselves as having careers beyond the organization, like doctors, lawyers, and architects before them. "My MBA is my certificate of competence and my passport," one told me. She had still to learn that a professional's reputation is built on work completed, not on certificates obtained, but her starting motivation was clear. Such people want an organization that recognizes their individual talents and provides space for their individual contributions. They prefer small, autonomous work groups based on reciprocal trust between leader and led, groups responsible, as far as possible, for their own destiny. They would like to have it both ways, of course, preferring those autonomous groups to be part of a larger family that can provide resources, career opportunities, and the leverage that comes with size. Federalism to them is thus a way to make it big while keeping it small—and independent.

Faced with these simultaneous pressures, businesses are adapting and experimenting. In so doing, they might save themselves some pain by understanding the basic principles that have defined federalism over the centuries. For these five principles—well-established though not always well-applied—translate readily into the world of business where they can provide an organizational framework for the way the company goes about its work.

Subsidiarity is the most important of federalism's principles. It is a pity only that it is such an ugly and uncomfortable word. It means that power belongs to the lowest possible point in the organization. "A higher order body should not take unto itself responsibilities which properly belong to a lower order body" is how a 1941 papal encyclical puts it, because subsidiarity has long been part of the doctrine of the Catholic Church. The state should not do what the family can do better is one example of the principle turned into practice. "Stealing people's decisions is wrong" might be another way of putting it, something parents wrestle with as their children grow up.

All managers are tempted to steal their subordinates' decisions. Subsidiarity requires, instead, that they enable those subordinates, by training, advice, and support, to take those decisions better. Only if the decision would substantially damage the organization is the manager entitled to intervene. In aviation, the trainer allows the trainee pilot to get it wrong provided that the mistake will not crash the plane. It is the only way the trainee will learn to fly alone.

In the current European debate, subsidiarity means that power resides within the individual countries of the Community. Only with their agreement can Brussels exercise any authority. It is a form of reverse delegation. British Petroleum, which in effect went federal in 1990, devolving authority and responsibility to its separate businesses, had to decide which powers the center would retain. The center came up with a list of 22 "reserve powers" but, after discussions with the separate businesses, these were pruned down to the 10 most essential to the future direction of the company. In a federal system, the center governs only with the consent of the governed.

Subsidiarity, therefore, is the reverse of empowerment. It is not the center giving away or delegating power. Instead, power is assumed to lie at the lowest point in the organization and it can be taken away only by agreement. The Catholic Church works on this holistic premise when it says that every priest is a pope in his own parish. Robert Galvin does the same when he tells Motorola's sales force that they have all the authority of the chairman when they are with customers. Taken seriously, subsidiarity is an awesome responsibility because it imposes on the individual or the group what might be called "type two accountability."

This follows the distinction in statistics between a type one error, which, simply put, means getting it wrong, and a type two error, which is not getting it as right as it could have been. Traditionally, we have run organizations on the basis of type one accountability, making sure that no mistakes are made. Under subsidiarity, people are also judged against their type two accountability—did they seize every opportunity, did they make all the possible improvements?

To be effective, subsidiarity has to be formalized. Federal states have constitutions, negotiated contracts that set the boundaries of each group's powers and responsibilities. Organizations need contracts too. It has to be clear who can do what, how power is to be balanced, and whose authority counts where. Leave all this to chance or to personal goodwill and the powerful will steal more than they should and unbalance the whole.

Finally, subsidiarity requires intelligence and information, real-time data that is broad enough to give a total picture but detailed enough to pinpoint decision points. Before the days of electronic data interchange, true holism in business was a sham. If people are to exercise their responsibility taking account of the interests of the whole, they must have both the information that allows them to do so and enough training and knowledge to interpret the information. How else could Motorola's salespeople represent the chairman?

The center, then, should be small and can be small because of the possibilities of information technology. Because it is small, it cannot involve itself in too much detail and will not be able to control the operating companies day to day. Subsidiarity, therefore, is self-reinforcing. In 1990, Robert Horton's first decision as chairman of British Petroleum was to move the head office out of its tower block in the city of London and to cut its numbers by more than half. The symbolism of the move was important; so was the new language for the people in the new center (no longer the head office)—team leaders, coordinators, and advisers. British Petroleum could, and probably will, go farther and disperse some of that center to the operating units to reinforce the next principle of federalism.

The states of a federation stick together because they need one another as much as they need the center. In that sense a federation is different from a confederation, where the individual states yield no sovereignty to the center and try to need nothing from their neighbors. They agree only to collaborate on certain important issues. Such things fall apart, as the new Commonwealth of Independent States in what used to be the Soviet Union may soon discover.

Interdependence is achieved partly through the reserve powers of the center, partly by locating services or facilities needed by all in the territory of one or two. Research and development, for instance, can be located in Germany, the United States, and Japan but serve the world. The European computing center may be run by and from France but serve all the European operating companies. In political science, this is called pluralism—many centers of power and expertise.

Federalism encourages combination when and where appropriate but not centralization. Unilever, for instance, has pulled back its European detergent manufacturing from the individual countries into one location to achieve the economies of scale possible in producing what is now a commodity. Gillette combined its European and North American marketing management in one office in Boston as a prelude to a simultaneous launch of its new Sensor razor. It is only when combination becomes excessive or is located all in one place that it offends against the principle of pluralism.

Pluralism is a key element of federalism because it distributes power, avoiding the risks of autocracy and the overcontrol of a central bureaucracy. It ensures a measure of democracy in the larger organizations because the wishes of the different players cannot be ignored. The result is the new "dispersed center" of federalism, a center that is more a network than a place. There are, however, costs to this dispersion. The center still has to be a center, to meet and talk and share. Telephones and videoconferences are no substitutes for some real meetings. Airplanes and red-eyes become inevitable. The exhaustion is worth it. Paradoxically, the dispersion of the center bonds the whole together. Units who use each other need each other.

The result is a matrix of sorts. Not the traditional matrix of functions and businesses but one in which every operating unit is accountable both to its respective global business sector and to its local region and that also draws on communal resources and services, wherever they may be located. It is a complex mix for a complex world and a mix that will be constantly changing. Federalism is and must be flexible; it can never be static.

Interdependence is unlikely, if not impossible, without agreement on the basic rules of conduct, a common way of communicating, and a common unit of measurement. If Europe ever develops into a proper federation, these will be essential requirements, just as they are in America. In corporate terms, a common law means a basic set of rules and procedures, a way of doing business. ABB has an 18-page "bible" that is effectively its common law. Grand Metropolitan has a group of people based in the center but traveling the world who carry with them the standards, customs, and culture of Grand Met. They are popularly known as the "bag carriers," modern-day missionaries, promulgating the language and the law of the corporation.

A common language means not only, in most cases, American English but also a common information system so that everyone can talk—not just to one another's answering machines but also to their PCs. A common currency means simply that units of measurement must be agreed to so that oranges *can* be compared with apples around the world. Obvious though these things are, they are often forgotten in the haste to get on with the job. Too many mergers ignore them or leave them for later when they are far harder to create.

The United States and other federalist countries take this concept for granted, although it seldom percolates through to their business organizations. These, like old monarchical regimes, prefer to concentrate power wherever possible in the interests of getting things done. Federalist organizations, however, worry more that the things done by the center may not be the right things, and they do not like to see too much power in one place or group. Now that Germany has decided to make Berlin its capital, we may see that city becoming a magnet, pulling business, finance, and the arts, as well as government, into one place. Germany would then become noticeably less federalist.

Today the management, monitoring, and governance of a business are increasingly seen as separate functions to be done by separate bodies, even if some of the membership of those bodies overlaps. This is the corporate equivalent of the separation of powers. Management is the executive function, responsible for delivering the goods. Monitoring is the judicial function, responsible for seeing that the goods are delivered according to the laws of the land, that standards are met, and ethical principles observed. Governance is the legislative function, responsible for overseeing management and monitoring and, most important, for the corporation's future, for strategy, policy, and direction.

When these three functions are combined in one body, the short-term tends to drive out the long, with month-to-month management and monitoring issues stealing the time and attention needed for governance. The big decisions then go wrong. In the Lloyd's insurance business of London, a federation made up of 179 autonomous insurance syndicates, the three functions are currently combined by law. The chairman of Lloyd's has to be a practicing underwriter, that is, an executive, and Lloyd's is responsible for its own regulation. The result is a mess, a loss in 1992 of $3.7 billion for the 1989 year of account and more of the same to come. The "names," or private individuals who have to pay these losses, are understandably clamoring for reform. Lloyd's has broken one of the cardinal principles of federalism.

Most companies are going the other way. Many have now separated the roles of chairman and chief executive and created two-tier boards, although they do not call them that, preferring to refer to the executive board as a committee or team. They also have separate audit committees and, on occasion, separate committees for monitoring the company's environmental or community responsibilities. In Britain and North America, the top board, the one responsible for governance, is not as representative of the different stakeholders as it would be in Germany or Japan. But it is increasingly seen to be the duty, particularly of the nonexecutive directors, to take those interests into account. Governance in a federal system is ultimately democratic, accountable to all the interest groups on which it depends, not just to its financiers. In the long term it cannot afford to ignore those other interests.

In a federal country, everyone is a citizen of two states, his or her own and the Union. A Texan is also an American, and the Stars and Stripes can be found waving outside the house of many an ardent

Californian. A resident of Munich may be a Bavarian first and a German second, but he is both. Corporate letterheads likewise fly two flags. Some put "a member of the X group of companies" in small letters in the corner. Others, such as Shell, give the federal logo pride of place. The layout will say a lot about the distribution of power, but both flags will always be present.

Local citizenship seldom needs much reinforcement. Indeed, the "states" of a federal business are often themselves monarchical, led by a forceful baron. This is not inconsistent. The federal whole draws its strength from the strong leadership of the "states"—another of federalism's paradoxes but one that ensures a strong local identity.

Increasingly, it is the federal citizenship that requires emphasis if interdependence is to be fostered. To do this, corporations add their equivalent of a national anthem to the flag, issuing "mission statements" or "vision and value statements" that are regularly recited throughout the federation—if not always totally believed. These are useful, symbolically, because they remind people of the larger whole and of their wider citizenship. But at their best, these national anthems provide what *The Art of Japanese Management* authors Richard Pascale and Anthony Athos call "the spiritual fabric" of the corporation. As it happens, they are describing companies in present-day Japan. The tradition, however, is much older. In Elizabethan England, venturers went forth unfettered by authority and bound together only by their concern for "The Queen's Great Matter." That understanding built an empire.

Unilever has an annual occasion, popularly known as the "O Be Joyful" day, when its senior executives from around the world assemble to hear the annual results and, more subliminally, to celebrate their second citizenship. When corporations talk of "shared values" these days, they are recognizing that what bonds a federal system together has to be more than the need to improve the bottom line, essential though that is. It has to be some modern-day equivalent of the Queen's Great Matter. Finding that equivalent and articulating it is a major challenge for leadership.

A president also helps to bond a federation together by exemplifying the larger state and serving as its ambassador-at-large both to the outside world and, almost more important, to its own citizens. Sir John Harvey-Jones, the former chairman of ICI, understood this well. His face and laugh became familiar features in the British media and helped to give the big chemical company a human as well as a technological face. Akio Morita of Sony is another of these president ambassadors, endlessly reinforcing the core values of his federation of companies by speeches, articles, and personal visits.

Federalism is, on the face of it, a way of thinking about the structure and operations of large organizations. Leave it there and it does not make much difference to the executive or technician in Pittsburgh or Mannheim. But we cannot leave it there. The thinking about power and responsibility that animates federalism is pervasive in developed societies. The pull of professionalism ensures that this thinking reaches beyond an organization's structure into its processes, the way that individuals relate to one another and to the tasks they take on. As a result, the federal way of thinking can be extended into a set of maxims for managing in today's organizations.

Authority must be earned from those over whom it is exercised. This is the practical implication of subsidiarity. In the organizations dominated by the new professionals, you cannot tell people what to do unless they respect you, agree with you, or both. We used to teach that authority came from above, but that was when people were hired hands whose time had been bought to do the company's bidding. That day has long passed, but this so-called "instrumental contract" still applies in many places, particularly in times of recession. Yet as more people think of themselves as professionals, with careers that span companies, purely instrumental contracts become less and less effective.

Professionals require management by consent if they are to give their best; consent that is theirs to give or to withhold. This maxim may sound obvious, but two major and unsuspected implications follow from it. Units have to be small so that people can get to know one another well enough to earn their colleagues' respect through their records of achievement. And people have to be around long enough to build up those records. Reputation can and does precede one into a new role but then it has to be justified. We are talking, therefore, of units of less than 100 people, perhaps, and of 3- to 5-year tenures in jobs. Organizations that think of their people as role occupants, replaceable and moveable as long as the role is properly defined, are not thinking federally. Organizations that reward success with promotion every two years are making it difficult, if not impossible, to manage with respect and by consent.

People have both the right and the duty to sign their work. Subsidiarity requires that people take responsibility for their decisions by signing their work, both literally and metaphorically. The new as well as the old professionals do just that. Your doctor is an individual, not an anonymous "medical supervisor." Films and television programs end with long lists of names—the signatures of all, even the most junior, who contributed. Most journalists sign their work; so do architects, lawyers, professors, clothing designers, and artists. Consultancies' project teams now put the names of all their members on the title pages of their reports. Advertising agencies do the same. My new Swiss watch arrived with a label stating "Gerard made this." We may not want to know who these people are, but they want to tell us, and that is the important thing. It is a healthy trend in organizations, and it will spread as more work gets done in small, discrete groups.

A signature on one's work may be the best single recipe for quality. For reasons of personal pride, as well as fear of recrimination, few will want to sign their names to a dud product. Federal thinking insists, however, that one's signature is a right as well as a responsibility, a demonstration that the individual has made a personal contribution. The new chief executive of an art-printing business in Britain called his work force together after one month and said, "I am ashamed of much of the stuff that leaves this building, even if the customers seem to accept it. In future, every item will have a piece of paper headed 'we are proud to have done this work' and signed by every member of the work group." He expected an angry or at least a sullen response but instead he got cheers. "We were ashamed too" one worker said, "but we thought that was all you wanted, acceptable rubbish at the lowest cost. Now all you have to do is provide the equipment so that we can do the sort of work we will be proud to sign."

Those workers had a point. Encouraging people to sign their work does have implications. They have to have the right equipment. They have to be the right sort of people to begin with, properly trained and properly qualified. They have to know, by benchmarking or other means, what the right standards are.

Autonomy means managing empty spaces. Subsidiarity and signatures both imply a lot of individual discretion. Yet unbounded discretion can be frightening for the individual and dangerous for the organization. Groups and individuals therefore live within two concentric circles of responsibility. The inner circle contains everything they *have* to do or fail—their baseline. The larger circle marks the limits of their authority, where their writ ends. In between is their area of discretion, the space in which they have both the freedom and the responsibility to initiate action. This space exists for them to fill; it is their type two accountability.

Of necessity, individual initiatives can be judged only after the event. Organizations prefer to control and judge things before they happen. It is safer that way. It is also slower, more expensive, and it assumes that those who are higher up and farther away know better. The assumption behind federal thinking—and the empty space for individual initiative—is that those higher up may not know better. That assumption requires a lot of trust and a necessary forgiveness if the initiative turns out wrong. Where no mistakes are tolerated, no initiative will be risked. "Forgiveness provided one learns" is a necessary part of federalist thinking. It can be a hard part to practice.

Management by trust, empathy, and forgiveness sounds good. It also sounds soft. It is, in practice, tough. Organizations based on trust have, on occasion, to be ruthless. If someone can no longer be trusted, he or she cannot be given an empty space. To keep the spirit of subsidiarity intact, those who do not merit trust must go elsewhere, quickly.

This poses a dilemma for organizations that have thought it right to guarantee jobs and careers for life to all whom they employ. If they have chosen wrongly, if trust turns out to be misplaced, they must either break the guarantee or close up the empty space professionals value so highly. It seems probable that organizations will start to require long probationary periods before they give these lifetime guarantees. Either that or they will move to more fixed-term contracts. Leaders, too, will need to be tough as well as trusting and forgiving— another federal paradox.

Twin hierarchies are necessary and useful. Twin hierarchies demonstrate the principle of interdependence at the work-group level. There is, in every organization, a clear status hierarchy. Some people are justifiably senior to others and are paid more than others because of their knowledge, experience, or proven ability. Traditionally, the most senior person in the status hierarchy leads any group on any task. That, however, makes no sense where the task requires a group of people with different skills and where one particular skill must take the lead. In an advertising agency, for instance, the young account director may be properly deferential to the wise old media buyer, but there is never any doubt about who is in the chair. In the task hierarchy, the role dictates who is who. Outside the meeting, however, the status hierarchy reasserts itself in the accustomed way.

Twin hierarchies are commonplace in professional organizations. They have to be. They are rarer in business. But they will become more common as skills become more specialized and as task groups realize that they are temporary alliances of expertise that need to make the best use of one another to get the work done—interdependence in practice. The concept has important side effects, however: by allowing the young specialist to demonstrate his or her expertise to the rest of the organization, it provides great encouragement for making that expertise as good as it can be and exposes him or her to the realities of the business. At the same time, it takes some getting used to. Not least it requires notable self-confidence from those senior in the status hierarchy if they are, on occasion, to work under the direction of their juniors.

Distinguishing between status and task hierarchies allows organizations to become much flatter without losing efficiency. The older professional organizations typically have only four levels from trainee to partner, or medical consultant, or professor, or whatever the top layer is called. The Catholic Church has bishops, priests, and deacons—and a pope who is its president ambassador. Business organizations are following suit, especially those staffed largely by knowledge workers. Four layers of status are enough, they find, as more of their work is organized in teams, each with its appropriate task hierarchy.

What is good for me should be good for the corporation. This is the twin citizenship principle brought down to the level of the individual. Professionals believe in what the Japanese call "self-enlightenment," knowing that if they do not continually invest in their own learning and development they will be a wasting asset. What they ask of the organization is that it facilitate and encourage this process of continual learning by paying any costs and providing leaves of absence. In return, they own a loyalty to the larger state, the organization. But as in the larger federal structures, this loyalty can no longer be taken for granted. It has to be earned and continually reinforced. If the corporation reneges on the implicit, and sometimes explicit, contract that facilitates individual development, or if it fails to recognize or take advantage of a significant piece of learning—a new qualification perhaps—the individual will feel released from any sense of obligation.

But this individualism, which provides the best guarantee of professional standards and the best engine for personal achievement, has to be harnessed to a cause that is greater than itself if it is to be truly useful. It is that larger and wider loyalty or citizenship that needs special emphasis, as it always does in federalism. Saint Augustine once said that the worst of sins was to be "turned in on oneself." It is still true today. Without that wider citizenship, the prized individualism of the new professionals can look remarkably like selfishness.

Federalism reverses a lot of traditional management thinking. In particular, it assumes that most of the energy is out there, away from the center, and down there, away from the top. Power, in federalist thinking, is redistributed because no one person and no one group can be all-wise, all-knowing, all-competent. Monarchy is risky, acceptable only in times of crisis, as once at Chrysler. Bureaucracy is stifling. Better to let 1,000 flowers bloom, even if some of them turn out to be weeds. Paradoxically, although federalism wants no all-powerful monarch at its center, it needs strong leaders in its parts. Choosing those leaders and developing them will always be one of the center's closely guarded reserve powers. You cannot, however, make a federation strong and keep it growing just by keeping it small. The independent bits, be they individuals, clusters, business units, or separate companies have to feel and be part of a greater whole.

Federalism is not simple. It matches complexity with complexity. It is always tempting to seek to impose a unitary authority and a unitary system on a set of complex purposes; but to do so ignores the necessary variety of the bigger world in which all corporations today are players. It would be akin to turning harmony into unison. Federalism is in tune with the times—times that want to value and respect diversity and difference, times in which people want to do their own thing and yet be part of something bigger, times in which they look for structure but not imposed authority.

Tried and tested, often to the point of failure, in the political world, federalism has great added value as an organizational concept. The wheel does not have to be reinvented for our corporations. We know how federalism is supposed to work. Making it happen, however, is something else again. History is not overfull of examples of monarchies or oligarchies voluntarily turning themselves into federations. Federations typically arise when smaller states need to combine and yet retain their identity. Only after war or revolution do oligarchies turn federal. Here, therefore, there are no good models. We must proceed as best we may.

To do so requires determination at the top, the will to give some power away in order to gain momentum. That will be easier if all concerned know what is happening and why, if they understand the thinking that lies behind the changes. Understanding is always a good lubricant for change. With that determination and that understanding our corporations may yet add a chapter to the textbooks of political science by providing examples of voluntary federalism.

14

Predators and Prey: A New Ecology of Competition

James F. Moore

For most companies today, the only truly sustainable advantage comes from out-innovating the competition. Successful businesses are those that evolve rapidly and effectively. Yet innovative businesses can't evolve in a vacuum. They must attract resources of all sorts, drawing in capital, partners, suppliers, and customers to create cooperative networks.

Much has been written about such networks, under the rubric of strategic alliances, virtual organizations, and the like. But these frameworks provide little systematic assistance for managers who seek to understand the underlying strategic logic of change. Even fewer of these theories help executives anticipate the managerial challenges of nurturing the complex business communities that bring innovations to market.

How is it that a company can create an entirely new business community—like IBM in personal computers—and then lose control and profitability in that same business? Is there a stable structure of community leadership that matches fast-changing conditions? And how can companies develop leadership that successfully adapts to continual waves of innovation and change? These questions remain unanswered because most managers still frame the problem in the old way: companies go head-to-head in an industry, battling for market share. But events of the last decade, particularly in high-technology businesses, amply illustrate the limits of that understanding.

In essence, executives must develop new ideas and tools for strategizing, tools for making tough choices when it comes to innovations, business alliances, and leadership of customers and suppliers.

Anthropologist Gregory Bateson's definition of *co-evolution* in both natural and social systems provides a useful starting place. In his book *Mind and Nature,* Bateson describes co-evolution as a process in which interdependent species evolve in an endless reciprocal cycle—in which "changes in species A set the stage for the natural selection of changes in species B"—and vice versa. Consider predators and their prey, for instance, or flowering plants and their pollinators.

Another insight comes from biologist Stephen Jay Gould, who has observed that natural ecosystems sometimes collapse when environmental conditions change too radically. Dominant combinations of species may lose their leadership. New ecosystems then establish themselves, often with previously marginal plants and animals at the center. For current businesses dealing with the challenges of innovation, there are clear parallels and profound implications.

Automobiles: An Old-Fashioned Timeline

An ecological approach can be used to analyze the evolution of any major business. However, a look at how the old-line automobile companies evolved reveals a different time scale than that of almost any new business today. Historically, the evolutionary stages of an established ecosystem like Ford's or GM's often took decades to play out; but now businesses can be born and die in a matter of years. Managers used to focus on directing the action within a particular stage rather than on how to move from one stage to another. Yet transition between stages has currently become a managerial fact of life.

The major U.S. automobile ecosystems took about three-quarters of a century to evolve, a phenomenal length of time compared with the rise and fall of high-tech businesses like personal computers. However, early automobile executives were well aware of the need to forge a community of suppliers and customers.

Birth of the Horseless Carriage. The late 1800s were a time of experimentation, as the first automobile pioneers struggled to grasp the potential of individualized, motorized transportation. Ranson E. Olds and a handful of others established viable automobile business ecosystems by the turn of the century. Their machines worked reasonably well, were accepted by a small but dedicated number of customers, and could be profitably produced.

Expansion Battles. The next 20 years carried the automobile business deep into the second state of ecological competition. In 1904, William C. Durant began building what would become General Motors. Henry Ford founded the Ford Motor Company, and, in 1908, he introduced his mass-produced, mass-marketed Model T. Near-legendary battles between Ford and GM ensued—struggles as much for soul and future definition of the business as for simple market share.

Ford's approach was based on vertical integration, carefully engineered production, and product simplicity. Ford's ecosystem had what we now would call "scalability"; by 1914, his company produced over 267,000 cars and held 48% of the market.

Durant's strategy for GM, however, was based on acquisitions of early companies, marketing might, sales coverage, and product variety. Durant's ecosystem captured market share by pooling and integrating the markets and the production facilities of a variety of smaller companies. However, by 1920, General Motors had nearly collapsed because of the inability of Durant's management systems to control such a complex collection of business entities.

From about 1910 to 1930, industry leaders directed the large expansion of the automobile market, reconfiguring the major ecosystems in the process. Alfred P. Sloan's design for General Motors, initiated in 1920, is most notable and involved the simultaneous ouster of Durant. Sloan's design specifically allowed for the management of a complex business ecosystem by breaking up the diverse company into product lines, which, in turn, could be focused like Ford's mass-produced lines. Sloan also centralized financial oversight of decentralized product lines, and GM became the prototype of the modern multidivisional company.

Community Leadership. By the 1930s, battles for community leadership and bargaining power revolved around the principal supplier to the auto industry: labor. In the late 1920s, around 500,000 people worked in the Detroit area car factories. Working conditions were dangerous; one auto body plant was known as "the slaughterhouse." But by the mid-1930s, the United Auto Workers Union had formed. In 1937, the UAW achieved a landmark victory when GM recognized the union as an official representative of its employees.

Over time, organized labor brought workers crucial bargaining power, which the union used to force the companies to share the spoils of victory. The tug-of-war between workers and companies continued for decades, mediated with varying effectiveness by the U.S. government. While it protected workers, this form of ecosystem struggle also carried with it high costs: work-rule rigidity and the polarization of workers and management. These costs would come back to haunt the U.S. automobile business in the next stage of ecosystem development.

The Threat of Obsolescence. Labor-management struggles continued into the 1970s, until both sides were driven together by a much deeper crisis: the obsolescence of the management approaches, business practices, and systems of production that had been only incrementally improved since the 1920s. The near collapse of the U.S. automobile business came, of course, at the hands of the Japanese. The Toyota ecosystem, for one, was capable of unheard-of levels of product variety, quality, and efficiency at the time. This powerful new business ecosystem was based on a combination of customer-focused design, concurrent engineering, flexible manufacturing, dedicated workers, and networks of suppliers, all tied together through statistically refined management practices.

Therefore, the automobile industry, as traditionally defined, found itself in a full-fledged ecological war, defending against a new wave of business ecosystems. Self-renewal proved difficult, and companies like Ford and Chrysler had nearly collapsed by the late 1970s. The superiority of Japanese approaches ultimately forced the transformation of the world automobile business into what we know today.

To extend a systematic approach to strategy, I suggest that a company be viewed not as a member of a single industry but as part of a *business ecosystem* that crosses a variety of industries. In a business ecosystem, companies co-evolve capabilities around a new innovation: they work cooperatively and competitively to support new products, satisfy customer needs, and eventually incorporate the next round of innovations.

For example, Apple Computer is the leader of an ecosystem that crosses at least four major industries: personal computers, consumer electronics, information, and communications. The Apple ecosystem encompasses an extended web of suppliers that includes Motorola and Sony and a large number of customers in various market segments.

Apple, IBM, Ford, Wal-Mart, and Merck have all been or still are the leaders of business ecosystems. While the center may shift over time, the role of the leader is valued by the rest of the community. Such leadership enables all ecosystem members to invest toward a shared future in which they anticipate profiting together.

Yet in any larger business environment, several ecosystems may vie for survival and dominance: the IBM and Apple ecosystems in personal computers, for example, or Wal-Mart and Kmart in discount retailing. In fact, it's competition among business ecosystems, not individual companies, that's largely fueling today's industrial transformation. Managers can't afford to ignore the birth of new ecosystems or the competition among those that already exist.

Whether that means investing in the right new technology, signing on suppliers to expand a growing business, developing crucial elements of value to maintain leadership, or incorporating new innovations to fend off obsolescence, executives must understand the stages that all business ecosystems pass through—and, more important, how to direct the changes.

A business ecosystem, like its biological counterpart, gradually moves from a random collection of elements to a more structured community. Think of a prairie grassland that is succeeded by stands of conifers, which in turn evolve into a more complex forest dominated by hardwoods. Business ecosystems condense out of the original swirl of capital, customer interest, and talent generated by a new innovation, just as successful species spring from the natural resources of sunlight, water, and soil nutrients.

Every business ecosystem develops in four distinct stages: birth, expansion, leadership, and self-renewal—or, if not self-renewal, death. In reality, of course, the evolutionary stages blur, and the managerial challenges of one stage often crop up in another. Yet I've observed the four stages in many companies over time, across businesses as diverse as retailing, entertainment, and pharmaceuticals. What remains the same from business to business is the process of co-evolution: the complex interplay between competitive and cooperative business strategies (see Exhibit I).

During Stage 1 of a business ecosystem, entrepreneurs focus on defining what customers want, that is, the value of a proposed new product or service and the best form for delivering it. Victory at the birth stage, in the short term, often goes to those who best define and implement this customer value proposition. Moreover, during Stage 1 of a business ecosystem, it often pays to cooperate. From the leader's standpoint, in particular, business partners help fill out the full package of value for customers. And by attracting important "follower" companies, leaders may stop them from helping other emerging ecosystems.

The rise of the personal computer is a revealing example of ecological business development. In the early 1970s, a new technology—the microprocessor—emerged with the potential to spawn vast new

Exhibit I. The evolutionary stages of a business ecosystem

	Cooperative challenges	Competitive challenges
Birth	Work with customers and suppliers to define the new value proposition around a seed innovation.	Protect your ideas from others who might be working toward defining similar offers. Tie up critical lead customers, key suppliers, and important channels.
Expansion	Bring the new offer to a large market by working with suppliers and partners to scale up supply and to achieve maximum market coverage.	Defeat alternative implementations of similar ideas. Ensure that your approach is the market standard in its class through dominating key market segments.
Leadership	Provide a compelling vision for the future that encourages suppliers and customers to work together to continue improving the complete offer.	Maintain strong bargaining power in relation to other players in the ecosystem, including key customers and valued suppliers.
Self-renewal	Work with innovators to bring new ideas to the existing ecosystem.	Maintain high barriers to entry to prevent innovators from building alternative ecosystems. Maintain high customer switching costs in order to buy time to incorporate new ideas into your own products and services.

applications and dramatically reduce the cost of computing. Yet this innovation sat dormant for several years. By 1975, hobbyist machines like the Altair and IMSAI had penetrated a narrow market. But these computers were not products that could be used by the average person.

Starting in the late 1970s, Tandy Corporation, Apple, and others introduced early versions of what would eventually become the personal computer. The seed innovation they all chose was the microprocessor, but these first designers also recognized that other products and services had to be created to bring the whole package together. These ranged from hardware components to software to services like distribution and customer support.

Apple and Tandy each had a different strategy for creating a full, rich ecosystem. Apple worked with business partners and talked about "evangelizing" to encourage co-evolution. While the company tightly controlled its basic computer design and operating system software, it encouraged independent software developers to write programs for its machine. Apple also cooperated with independent magazines, computer stores, and training institutions—and even seeded a number of school districts with Apple IIs.

Tandy, on the other hand, took a more vertically integrated approach. It attempted to buy and then own its software, ranging from the operating system to programming languages and applications like word processors. The company controlled sales, service, support and training, and market development by selling exclusively through its Radio Shack stores. At the same time, it discouraged independent magazines devoted to its TRS-80 machines. Therefore, Tandy's simpler and more tightly controlled ecosystem did not build the excitement, opportunities, and inner rivalries of Apple's, nor did it harness as much capital and talent through the participation of other companies.

Tandy's approach got the company out front fast; in 1979, it had sales of $95 million compared with Apple's $47.9 million. However, Tandy's tight control of its ecosystem ultimately led to slower growth at a time when establishing market share and a large user base was essential to success. By 1982, Apple's $583.1 million in sales had decisively passed Tandy's $466.4 million.

Meanwhile, a third business ecosystem emerged in the early days of personal computing. It never rivaled Apple's or Tandy's in size, but it did help IBM enter the fray. This third ecosystem centered around two software companies: Digital Research and Micropro. In 1977, Digital Research made its software operating system CP/M available independent of hardware. That separation allowed almost any small manufacturer to assemble components and put out a usable personal computer. Overnight, a variety of small companies entered the business, building on the same Zilog microprocessor used in the early Tandy machines.

In 1979, Micropro brought out a word processor that ran on CP/M-based machines. Wordstar was the first truly powerful word processor, and it took an important group of potential PC customers—writers and editors—by storm. Demand for CP/M machines soared, fueling the growth if not the fortunes of small companies like Morrow and Kaypro.

But during the first stage of any business ecosystem, co-evolving companies must do more than satisfy customers; a leader must also emerge to initiate a process of rapid, ongoing improvement that draws the entire community toward a grander future. In the Apple and Tandy ecosystems, the hardware companies provided such leadership by studying the market, defining new generations of functionality, and orchestrating suppliers and partners to bring improvements to market. In the CP/M ecosystem, however, the hardware companies were bedeviled by rivalry among themselves. Infighting kept down prices and profit margins, and none of the CP/M companies could afford heavy advertising programs.

In Stage 1, established companies like IBM are often better off waiting and watching carefully as a new market sorts itself out. The iterative process of trying out innovative ideas and discovering which solutions are attractive to customers is hard to accomplish in a traditional corporate culture. And the diverse experimentation that thrives in an entrepreneurial scene provides more "genetic diversity" from which the market can ultimately select the fittest offering.

Established companies can subsequently replicate successful ideas and broadcast them across a wider market. In other words, they can enter the market at Stage 2 by appropriating the developmental work of others. Meanwhile, original ecosystems that succeed, like Apple's, do so by consciously nurturing a full community of partners and suppliers right from the start.

In Stage 2, business ecosystems expand to conquer broad new territories. Just as grasses and weeds rapidly cover the bare, scorched ground left after a forest fire, some business expansions meet little resistance. But in other cases, rival ecosystems may be closely matched and choose to attack the same territory. Direct battles for market share break out. Fighting can get ugly as each ecosystem tries to exert pressure on suppliers and customers to join up.

In the end, one business ecosystem may triumph, or rival ecosystems may reach semistable accommodations. Think of a hardwood forest that borders a grassland. The zone of conflict at the boundary may shift from year to year, but it never completely wipes out either ecosystem.

In general, two conditions are necessary for Stage 2 expansion: (1) a business concept that a large number of customers will value; and (2) the potential to scale up the concept to reach this broad market. During the expansion stage, established companies can exercise enormous power in marketing and sales, as well as in the management of large-scale production and distribution, literally crushing smaller ecosystems in the process.

IBM, for example, entered the personal computer business in 1981. In contrast to its own history and culture of vertical integration, IBM followed and extended the Apple model of building a community of supporters. IBM took on partners and opened its computer architecture to outside suppliers. Moreover, it adopted a microprocessor from Intel that incorporated all of the instructions available in the Zilog microprocessor in Tandy and CP/M machines. And IBM licensed MS-DOS, a software operating system from then tiny Microsoft, which was almost a near clone of CP/M. As a result, Wordstar and other popular application programs could easily be ported over to the IBM PC.

One of the most important managerial challenges in Stage 2 is to stimulate market demand without greatly exceeding your ability to meet it. IBM certainly stimulated demand for its new machine through a combination of heavy brand advertising, distribution through Sears and other channels, and building its own network of specialty stores. By anyone's measure, IBM's approach to expanding its PC ecosystem was a major success. Its personal computing business grew from $500 million in 1982 to $5.65 billion by 1986, and IBM's ecosystem rapidly dominated the market.

However, IBM also generated much more demand than it could meet. The company maintained high prices, which encouraged others to enter the market by setting a high price umbrella under which they could thrive. Compaq, for example, became the fastest company to join the Fortune 500 based on supplying machines to meet demand in the IBM ecosystem.

IBM did its best to keep up with demand. In the early 1980s, it invested directly in several key suppliers to help it grow fast enough to meet the market. Intel, for example, received $250 million from IBM in 1983. Concerned about its image as an insensitive behemoth, as well as possible antitrust objections, IBM managers carefully assured these suppliers that the help came without any strings attached.

IBM's relationships with suppliers were basically nonexclusive. Obviously, suppliers like Intel, Microsoft, and Lotus were happy to help the success of Compaq and others because it allowed them to diversify the risk of overdependence on IBM. For its part, IBM was flush with more demand and success than it knew what to do with. Top managers didn't focus on slowing the development of clone makers and nonexclusive suppliers—or keeping crucial elements of value like the microprocessor in-house. At first, IBM didn't attack new competitors within its ecosystem through the courts, through special promotions, or by lowering its own prices.

However clear the threat from the rest of the pack appears to us now, at the time, IBM and its business partners were pleased. By 1986, the combined revenues of companies in the IBM ecosystem were approximately $12 billion, dwarfing the Apple ecosystem's revenues of approximately $2 billion. IBM's leadership also forced Tandy and essentially every other non-Apple maker of personal computers to dump their proprietary designs and offer IBM PC compatibles.

In contrast with IBM, the story of Wal-Mart's retailing ecosystem shows how top management can take the right precautions when a business is expanding (see "The Evolution of Wal-Mart: Savvy Expansion and Leadership"). In general, Stage 2 rewards fast expansion that squeezes competing ecosystems to the margin. But managers must also prepare for future leadership and leverage in the next stage. To do so, companies need to maintain careful control of customer relationships and core centers of value and innovation. Moreover, they must develop relationships with their suppliers that constrain these followers from becoming leaders in Stage 3.

The Evolution of Wal-Mart: Savvy Expansion and Leadership

An ecological analysis of Wal-Mart reveals how a relatively small company, starting in a rural area of the United States, could turn its original isolation to advantage by creating a complete business ecosystem. Wal-Mart developed and continues to refine an offer that customers find nearly irresistible: low prices on a variety of brands as diverse as Gitano jeans and Yardman lawn mowers. Moreover, CEO Sam Walton managed the company's expansion superbly and increased bargaining power during the leadership stage.

The Birth of Discounting. In the early 1960s, Kmart, Wal-Mart, and other discounters recognized that the Main Street five-and-dime was giving way to the variety store. And variety stores, in turn, were threatened by the large discount store. In order to buy a wide range of goods at low prices in one location, customers were increasingly willing to get into cars and drive to malls or other non–Main Street locations.

Kmart and Wal-Mart appeared on the discount scene at about the same time. The Kmart stores were actually owned by old-style S.S. Kresge, which reinvented itself as a suburb-oriented discount retailer, with big stores located near existing malls and towns of more than 50,000 people. Kmart stores carried items aimed at the lower end of suburban tastes.

By the late 1960s Wal-Mart had worked out the basic structure of its own business ecosystem: Wal-Mart stores, which supplied a variety of well-known brands, were located in relatively sparsely populated areas. The company went into towns of 5,000 people, particularly where several of these towns might be served by one store. Wal-Mart products were up to 15% cheaper than those available in "mom-and-pop" stores.

While the original Wal-Mart locations could support one store, the customer population wasn't large enough to maintain two rival discounters. Thus once Wal-Mart established a store in a particular area and had beaten back weak local retailers, it was seldom threatened with future local competition from other discounters, including Kmart.

Expansion: Planning for a Chokehold. Once its business strategy was up and running in a number of discount stores in the American South and Mid-West, Wal-Mart's top executives concentrated on developing organizational capabilities that would let it scale up successfully. They were obsessed with three things:

- Building a set of incentives that would ensure employee commitment to local stores, which led to a complex system of training, oversight, bonuses, and stock-purchase plans for workers.

- Managing communication and control of a network of remotely located stores, which required close monitoring of a carefully drawn set of measures that were transmitted daily to Wal-Mart headquarters in Bentonville, Arkansas.

- Setting up an efficient distribution system that allowed for joint purchasing, shared facilities, systematic ordering, and store-level distribution of a large number of different goods. This third obsession ultimately became Wal-

Mart's trademark hub-and-spoke distribution system: warehouses served constellations of stores located no more than a day's drive from the center.

In 1970 Wal-Mart went public to raise funds for its expansion. That same year, the company built its first hub-and-spoke distribution center—embarking on a strategy of targeting a large geographic area, setting up a distribution center, and then populating the area with as many stores as the territory would support. Wal-Mart not only filled the needs of customers in small towns but also saturated entire regions, making it uneconomical for competitors to enter as either distributors or local store owners.

The number of Wal-Mart stores grew rapidly, from 32 in 1970 to 195 in 1978—when the first fully automated distribution center opened—to 551 in 1983—when Wal-Mart launched its own satellite, creating a communication network to keep in daily touch with its now far-flung empire.

Leadership: Building Bargaining Power. By 1984, Wal-Mart's managerial agenda changed. What was in the birth and expansion stages a race to develop systems and conquer territory now became a concerted effort to build bargaining power. As the leaders of a highly successful and visible business ecosystem, Wal-Mart managers worked on continuing to assert the company's vision over other community members, including suppliers like Procter & Gamble, Rubbermaid, and Helene Curtis Industries.

First, Wal-Mart resisted the temptation to charge higher prices in the markets and regions it dominated. Instead, top managers still viewed each market as "contestable"—as a potential opening for rivals if Wal-Mart ceased to give the maximum possible value to customers. Continued customer leadership, in turn, enhanced the Wal-Mart brand and further cemented the company's place in the minds and buying habits of consumers. Wal-Mart's system of "everyday low prices," in which there's no need for weekly sales or special promotions, has now become a standard in discount retailing.

Second, Wal-Mart—now a very large and powerful channel to customers—started putting heavy pressure on suppliers to keep their prices down. Moreover, Wal-Mart compelled its suppliers to set up cross-company distribution systems to attain maximum manufacturing efficiency. For example, in 1987, Wal-Mart and Procter & Gamble reached an unprecedented accord to work together through extensive electronic ordering and information sharing between the companies. In return, Wal-Mart gives better payment terms than the rest of the retailing industry: on average, Wal-Mart pays its suppliers within 29 days; Kmart within 45 days.

Third, Wal-Mart continued to invest in and enhance its own fundamental economies of scale and scope in distribution. By the leadership stage, distribution had become the crucial ecological component of the Wal-Mart ecosystem. In fact, Wal-Mart's distribution chokehold has allowed the ecosystem as a whole to triumph over others like Kmart's. While suppliers, big and small, may chafe under Wal-Mart's heavy hand, it's also clear that most of them need this particular leader to survive. Exhibit II is a testament to the company's dominance and bargaining power in the leadership stage.

Finally, Wal-Mart has extended its reach into adjacent territories and ecosystems. In 1983, Wal-Mart entered the membership discount market with its Sam's Club, which by 1992 included 208 clubs that contributed over $9.4 billion in revenues. In 1990, Wal-Mart incorporated another ecosystem by acquiring McLane Company, the nation's largest distributor to the convenience store industry. McLane, under Wal-Mart's control, now serves about 30,000 retail stores, including 18,000 convenience stores. And in 1992, Wal-Mart also acquired the distribution and food processing divisions of Southland Corporation. Southland operates a large chain of 7-Eleven convenience stores, and this acquisition added as many as 5,000 more 7-Eleven stores to the McLane/Wal-Mart customer base.

While the lion and antelope are both part of a healthy savanna ecosystem, they also struggle with each other to determine to what extent each species expands within it. Similarly, in business ecosystems, two conditions contribute to the onset of the leadership struggles that are the hallmark of Stage 3. First, the ecosystem must have strong enough growth and profitability to be considered worth fighting over. Second, the structure of the value-adding components and processes that are central to the business ecosystem must become reasonably stable.

This stability allows suppliers to target particular elements of value and to compete in contributing them. It encourages members of the ecosystem to consider expanding by taking over activities from those closest to them in the value chain. Most of all, it diminishes the dependence of the whole ecosystem on the original leader. It's in Stage 3 that companies become preoccupied with standards, interfaces, "the modular organization," and customer-supplier relations.

For example, by the mid-1980s, the IBM PC technical architecture defined the de facto business structure for the personal computer business as a whole. Virtually any company could figure out how to make components and services that would dovetail effectively with other elements of the PC ecosystem. Of course, this was a mixed

Exhibit II. Wal-Mart takes off

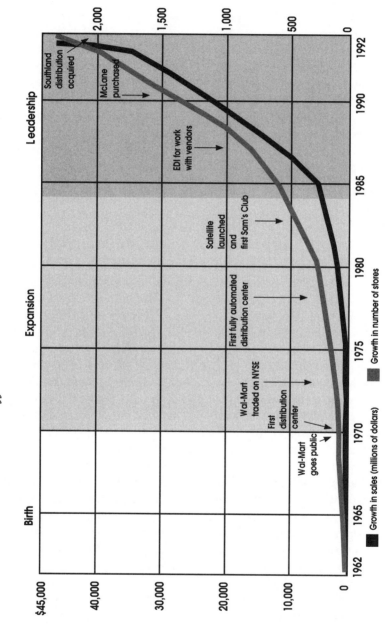

Birth

Expansion

Leadership

Wal-Mart
goes public

First
distribution
center

Wal-Mart
traded on NYSE

First fully automated
distribution center

Satellite
launched
and
first Sam's Club

EDI for work
with vendors

McLane
purchased

Southland
distribution
acquired

Growth in sales (millions of dollars)

Growth in number of stores

blessing for IBM. The openness of its computer architecture encouraged third parties to support it, dramatically accelerating the ecosystem's growth. Yet this same openness decreased the dependence of suppliers on IBM's leadership, laying the foundations for Stage 3 "clone wars."

Lotus, Intel, Microsoft, and other suppliers started working together to determine common standards for hardware and software, with and without IBM's involvement. Other ecosystem members welcomed this new leadership since it seemed fairer to suppliers and more innovative than IBM's.

Belatedly, IBM sought to enforce its patents against clone makers, seeking licenses from major players—one of the many strategies that failed. A grim milestone of sorts was achieved in 1989 when clone shipments and product shipments from other smaller companies bypassed those of major personal computer manufacturers. Thus IBM was relegated to competing head-on with myriad "box makers." IBM still retained a large share of the market but only through offering extensive discounts to large volume purchasers.

Which brings us to the new structure of today's "Microsoft-Intel" ecosystem: Microsoft, with gross margins estimated at 80%; Intel, with gross margins of 40% and 50% on its new chips; and IBM's PC business with margins of about 30%, a far cry from the 70% to 90% margins in its mainframe business.

In Stage 3, bargaining power comes from having something the ecosystem needs and being the only practical source. Sometimes this sole-source status can be established contractually or through patent protection. But fundamentally, it depends on constant innovation—on creating value that is critical to the whole ecosystem's continued price/performance improvement. During expansion, IBM didn't find a way to keep innovating or even to achieve economies of scale. Power shifted to chips and software, areas in which IBM did not excel.

Now both Intel and Microsoft have bargaining power through control of a critical component. Each is a strong leader and plays the role of *central ecological contributor.* Central contributors maintain the much-coveted chokehold within a business ecosystem. In short, other members can't live without them. This central position enables them to bargain for a higher share of the total value produced by the ecosystem. For example, Intel and Microsoft have gross margins that are almost double the average for their whole ecosystem.

Central contributor status is maintained in part by the investments others have made in being followers. Hardware and software vendors have made heavy investments in Microsoft operating systems and in applications that work with Intel chips. Switching to other vendors would be risky and expensive; if possible, other co-evolving companies don't want the burden of learning how to work with a new leader.

In addition, central companies reinforce their roles by making important innovative contributions to the performance of the ecosystem as a whole. Intel, for instance, has enormous scale advantages in the fabrication of microprocessors. Its chip volumes allow it to work out fabrication-process advances sooner than other chip vendors. Ironically, IBM held a license to manufacture Intel-designed microprocessors. With its large volumes during the expansion stage, IBM could have been the one taking the fabrication and price/performance lead in chips—and it could have denied Intel the scale to keep up.

Finally, followers value a central contributor because of its grip on customers. End users are drawn to Microsoft operating systems and Intel chips because so many software applications are available for them. In turn, developers keep turning out such applications because they know Microsoft and Intel are customer gateways.

To some extent, these two companies achieved their current central position by being in the right place at the right time—that is, by serving IBM. Intel and Microsoft clearly appreciate what they have now and are working effectively to maintain their central contributions. Still, some companies like Wal-Mart have systematically gone about building a strong ecosystem, one that guarantees a leading role for themselves.

In any case, for dominant companies, the expansion and leadership stages of an ecosystem can make or break them. In Stage 3, lead producers must extend control by continuing to shape future directions and the investments of key customers and suppliers. And for healthy profits, any company in the ecosystem—leader or follower—must maintain bargaining power over other members.

Stage 4 of a business ecosystem occurs when mature business communities are threatened by rising new ecosystems and innovations. Alternatively, a community might undergo the equivalent of an earthquake: sudden new environmental conditions that include changes in government regulations, customer buying patterns, or macroeconomic conditions. Moreover, these two factors reinforce each other. An altered environment is often more hospitable to new or formerly marginal business ecosystems.

In fact, how a dominant company deals with the threat of obsolescence is the ultimate challenge. Just because Microsoft and Intel are leaders now doesn't mean their current ecosystem is immortal. Nor does it mean that Microsoft NT ("New Technology" operating software) will form the basis for its successor. After all, Novell and UNIX Systems Laboratories have merged and will put forth a new generation of software, looking to strengthen a new ecosystem. Both Hewlett-Packard and Sun Microsystems remain strongly entrenched. And Motorola is now manufacturing a new generation microprocessor to be sold by both IBM and Apple, along with a jointly developed new software operating system.

Leading successive generations of innovation is clearly crucial to an ecosystem's long-term success and its ability to renew itself. Today's pharmaceutical companies provide some interesting insights into three general approaches to self-renewal, which can be used alone or in combination: (1) dominant companies can seek to slow the growth of a new ecosystem; (2) they can try to incorporate new innovations into their own ecosystems; or (3) they can fundamentally restructure themselves to try coping with a new reality.

During the past few decades, pharmaceutical companies have operated under a relatively consistent, if largely implicit, social compact with government regulators. In exchange for investing heavily in product and process innovation, drug companies have been allowed comparatively high margins and protection from competition through patent laws and lengthy approval processes. Traditional pharmaceutical ecosystems, therefore, have evolved around three major functions: R&D, testing and approval management, and marketing and sales. Each of these functions is expensive, hard to perfect, and thus presents a barrier to new competitors. In the past, these functions were carried out within large, vertically integrated companies that did not, until recently, consider themselves networked organizations.

In the 1980s, generic drug manufacturers that specialized in producing off-patent drugs posed a threat to the established pharmaceutical houses. The dominant companies responded by blocking these rival ecosystems in order to minimize their expansion. This included lobbying to slow generic-drug enabling legislation and to reinforce the natural conservatism of the U.S. Food and Drug Administration. Well-funded marketing and sales efforts convinced thousands of individual physicians to continue prescribing mostly branded drugs. While the generic drug manufacturers were able to establish alternative ecosystems, their penetration of the market has been held to about 30%, with little price cutting by the dominant companies.

Meanwhile, a variety of small biotechnology start-ups posed an even greater threat to the traditional pharmaceutical powerhouses. In general, biotech researchers concentrate on isolating complex substances that already exist in the human body and finding ways to manufacture them—for example, human insulin and human growth hormone. As many as one biotech try in ten may prove successful, which keeps the R&D cost down to between $100 million and $150 million per marketable product. Compare this with the traditional pharmaceutical average of 10,000 chemical tries to identify one marketable drug—and R&D costs of $250 million to $350 million per product.

Many of the founders of and investors in biotechnology start-ups believed that low R&D costs would provide the basis for creating whole new business ecosystems that could compete with the established drug companies. For example, Genentech, one of the pioneering biotech companies, clearly intended to establish itself as a full competitor. By the mid-1980s, Genentech had five products in the market and was marketing three itself. It licensed its first two products: alpha-interferon to Hoffmann-La Roche and insulin to Eli Lilly. Using the cash from these licenses, Genentech sought to manufacture and market human growth hormone and tissue plasminogen activator on its own. Yet in 1990, 60% of Genentech was sold to Hoffmann-La Roche for $2.1 billion. A similar fate has befallen almost all of the original biotech companies.

In essence, these companies misjudged the difficulties of mastering the testing and approval process. The first biotech managers bet on the assumption that testing and approval would, like R&D, be less expensive and problematic than it was for their traditional competitors. Since biotech products were existing molecules already resident in the human body, these products would presumably require much less testing than synthetic chemical compounds. However, the FDA approval process in the United States, which grants access to the most important market worldwide, has not borne this out. From 1981 to 1991, only 12 biotech products were approved for general marketing.

Strapped for cash and unable to raise much more from their original investors, most biotech companies ended the 1980s in no position to lead their own business ecosystems. Biotech managers and investors were attracted to alliances with traditional companies and thus merged new business ecosystems with powerful existing ones. In turn, dominant companies like Merck, Eli Lilly, and Bristol-Myers began to think like business ecosystem builders. In order to snap up licenses, patents, and talent to strengthen their own R&D, these companies affiliated themselves with the biotech companies rather than simply blocking their new rivals.

Of course, the leaders of a mature business ecosystem sometimes have no choice but to undertake profound structural and cultural changes. Pharmaceutical ecosystems now face new threats and a profoundly altered environment. The social compact to protect drug company profits in exchange for product and process innovation is breaking down. The public, government, and corporations all want health care costs reduced. Drug company leaders see lean times ahead as they confront the possibility of price and profit caps, as well as consolidated purchasing of drugs by HMOs and government agencies.

Responding to this environmental shift will force changes across all major functions. Companies will probably have to limit R&D spending and focus it carefully. Managers are likely to design a testing and approval process that highlights not only efficacy but also cost/benefit performance of new treatments. Finally, companies will probably market and sell less directly to individual physicians, focusing instead on negotiations with experts who represent third-party payers and government.

But despite the difficulties of such a complex business environment, managers can design longevity into an ecosystem. During the expansion and leadership stages, for instance, companies can work hard to micro-segment their markets, creating close, supportive ties with customers. These customers will then remain committed to a particular ecosystem long enough for its members to incorporate the benefits of new approaches.

And visionary executives like Merck's Roy Vagelos can sometimes lead an ecosystem so that it rapidly and effectively embraces anticipated developments—be they new technologies, regulatory openings, or consumer trends. Ultimately, there is no substitute for eternal vigilance. As Intel's Andy Grove noted recently, "Only the paranoid survive."

Clearly, pharmaceutical companies—and any other venture threatened by continual innovations—can no longer allow their particular ecosystems to evolve without direction. Using an ecological approach, executives can start making strategic changes by systematically questioning their company's current situation: Is the company linked with the very best suppliers and partners? Is the company betting its future on the most promising new ideas? Are suppliers leading the way in commercializing innovation? Over the long run, how will the company maintain sufficient bargaining power and autonomy to guarantee good financial returns?

Examining a company's key competitors from a business ecological point of view is also important: What hidden web of customer and supplier relationships have competitors worked to develop? Who do they depend on for ideas and supplier support? What are the nature and benefits of those relationships? How do these compare with what the company has?

And to prepare the ground for organizational breakthroughs, managers need to consider how the work of their company might be radically different: What seed innovations might make current businesses obsolete? What would it take to catalyze a cluster of ideas into a new and vital business ecosystem? What type of community would be required to bring these new ideas to the widest possible market?

Asking these questions, let alone acting on the answers, has become a difficult necessity for all companies. Superficially, competition among business ecosystems is a fight for market share. But below the surface, these new competitive struggles are fights over who will direct the future.

Yet it's precisely in the role of conscious direction that a strictly biological metaphor is no longer useful. Business communities, unlike biological communities of co-evolving organisms, are social systems. And social systems are made up of real people who make decisions; the larger patterns are maintained by a complex network of choices, which depend, at least in part, on what participants are aware of. As Gregory Bateson noted, if you change the ideas in a social system, you change the system itself.

I anticipate that as an ecological approach to management becomes more common—as an increasing number of executives become conscious of co-evolution and its consequences—the pace of business change itself will accelerate. Executives whose horizons are bounded by traditional industry perspectives will find themselves missing the real challenges and opportunities that face their companies. Shareholders and directors, sensing the new reality, will eventually remove them. Or, in light of the latest management shifts, they may have already done so.

Unfortunately for employees and investors, this often occurs only after the companies involved have been deeply damaged. Companies that once dominated their industries, as traditionally defined, have been blindsided by new competition. Whether such companies can find the appropriate leadership to renew the ecosystems on which their future depends remains an open question. If they cannot, they'll be supplanted by other companies, in other business ecosystems, that will expand and lead over the next few years.

For the individuals caught up in these ecosystem struggles, the stakes are high. As a society, we must find ways of helping members of dying ecosystems get into more vital ones while avoiding the temptation of propping up the failed ecosystems themselves. From an ecological perspective, it matters not which particular ecosystems stay alive; rather, it's only essential that competition among them is fierce and fair—and that the fittest survive.

15
Good Communication That Blocks Learning

Chris Argyris

Twenty-first-century corporations will find it hard to survive, let alone flourish, unless they get better work from their employees. This does not necessarily mean harder work or more work. What it does necessarily mean is employees who've learned to take active responsibility for their own behavior, develop and share first-rate information about their jobs, and make good use of genuine empowerment to shape lasting solutions to fundamental problems.

This is not news. Most executives understand that tougher competition will require more effective learning, broader empowerment, and greater commitment from everyone in the company. Moreover, they understand that the key to better performance is better communication. For 20 years or more, business leaders have used a score of communication tools—focus groups, organizational surveys, management-by-walking-around, and others—to convey and to gather the information needed to bring about change.

What *is* news is that these familiar techniques, used correctly, will actually inhibit the learning and communication that twenty-first-century corporations will require not just of managers but of every employee. For years, I have watched corporate leaders talking to subordinates at every level in order to find out what actually goes on in their companies and then help it go on more effectively. What I have observed is that the methods these executives use to tackle relatively simple problems actually prevent them from getting the kind of deep information, insightful behavior, and productive change they need to cope with the much more complex problem of organizational renewal.

Years ago, when corporations still wanted employees who did only what they were told, employee surveys and walk-around management were appropriate and effective tools. They can still produce useful information about routine issues like cafeteria service and parking privileges, and they can still generate valuable quantitative data in support of programs like total quality management. What they do *not* do is get people to reflect on their work and behavior. They do not encourage individual accountability. And they do not surface the kinds of deep and potentially threatening or embarrassing information that can motivate learning and produce real change.

Let me give an example of what I mean. Not long ago, I worked with a company conducting a TQM initiative. TQM has been highly successful at cutting unnecessary costs, so successful that many companies have raised it to the status of a management philosophy. In this particular case, a TQM consultant worked with top management to carry out a variety of surveys and group meetings to help 40 supervisors identify nine areas in which they could tighten procedures and reduce costs. The resulting initiative met its goals one month early and saved more money than management had anticipated. The CEO was so elated that he treated the entire team to a champagne dinner to celebrate what was clearly a victory for everyone involved.

I had regular conversations with the supervisors throughout the implementation, and I was struck by two often-repeated comments. First, the supervisors told me several times how easy it had been to identify the nine target areas since they knew in advance where the worst inefficiencies might be found. Second, they complained again and again that fixing the nine areas was long overdue, that it was high time management took action. As one supervisor put it, "Thank God for TQM!"

I asked several supervisors how long they had known about the nine problem areas, and their responses ranged from three to five years. I then asked them why, if they'd known about the problems, they'd never taken action themselves. "Why 'Thank God for TQM'?" I said. "Why not 'Thank God for the supervisors'?"

None of the supervisors hesitated to answer these questions. They cited the blindness and timidity of management. They blamed interdepartmental competitiveness verging on warfare. They said the culture of the company made it unacceptable to get others into trouble for the sake of correcting problems. In every explanation, the responsibility for fixing the nine problem areas belonged to someone else.

The supervisors were loyal, honest managers. The blame lay elsewhere.

What was really going on in this company? To begin with, we can identify two different problems. Cost reduction is one. The other is a group of employees who stand passively by and watch inefficiencies develop and persevere. TQM produces the simple learning necessary to effect a solution to the first problem. But TQM will not prevent a recurrence of the second problem or cause the supervisors to wonder why they never acted. To understand why this is so, we need to know more about how learning takes place and about at least two mechanisms that keep it from taking place at all.

As I have emphasized in my previous articles on learning in the workplace, learning occurs in two forms: single-loop and double-loop. Single-loop learning asks a one-dimensional question to elicit a one-dimensional answer. My favorite example is a thermostat, which measures ambient temperature against a standard setting and turns the heat source on or off accordingly. The whole transaction is binary.

Double-loop learning takes an additional step or, more often than not, several additional steps. It turns the question back on the questioner. It asks what the media call follow-ups. In the case of the thermostat, for instance, double-loop learning would wonder whether the current setting was actually the most effective temperature at which to keep the room and, if so, whether the present heat source was the most effective means of achieving it. A double-loop process might also ask why the current setting was chosen in the first place. In other words, double-loop learning asks questions not only about objective facts but also about the reasons and motives behind those facts.

Here is a simple illustration of the difference between these two kinds of learning: A CEO who had begun to practice his own form of management-by-walking-around learned from his employees that the company inhibited innovation by subjecting every new idea to more than 275 separate checks and sign-offs. He promptly appointed a task force to look at this situation, and it eliminated 200 of the obstacles. The result was a higher innovation rate.

This may sound like a successful managerial intervention. The CEO discovers a counterproductive process and, with the cooperation of others, produces dramatic improvement. Yet I would call it a case of single-loop learning. It addresses a difficulty but ignores a more fundamental problem. A more complete diagnosis—that is to say, a double-loop approach to this situation—would require the CEO to ask the employees who told him about the sign-offs some tougher questions about company culture and their own behavior. For example, "How long have you known about the 275 required sign-offs?" Or "What goes on in this company that prevented you from questioning these practices and getting them corrected or eliminated?"

Why didn't the CEO ask these questions of the supervisor? And why didn't the 40 supervisors ask these questions of themselves? There are two closely related mechanisms at work here—one social, the other psychological.

The social reason that the CEO did not dig deeper is that doing so might have been seen as putting people on the spot. Unavoidably, digging deeper would have uncovered the employees' collusion with the inefficient process. Their motives were probably quite decent— they didn't want to open Pandora's box, didn't want to be negative. But their behavior—and the behavior of the CEO in ignoring this dimension of the problem—combined with everyone's failure to examine his or her individual behavior and blocked the kind of learning that is crucial to organizational effectiveness.

In the name of positive thinking, in other words, managers often censor what everyone needs to say and hear. For the sake of "morale" and "considerateness," they deprive employees and themselves of the opportunity to take responsibility for their own behavior by learning to understand it. Because double-loop learning depends on questioning one's own assumptions and behavior, this apparently benevolent strategy is actually *anti*learning. Admittedly, being considerate and positive can contribute to the solution of single-loop problems like cutting costs. But it will never help people figure out why they lived with problems for years on end, why they covered up those problems, why they covered up the cover-up, why they were so good at pointing to the responsibility of others and so slow to focus on their own. The 40 supervisors said it was high time that management took steps. None of them asked why they themselves had never even drawn management's attention to nine areas of waste and inefficiency.

What we see here is managers using socially "upbeat" behavior to inhibit learning. What we do not see, at least not readily, is why anyone should want to inhibit learning. The reason lies in a set of deeper and more complex psychological motives.

Consider again the story of the 40 supervisors. TQM's rigorous, linear reasoning solves a set of important, single-loop problems. But while we see some effective single-loop learning, no double-loop learning occurs at all. Instead, the moment the important problems involve potential threat or embarrassment, rigorous reasoning goes right out the window and *defensive reasoning* takes over. Note how the supervisors deftly sidestep all responsibility and defend themselves against the charge of inaction—or worse, collusion—by blaming others. In fact, what I call defensive reasoning serves no purpose except self-protection, though the people who use it rarely acknowledge that they are protecting themselves. It is the group, the department, the organization that they are protecting, in the name of being positive. They believe themselves to be using the kind of rigorous thinking employed in TQM, which identifies problems, gathers objective data, postulates causes, tests explanations, and derives corrective action, all along relatively scientific lines. But the supervisors' actual techniques—gathering data selectively, postulating only causes that do not threaten themselves, testing explanations in ways that are sloppy and self-serving—are a parody of scientific method. The supervisors are not protecting others; they are blaming them. They have learned this procedure carefully over time, supported at each step by defensive organizational rationalizations like "caring" and "thoughtfulness."

The reason the supervisors fail to question their own rather remarkable behavior—the reason they so instinctively and thoroughly avoid double-loop learning—is psychological. It has to do with the mental models that we all develop early in life for dealing with emotional or threatening issues.

In the process of growing up, all of us learn and warehouse master programs for dealing with difficult situations. These programs are sets of rules we use to design our own actions and interpret the actions of others. We retrieve them whenever we need to diagnose a problem or invent or size up a solution. Without them, we'd have to start from scratch each time we faced a challenge.

One of the puzzling things about these mental models is that when the issues we face are embarrassing or threatening, the master programs we actually use are rarely the ones we think we use. Each of us has what I call an *espoused theory of action* based on principles and precepts that fit our intellectual backgrounds and commitments. But most of us have quite a different *theory-in-use* to which we resort in moments of stress. And very few of us are aware of the contradiction between the two. In short, most of us are consistently inconsistent in the way we act.

Espoused theories differ widely, but most theories-in-use have the same set of four governing values. All of us design our behavior in order to remain in unilateral control, to maximize winning and minimize losing, to suppress negative feelings, and to be as rational as possible, by which we mean laying out clear-cut goals and then evaluating our own behavior on the basis of whether or not we've achieved them.

The purpose of this strategy is to avoid vulnerability, risk, embarrassment, and the appearance of incompetence. In other words, it is a deeply defensive strategy and a recipe for ineffective learning. We might even call it a recipe for antilearning, because it helps us avoid reflecting on the counterproductive consequences of our own behavior. Theories-in-use assume a world that prizes unilateral control and winning above all else, and in that world, we focus primarily on controlling others and on making sure that we are not ourselves controlled. If any reflection does occur, it is in the service of winning and controlling, not of opening ourselves to learning.

Defensive strategies discourage reflection in another way as well. Because we practice them most of our lives, we are all highly skilled at carrying them out. Skilled actions are second nature; we rarely reflect on what we take for granted.

In studies of more than 6,000 people, I have found this kind of defensive theory-in-use to be universal, with no measurable difference by country, age, sex, ethnic identity, education, wealth, power, or experience. All over the world, in every kind of business and organization, in every kind of crisis and dilemma, the principles of defensive reasoning encourage people to leave their own behavior unexamined and to avoid any objective test of their premises and conclusions.

As if this individual defensive reasoning were not enough of a problem, genuine learning in organizations is inhibited by a second universal phenomenon that I call *organizational defensive routines*. These consist of all the policies, practices, and actions that prevent human beings from having to experience embarrassment or threat and, at the same time, prevent them from examining the nature and causes of that embarrassment or threat.

Take face-saving. To work, it must be unacknowledged. If you tell your subordinate Fred that you are saving his face, you have defeated your own purpose. What you do tell Fred is a fiction about the success of his own decision and a lie about your reasons for rescinding it. What's more, if Fred correctly senses the mixed message, he will almost certainly say nothing.

The logic here, as in all organizational defensive routines, is unmistakable: send a mixed message ("Your decision was a good one, and I'm overruling it"); pretend it is not mixed ("You can be proud of your contribution"); make the mixed message and the pretense undiscussable ("I feel good about this outcome, and I'm sure you do too"); and, finally, make the undiscussability undiscussable ("Now that I've explained everything to your satisfaction, is there anything *else* you'd like to talk about?").

Defensive reasoning occurs when individuals make their premises and inferences tacit, then draw conclusions that cannot be tested except by the tenets of this tacit logic. Nothing could be more detrimental to organizational learning than this process of elevating individual defensive tactics to an organizational routine.

Yet whenever managers are trying to get at the truth about problems that are embarrassing or threatening, they are likely to stumble into the same set of predictable pitfalls. Asked to examine their own behavior or the behavior of subordinates, people in this situation are likely:

- To reason defensively and to interact with others who are reasoning defensively;
- To get superficial, single-loop responses that lead to superficial, single-loop solutions;
- To reinforce the organizational defensive routines that inhibit access to valid information and genuine learning;
- To be unaware of their own defenses because these are so skilled and automatic; and
- To be unaware that they are producing any of these consequences, or, if they *are* aware of defensiveness, to see it only in others.

Given all these built-in barriers to self-understanding and self-examination under threatening conditions, it is a wonder that organizational learning takes place at all. It is an even greater wonder when we realize that many of the forms of communication that management works so hard to perfect actually reinforce those barriers. Yet this is exactly what they do.

We have seen a couple of examples of management's "benevolent" censorship of true but negative messages. In addition, we have looked at the psychological mechanisms that lead employees, supervisors, managers, and executives to engage in personal and collective defensive routines. The question we still have to answer is precisely how modern corporate communications succeed in actually contributing to this censorship and these defensive routines.

They do so in two explicit ways. First, they create a bias against personal learning and commitment in the way they parcel out roles and responsibilities in every survey, dialogue, and conversation. Second, they open a door to defensive reasoning—and close one on individual self-awareness—in the way they continuously emphasize extrinsic as opposed to intrinsic motivation.

First, consider the way roles and responsibilities are assigned in manager-employee (or leader-subordinate) conversations, interviews, and surveys. There seem to be two rules. Rule number one is that employees are to be truthful and forthcoming about the world they work in, about norms, procedures, and the strengths and weaknesses of their superiors. All other aspects of their role in the life of the organization—their goals, feelings, failings, and conflicted motives—are taken for granted and remain unexamined. Rule number two is that top-level managers, who play an intensely scrutinized role in the life of the company, are to assume virtually all responsibility for employee well-being and organizational success. Employees must tell the truth as they see it; leaders must modify their own and the company's behavior. In other words, employees educate, and managers act.

Take the case of Acme, a large, multinational energy company with 6,000 employees. Under increasing competitive pressure, the company was forced to downsize, and to no one's surprise, morale was failing fast. To learn as much as possible about its own shortcomings and how to correct them, Acme management designed and conducted an employee survey with the help of experts, and 95% of employees responded. Of those responding, 75% agreed on five positive points:

- They were proud to work for Acme.
- Their job satisfaction was very high.
- They found their immediate supervisors fair and technically competent.
- They believed management was concerned for their welfare.
- They felt competent to perform their own jobs.

Some 65% of the respondents also indicated some concerns:

- They were skeptical about management's capacity to take initiative, communicate candidly, and act effectively.
- They described Acme's corporate culture as one of blame.
- They complained that managers, while espousing empowerment, were strongly attached to their own unilateral control.

The CEO read the first set of findings to mean that employees were basically satisfied and loyal. He saw the second set as a list of problems that he must make a serious effort to correct. And so the CEO replaced several top managers and arranged for the reeducation of the whole management team, including himself and his direct reports. He announced that Acme would no longer tolerate a culture of blame. He introduced training programs to make managers more forthright and better able to take initiative. And he promised to place greater emphasis on genuine empowerment.

The CEO's logic went like this: My employees will identify the problems. I'll fix them by creating a new vision, defining new practices and policies, and selecting a top management team genuinely committed to them. Change will inevitably follow.

I think most managers would call this a success story. If we dig deeper, however, we see a pattern I've observed hundreds of times. Underneath the CEO's aggressive action, important issues have been bypassed, and the bypass has been covered up.

When the CEO took his new team on a five-day retreat to develop the new strategy and plan its implementation, he invited me to come along. In the course of the workshop, I asked each participant to write a simple case in a format I have found to be a powerful tool in predicting how executives will deal with difficult issues during implementation. The method also reveals contradictions between what the executives say and what they do and highlights their awareness of these discrepancies.

I asked each member of the team to write one or two sentences describing one important barrier to the new strategy and another three or four sentences telling how they would overcome that barrier. Then I asked them to split the rest of the page in half. On one side, they were to write an actual or imagined dialogue with a subordinate about the issue in question. On the other side, they were to note any unsaid or unsayable thoughts or feelings they might have about this conversation. I asked them to continue this script for several pages. When they were finished, the group as a whole discussed each case at some length, and we recorded the discussions. The ability to replay key sections made it easier for the participants to score themselves on candor, forthrightness, and the extent to which their comments and behavior encouraged genuine employee commitment—the three values that the CEO had directed the executives to foster.

All of the executives chose genuinely important issues around resistance to change. But all of them dealt with the resistance they expected from subordinates by easing in, covering up, and avoiding candor and plain speaking. They did so in the name of minimizing subordinates' defensiveness and in hopes of getting them to buy into change. The implicit logic behind their scripts went something like this:

- Hide your fears about the other person's likely resistance to change. Cover this fear with persistent positiveness. Pretend the two of you agree, especially when you know you don't.
- Deal with resistant responses by stressing the problem rather than the resistance. Be positive. Keep this strategy a secret.
- If this approach doesn't work, make it clear that you won't take no for an answer. After all, you're the boss.

Imagine this kind of logic applied to sensitive issues in hundreds of conversations with employees. It's not hard to guess what the response will be, and it certainly isn't buy-in.

What happened to candor, forthrightness, and commitment building? All the executives failed to walk their talk, and all were unaware of their own inconsistency. When I pointed out the gap between action and intention, most saw it at once. Most were surprised that they hadn't seen it before. Most were quick to recognize inconsistency in others, but their lack of awareness with regard to their own inconsistency was systematic.

I know of only one way to get at these inconsistencies, and that is to focus on them. In the Acme case, the CEO managed to ignore the fact that the survey results didn't compute: on the one hand, employees said they were proud to work for the company and described management as caring; on the other, they doubted management's candor and competence. How could they hold both views? How could they be proud to work for a company whose managers were ineffective and inconsistent?

The CEO did not stop to explore any of these contradictions before embarking on corrective action. Had he done so, he might have discovered that the employees felt strong job satisfaction precisely *because* management never asked them to accept personal responsibility for Acme's poor competitive performance. Employees could safely focus their skepticism on top management because they had learned to depend on top management for their welfare. They claimed to value empowerment when in reality they valued dependence. They claimed commitment to the company when in reality they were committed only to the principle that management should make all the tough decisions, guarantee their employment, and pay them fairly. This logic made sense to employees, but it was *not* the kind of commitment that management had in mind.

None of these issues was ever discussed with employees, and none was raised in the leadership workshops. No effort was made to explore the concept of loyalty that permitted, indeed encouraged, managers to think one thing and say another. No attempt was made to help employees understand the role they played in the "culture of blame" that they'd named in the survey as one of their chief concerns. Above all, no one tried to untangle the defensive logic that contributed so mightily to these inconsistencies and that so badly needed critical examination. In fact, when I asked the management team why they had not discussed these questions, one person told me, "Frankly, until you started asking these questions, it just didn't occur to us. I see your point, but trying to talk to our people about this could be awfully messy. We're really trying to be *positive* here, and this would just stir things up."

The Acme story is a very common one: lots of energy is expended with little lasting progress. Employee surveys like the one Acme conducted—and like most other forms of leader-subordinate communication—have a fundamentally antimanagement bias whenever they deal with double-loop issues. They encourage employees *not* to reflect on their own behavior and attitudes. By assigning all the responsibility for fixing problems to management, they encourage managers *not* to relinquish the top-down, command-and-control mind-set that prevents empowerment.

The employees at Acme, like the 40 supervisors who were wined and dined for their TQM accomplishments, will continue to do what's asked of them as long as they feel adequately rewarded. They will follow the rules, but they will not take initiative, they will not take risks, and they are very unlikely to engage in double-loop learning. In short, they will not adopt the new behaviors and frames of reference so critical to keeping their companies competitive.

Over the last few years, I have come in contact with any number of companies struggling with this transition from command-and-control hierarchy to employee empowerment and organizational learning, and every one of them is its own worst enemy. Managers embrace the language of intrinsic motivation but fail to see how firmly mired in the old extrinsic world their communications actually are. This is the second explicit way in which corporate communications contribute to nonlearning.

Take the case of the 1,200-person operations division of what I'll call

Europabank, where employee commitment to customer service was about to become a matter of survival. The bank's CEO had decided to spin off the division, and its future depended on its ability to *earn* customer loyalty. Europabank's CEO felt confident that the employees could become more market-oriented. Because he knew they would have to take more initiative and risk, he created small project groups to work out all the implementation details and get employees to buy into the new mission. He was pleased with the way the organization was responding.

The vice president for human resources was not so pleased. He worried that the buy-in wasn't genuine and that his boss was overly optimistic. Not wanting to be negative, however, he kept his misgivings to himself.

In order to assess what was really going on here, I needed to know more about the attitudes behind the CEO's behavior. I asked him for some written examples of how he would answer employee concerns about the spin-off. What would he say to allay their doubts and build their commitment? Here are two samples of what he wrote:

- "If the employees express fear about the new plan because the 'old' company guaranteed employment, say: 'The new organization will do its utmost to guarantee employment and better prospects for growth. I promise that.'"
- "If the employees express fear that they are not used to dealing with the market approach, say: 'I promise you will get the education you need, and I will ensure that appropriate actions are rewarded.'"

When these very situations later arose and he made these very statements to employees, their reactions were positive. They felt that the CEO really cared about them.

But look at the confusion of messages and roles. If the CEO means to give these employees a sense of their own power over their own professional fate—and that was his stated intent—then why emphasize instead what *he* will do for *them?* Each time he said, "I promise you," the CEO undermined his own goal of creating internal commitment, intrinsic motivation, and genuine empowerment.

He might have begun to generate real buy-in by pointing out to employees that their wishes were unreasonable. They want management to deal with their fears and reassure them that everything will turn out for the best. They want management to take responsibility for a challenge that is theirs to face. In a market-driven business, the CEO cannot possibly give the guarantees these employees want. The employees see the CEO as caring when he promises to protect and reward them. Unfortunately, this kind of caring disempowers, and someday it will hurt both the employees and the company.

Once employees base their motivation on extrinsic factors—the CEO's promises—they are much less likely to take chances, question established policies and practices, or explore the territory that lies beyond the company vision as defined by management. They are much less likely to learn.

Externally committed employees believe that management manipulates them and see loyalty as allowing the manipulation to take place. They will give honest responses to a direct question or a typical employee survey because they will be glad to tell management what's wrong. They will see it as a loyal act. What they are *not* likely to do is examine the risky issues surrounding their dependence, their ambivalence, and their avoidance of personal responsibility. Employees will commit to TQM, for example, if they believe that their compensation is just and that their managers are fair and trustworthy. However, these conditions, like the commitment they produce, come from an outside source: management.

This is external commitment, and external commitment harnesses external motivation. The energy available for work derives from extrinsic factors like good pay, well-designed jobs, and management promises. Individuals whose commitment and motivation are external depend on their managers to give them the incentive to work.

I recently watched a videotape of the CEO of a large airline meeting with relatively upper-level managers. The CEO repeatedly emphasized the importance of individual empowerment at all levels of the organization. At one point in the tape, a young manager identified a problem that top managers at the home office had prevented him from resolving. The CEO thanked the man and then asked him to go directly to the senior vice president who ran the department in question and raise the issue again. In the meantime, he said, he would pave the way. By implication, he encouraged all the managers present to take the initiative and come to him if they encountered bureaucratic barriers.

I watched this video with a group of some 80 senior executives. All but one praised the CEO for empowering the young manager. The single dissenter wondered out loud about the quality of the empowerment, which struck him as entirely external, entirely dependent on the action of the CEO.

I agreed with that lonely voice. The CEO could have opened a window into genuine empowerment for the young manager by asking a few critical questions: What had the young man done to communicate his sense of disempowerment to those who blocked him? What fears would doing so have triggered? How could the organization redesign itself to give young managers the freedom and safety to take such initiatives? For that matter, the CEO could have asked these same questions of his senior vice presidents.

By failing to explore the deeper issues—and by failing to encourage his managers to do the same—all the CEO did was promise to lend the young manager some high-level executive power and authority the next time he had a problem. In other words, the CEO built external commitment and gave his manager access to it. What he did *not* do was encourage the young man to build permanent empowerment for himself on the basis of his own insights, abilities, and prerogatives.

Companies that hope to reap the rewards of a committed, empowered work force have to learn to stop kidding themselves. External commitment, positive thinking at any price, employees protected from the consequences and even the knowledge of cause and effect—this mind-set may produce superficial honesty and single-loop learning, but it will never yield the kind of learning that might actually help a company change. The reason is quite simply that for companies to change, employees must take an active role not only in describing the faults of others but also in drawing out the truth about their *own* behavior and motivation. In my experience, moreover, employees dig deeper and harder into the truth when the task of scrutinizing the organization includes taking a good look at their own roles, responsibilities, and potential contributions to corrective action.

The problem is not that employees run away from this kind of organizational self-examination. The problem is that no one asks it of them. Managers seem to attach no importance to employees' feelings, defenses, and inner conflicts. Moreover, leaders focus so earnestly on "positive" values—employee satisfaction, upbeat attitude, high morale—that it would strike them as destructive to make demands on employee self-awareness.

But this emphasis on being positive is plainly counterproductive. First, it overlooks the critical role that dissatisfaction, low morale, and negative attitudes can play—often *should* play—in giving an accurate picture of organizational reality, especially with regard to threatening or sensitive issues. (For example, if employees are helping to eliminate their own jobs, why should we expect or encourage them to display high morale or disguise their mixed feelings?) Second, it condescendingly assumes that employees can only function in a cheerful world, even if the cheer is false. We make no such assumption about senior executives. We expect leaders to stand up and take their punches like adults, and we recognize that their best performance is often linked to shaky morale, job insecurity, high levels of frustration, and a vigilant focus on negatives. But leaders have a tendency to treat everyone below the top, including many of their managers, like members of a more fragile race, who can be productive only if they are contented.

Now, there is nothing wrong with contented people, if contentment is the only goal. My research suggests it is possible to achieve quite respectable productivity with middling commitment and morale. The key is a system of external compensation and job security that employees consider fair. In such a system, superficial answers to critical questions produce adequate results, and no one demands more.

But the criteria for effectiveness and responsibility have risen sharply in recent years and will rise more sharply still in the decades to come. A generation ago, business wanted employees to do exactly what they were told, and company leadership bought their acquiescence with a system of purely extrinsic rewards. Extrinsic motivation had fairly narrow boundaries—defined by phrases like "That's not my job"—but it did produce acceptable results with a minimum of complication.

Today, facing competitive pressures an earlier generation could hardly have imagined, managers need employees who think constantly and creatively about the needs of the organization. They need employees with as much *intrinsic* motivation and as deep a sense of organizational stewardship as any company executive. To bring this about, corporate communications must demand more of everyone involved. Leaders and subordinates alike—those who ask and those who answer—must all begin struggling with a new level of self-awareness, candor, and responsibility.

About the Contributors

William J. Abernathy held the William Barclay Harding Professorship of the Management of Technology at the Harvard Business School at the time of his death in 1983. One of the world' s foremost authorities on the management of technology, Abernathy focused his research on the relationships among technology, innovation, and productivity, and the managerial and organizational problems associated with technological change and long-term planning. He wrote several articles and books, including *The Productivity Dilemma: Roadblock to Innovation in the Automobile Industry*.

Chris Argyris is the James Bryant Conant Professor of Education and Organizational Behavior, Emeritus, at the Harvard Business School and the Graduate School of Education. He has consulted to numerous organizations, and has served as special consultant to the governments of such countries as England, France, Germany, Italy, and Sweden on problems of executive development and productivity. Professor Argyris is the author of 300 articles and 30 books, including *Knowledge for Action: A Guide to Overlooking Barriers to Organizational Change* and *On Organizational Learning*. He is on the board of editors for several scholarly journals, and in 1994 was the recipient of the Academy of Management's Award for lifetime contributions to the discipline of management.

Richard J. Boyle is a managing director and co-founder of Boyle Fleming & Company (BFC), a private investment and management firm. In 1994 BFC assumed strategic and operational management of Spinnaker Industries, a multi-industry manufacturing firm for which

Boyle now serves as chairman and chief executive officer. Involved in numerous business and community activities, Boyle is a member of the honorary engineering societies Tau Beta Pi and Eta Kappa Nu, serves on the board of directors of several companies, and was a governor of the Aerospace Industries Association for three years.

Kim B. Clark is the Harry E. Figgie, Jr., Professor of Business Administration at the Harvard Business School, where he serves as chair of the technology and operations management area and heads the Science and Technology Interest Group. Specializing in issues of technology, productivity, product development, and operations strategy, he is a frequent contributor to the *Harvard Business Review* and other management journals, and is the co-author with Steven C. Wheelwright of *Revolutionizing Product Development, Managing New Product and Process Development*, and *Leading Product Development*. He is also the co-author with Takahiro Fujimoto of *Product Development Performance: Strategy, Organization, and Management in the World Auto Industry* (Harvard Business School Press, 1991), which received the 1992 Nikkei Culture Award for economics publications, and co-editor with Steven C. Wheelwright of *The Product Development Challenge* (Harvard Business School Press, 1995).

David A. Garvin is the Robert and Jane Cizik Professor of Business Administration at the Harvard Business School and a former faculty chairman of the school's Manufacturing in Corporate Strategy program. His research interests lie in the areas of general management and strategic change, and he is especially interested in organizational learning, business and management processes, and the development of leading-edge organizations. Professor Garvin has taught in numerous corporate education programs and has consulted widely. His most recent article "Processes, Strategy, and Leading Change: A CEO Roundtable" appeared in the *Harvard Business Review*. He wrote *Operations Strategy: Text and Cases* and was a co-editor of *Education for Judgment: The Artistry of Discussion Leadership* (Harvard Business School Press, 1991).

Charles Handy is an independent writer, teacher, and broadcaster living in London and Italy. He has been an oil executive, a business economist, and a professor at the London Business School, where he holds the title of fellow. His interests lie in the changing role and shape of organizations in society, and the implications for those who live and work in and around those organizations. His best-selling books include

The Age of Paradox (Harvard Business School Press, 1994) and *The Age of Unreason* (Harvard Business School Press, 1991).

Shmuel Halevi is president and a founder of TurningPoint Associates, a Boston-based consulting firm that advises executives in the information technology, telecommunications, and software industries on business strategy, investment optimization, marketing, and new venture development. Mr. Halevi has twenty years of experience as a consultant, executive, entrepreneur, and engineer in the United States, Europe, and Japan. Before founding TurningPoint in 1995, he was executive vice president for The Technology Research Group (TRG), where he consulted to clients on issues of business formation and redefinition in the industrial, professional, and consumer markets worldwide.

Gary Hamel is a visiting professor of strategy and international management at the London Business School and president of the consulting firm Hamel, Inc. As a co-originator of such groundbreaking concepts as strategic intent, core competence, strategic architecture, and industry foresight, Professor Hamel has changed the focus and content of strategy in many of the world's most successful companies. He is the co-author with C.K. Prahalad of *Competing for the Future* (Harvard Business School Press, 1994) and is featured with Prahalad in the Harvard Business School Press Management Productions video (1995) of the same title. Twice a year Professor Hamel leads his Boot Camp for Industry Revolutionaries in the United States and Europe.

Robert H. Hayes holds the Philip Caldwell Professorship in Business Administration at the Harvard Business School, where he also serves as senior associate dean and director of faculty planning. His current research focuses on manufacturing competitiveness, technological development, and the integration of design with manufacturing. His book *Restoring Our Competitive Edge: Competing through Manufacturing*, co-authored with Steven C. Wheelwright, won the 1984 Association of American Publishers' Award for the best book on business, management, and economics published that year. Professor Hayes is also the co-author with Steven C. Wheelwright and Kim B. Clark of *Dynamic Manufacturing: Creating the Learning Organization* and co-editor with Gary P. Pisano of *Manufacturing Renaissance* (Harvard Business School Press, 1995).

Alan M. Kantrow is the chief knowledge officer of Monitor Company, an international strategy consulting firm based in Cambridge,

Massachusetts. Before joining Monitor, he was a partner at McKinsey & Company, where he was the editor of the *McKinsey Quarterly* and the director of communications for Europe and Asia-Pacific. He was also a senior editor at the *Harvard Business Review*. He is the author of several books and numerous articles on manufacturing strategy, product development, and the managerial uses of history.

James F. Moore is the founder and chairman of GeoPartners Research, Inc. He is a prominent expert in corporate strategy and alliance-based competition. He originated the business ecosystems approach to taking advantage of technology discontinuities and shaping industry evolution. Moore's ideas have been adopted by many of the world's leading companies in businesses as diverse as entertainment, computers, and heavy manufacturing.

Michael E. Porter is the C. Roland Christensen Professor of Business Administration at the Harvard Business School and a leading authority on competitive strategy. He has served as counselor on competitive strategy to many leading U.S. and international companies and speaks widely on issues of international competitiveness to business and government audiences throughout the world. Professor Porter is the author of 14 books, including *Competitive Advantage: Creating and Sustaining Superior Performance*, which won the Academy of Management's 1985 George R. Terry Book Award, and *The Competitive Advantage of Nations*. His most recent work in economic policy initiatives focuses on the development of America's inner cities.

C.K. Prahalad is the Harvey C. Fruehauf Professor of Corporate Strategy and International Business Administration at the University of Michigan's Graduate School of Business Administration. His research focuses on the role and value-added of top management in large, diversified, multinational corporations, and he has consulted with the top management of numerous firms worldwide. Professor Prahalad is the co-author with Yves Doz of *The Multinational Mission: Balancing Local Demands and Global Vision* and, most recently, the co-author with Gary Hamel of *Competing for the Future* (Harvard Business School Press, 1994). He is also featured with Hamel in the Harvard Business School Management Productions video *Competing for the Future* (1995).

James Brian Quinn is the William and Josephine Buchanan Professor of Management, Emeritus, at the Amos Tuck School at Dartmouth College. His research focuses on corporate strategy, managing intellect, management of technological change, and services industries. Professor Quinn is also a consultant to numerous leading U.S. and foreign corporations, the U.S. and foreign governments, and a number of small enterprises. He is the author of several articles and books, including *Intelligent Enterprise: Knowledge and Service-Based Strategies for Industry*, published in 1992, which won both the American Publishers Association Award as Book of the Year in Business and Scholarship and the American Academy of Management's Book of the Year Award for Outstanding Contribution to Advancing Management Knowledge.

Andrew S. Rappaport is a noted authority on business strategy for electronics technology companies, and has consulted to the management teams of more than 200 companies worldwide. His consulting practice focuses on assisting management teams to formulate successful strategic responses to changing technologies, market climates, and international economics, and to define and implement new and effective business and competitive models. Mr. Rappaport is an affiliate of Institutional Venture Partners, one of the country's leading early stage venture-capital funds. He also serves on numerous corporate and advisory boards and has founded several public and private hardware and software companies.

Wickham Skinner is the James E. Robison Professor of Business Administration, Emeritus, at the Harvard Business School. His work centers on the competitive position of U.S. industry, with a focus on manufacturing strategy—the basic, structural, long-range decisions that largely determine the performance of a manufacturing unit. Professor Skinner is the author of three books, including *Manufacturing: The Formidable Competitive Weapon* and co-author of ten case books; he has also written extensively for business magazines and journals. He currently serves on the boards of five corporations, including the Bath Iron Works, and four non-profit organizations, and is president of the Farnsworth Museum in Rockland, Maine.

George Stalk, Jr., is senior vice president of The Boston Consulting Group and has consulted to a variety of leading manufacturing and technology-oriented companies. He speaks regularly before business and industry associations on time-based competition and related topics and was recently identified by *Business Week* as one among a new generation of leading management gurus. He is the co-author of *Competing Against Time* and *Kaisha: The Japanese Corporation*, and has published articles in numerous business publications.

William Wiggenhorn is president of Motorola University and senior vice president of training and education at Motorola. Since Wiggenhorn joined Motorola in 1981, the company's training program has evolved into Motorola University, a world-class corporate training organization offering a broad range of products and services to Motorola operations and its key suppliers and customers around the world. Mr. Wiggenhorn was a participant in the White House Conference on Productivity and the White House Conference on Aging. He is chairman of the National Issues Committee of the American Society of Training and Development and a member of the National Alliance of Business Board of Directors.

McKinsey Award Second Place Winners

1980

World Oil and Cold Reality
André Bénard
November–December

Managing Your Boss
John J. Gabarro and John P. Kotter
January–February

1981

Behind Japan's Success
Peter F. Drucker
January–February

Why Japanese Factories Work
Robert H. Hayes
July–August

When Executives Burn Out
Harry Levinson
May–June

1982

Can Industry Survive the Welfare State?
Bruce R. Scott
September–October

1983

Moral Mazes: Bureaucracy and Managerial Work
Robert Jackall
September–October

1984

Yesterday's Accounting Undermines Production
Robert S. Kaplan
July–August

1985

Scenarios: Uncharted Waters Ahead
Pierre Wack
September–October

1986

I Thought I Knew What Good Management Was
William H. Peace
March–April

1987

Crafting Strategy
Henry Mintzberg
July–August

1988

The Power of Unconditional Service Guarantees
Christopher W.L. Hart
July–August

1989

Management Women and the New Facts of Life
Felice N. Schwartz
January–February

Eclipse of the Public Corporation
Michael C. Jensen
September–October

1990

Computers and the Coming of the U.S. Keiretsu
Charles H. Ferguson
July–August

The Core Competence of the Corporation
C.K. Prahalad and Gary Hamel
May–June

1991

Research That Reinvents the Corporation
John Seely Brown
January–February

1992

Emerson Electric: Consistent Profits, Consistently
Charles F. Knight
January–February

1993

Building a Learning Organization
David A. Garvin
July–August

1994

The Theory of the Business
Peter F. Drucker
September–October

INDEX

Abernathy, William J., 1, 25, 130
Absenteeism, 40
Accor, 266
Acme, 310–311, 312–313
Acquisition, diversification through, 150–154
Action program, for choosing corporate strategy, 165–167
Activities, sharing, as concept of corporate strategy, 159–163
Admiral, 26
Advanced Micro Devices, 247
Advantage, building layers of, 204–205
    See also Competitive advantage
Advisory committee, 94–95
Air compressor industry, 27
Air conditioner industry, 67–68, 82–83, 185, 187–189
    measuring quality of, 68–72
    sources of quality of, 72–82
Aircraft industry, 5, 108
Akers, John, 265
ALCO Standard, 138
Altair, 287
Altera, 251
Amdahl, 207
American Hospital Supply, 149
American Motors, 196
American Productivity Center, 16
American Standard, 132–133
Apollo, 258
Apple Computer, 117, 214, 250, 258, 297
    as business ecosystem, 284, 287, 288, 289, 290
    and Microsoft, comparison of, 243–246, 249

Appliance industry, 27–28
Application-specific integrated circuits (ASICs), 249–250, 251
Approaches, multiple, in large innovative companies, 114–115
Argyris, Chris, 303
Arizona State University, 237
Asea Brown Boveri (ABB), 265, 267–268, 273
Asia Pacific International University, 239
AST Research, 255–256
AT&T, 113, 114, 117, 119, 238, 253
    laptop computers of, 255
Athos, Anthony, The Art of Japanese Management (with R. Pascale), 275
Atlas Door, 189–191
Atmosphere, in large innovative companies, 112–113
Attractiveness test, 146, 147–148
Augustine, Saint, 279
Automobile industry, 10, 14, 30
    challenge to management in, 46–47
    character of new competition in, 28–29
    collaboration in, 208
    evolutionary stages of, 282–284
    industrial relations system in, 40
    Japanese, 28–29, 31–37, 46, 284
    technological renewal of, 41–46

Backward integration, 12–14
Baekelund, Leo, 114
Barnevik, Percy, 265, 267, 268
Bateson, Gregory, 300
    Mind and Nature, 282
Baxter Travenol, 149

327

Bearings industry, 173
Beatrice, 138
Bell Laboratories, 114
Benetton, 180
Better-off test, 146, 149
Big Three, 28, 32
Biotechnology industry, 117, 297–299
Boston Consulting Group, 120
Bowmar, 13
Boyle, Richard J., 89
Bricks, searching for loose, 204,
    205–206, 209
Bristol-Myers, 298–299
Britain, 154–155, 266, 277
    See also United Kingdom
British Petroleum, 266, 271, 272
BTR, 156
Bureau of Labor Statistics, 127
Burke, Edmund, 268
Business ecosystems, 284–285, 299–301
    Stage 1 of, 285–288
    Stage 2 of, 288–290
    Stage 3 of, 290, 293–296
    Stage 4 of, 296–299
    Wal-Mart as, 290–293, 296
Business unit(s), 137, 150
    and choosing corporate strategy, 163,
        165
    level, competition at, 139–146
    and portfolio management, 151
    and restructuring, 154, 156
    and sharing activities, 159, 160,
        162–163
    and transferring skills, 157–159
Business Week, 18–19

CAD/CAM, 131
Canada, 265
Canon, 196–198, 200, 206–207, 212, 216
Carter, Jimmy, 42
Cash-generating rate, 60
Caterpillar, 196, 197
Catholic Church, 270, 271, 279
CBS, 139, 167
Central ecological contributor, 294–296
Chemicals industry, 5
China, 256
Chips & Technologies, 251
Chrysler, 65, 196, 214, 280, 284
Ciba-Geigy, 265–266
Cirrus Logic, 251
Citizenship, twin, as principle of
    federalism, 279
City University of New York, 235
Claris, 246
Clark, Kim B., 25
Coca-Cola, 197, 264

Co-evolution, 282, 287, 300
Collaboration, competing through, 204,
    207–208
Commonwealth of Independent States,
    265, 272
Compaq, 243, 245, 289, 290
    laptop computers of, 253, 254, 255
Competition, character of new, in
    automobile industry, 28–29
Competitive advantage, 137, 171
    expanding concept of, 203–208
    and flexible factory, 175
    and focused factory, 173
    through low labor costs, 172
    time-based, 172, 179–180, 181, 183
Computer industry, 27, 241–243, 257,
    259, 260–263
    laptop, 241, 253–256
    Microsoft and Apple compared,
        243–246
    and semiconductor industry, 247, 248,
        249, 253
Computerless competition, 241–243
    new rules for, 257–260
Concurrent Design Environment, 243
Consolidated Foods, 154
Consumer Reports, 35
Controlled fusion industry, 117
Cooper Industries, 134
Copeland Corporation, 133, 134
Corporate portfolio management, 9–10
Corporate raiders, 137–138, 167
Corporate strategy, 137–138
    action program for, 165–167
    choosing, 163–167
    concepts of, 149–163
    and portfolio management, 150–154
    premises of, 139–146
    and restructuring, 154–156
    success or failure of, 138–139
    and transferring skills, 156–159
Corporate theme, creating, 167
Cost-of-entry test, 146, 148
Costs, of production, 31–33
Council on Competitiveness, 260–263
Coupling mechanisms, 95, 97
Courage Breweries, 155
CP/M, 287–288, 289
Cray Research, 241
Customer loyalty, 36, 312
Czechoslovakia, 265

Daewoo, 212
Davidson, J. Hugh, 11
De Benedetti, Carlo, 214
Decentralization, 211–213, 267
Deere & Company, 134

Defensive reasoning, 307, 308, 309, 310
Deterioration rate, 60–61
Dewey & Almy, 119
Digital Equipment Corporation (DEC), 115, 244, 258, 259
Digital Research, 287–288
Discounting, 66
  future, 55–58
  techniques, 51–52, 63, 64, 65
Disinvestment, 58
  logic of, 64–66
  spiral, reversing, 65–66
Diversification, 137–139, 146
  through acquisition, 150–154
  three essential tests for successful, 146–149, 155
  See also Corporate strategy
Divisionalization, 267
Domain operating system, 258
Domino's Pizza, 180
DRAM production, 241, 256
Draper, 26
Du Pont, 117, 138, 161
Durant, William C., 283

Ecosystems
  automobile, 282–284
  collapse of natural, 282
  See also Business ecosystems
Edison, Thomas, 110
Eguchi, Hideto, 179
Einstein, Albert, 121
Elders, 155
Electronics industry, 117, 230
Elf Aquitaine, 113
Eli Lilly, 298–299
Empowerment, 310–316 *passim*
Energy prices, rising, 61
Engagement, changing terms of, 204, 206–207
Entrepreneurs, *see* Inventor-entrepreneurs
Epson, 212
Espoused theory of action, 307
European Community, 265, 270–271
European managers, 20–21
Evans & Sutherland, 260
Ever Ready Batteries, 155
Exxon, 138

Fabs, 248, 250–251, 252
Factory
  flexible, 175–176, 177, 184–185
  focused, 173, 175, 177
  just-in-time, 190
Federal Express, 180

Federalism, 265–266
  five key principles of, 270–280
  and paradoxes of modern business, 266–269
  and pull of professionals, 269–270, 276
Ferguson, Charles, 254
Financial control, 9
Fisher, George, 234
Flexible factory, 175–176, 177, 184–185
Flexible manufacturing, 177, 180, 185, 205
Fluidity vs. stability, 43–44
Focused factory, 173, 175, 177
Food and Drug Administration (FDA), U.S., 109, 297, 298
Food service industry, 161–162
Ford, Henry, 10, 47, 283
Ford Motor Company, 29, 31, 33, 44, 65, 197
  as business ecosystem, 284
  Edsel of, 117–118
  evolutionary stages of, 282–283, 284
  global brand positions of, 212
  joint venture of, 208
  quality improvement at, 202
  Ranger trucks of, 82
Formality, excessive, 100
Forrester, Jay W., 181, 185, 186
"40 40 20" rule, 129
France, 1, 8, 20, 266
Fujitsu, 27, 199, 207, 212, 250, 259
  supercomputers of, 241

Galvin, Robert, 222–223, 226–227, 231, 234, 271
Garvin, David A., 51, 67
Genentech, 113, 117, 298
General Cinema, 156
General Electric (GE), 27–28, 134, 160, 211, 212, 213–214
  acquisitions of, 139
  federalism at, 266
  innovation at, 123–124
General Mills, 139
General Motors (GM), 32, 41, 44, 157, 208, 282–283
Generic drug manufacturers, 297
Germany, 1, 14, 20, 273
Gillette, 272
Gould, Stephen Jay, 282
Graham, Edward M., 42
Grand Metropolitan, 266, 273
Grayson, C. Jackson, 16–17
Grid Systems, 254, 255–256
Grove, Andy, 299
Gulf & Western, 154

Halevi, Shmuel, 241
Haloid, 117
Hamel, Gary, 193
Handy, Charles, 265
Hanson Trust, 154–155
Harvard Business Review, 147, 181, 254
Harvey-Jones, Sir John, 275–276
Hayes, Robert H., 1, 51
Heinz, 212
Helene Curtis Industries, 292
Hewlett-Packard, 82, 117, 118–119, 243,
    259, 297
Hierarchies, twin, 278–279
Hino, 180
Hipple, Eric von, 15
Hitachi, 27, 180, 205
Hoff, Ted, 115
Hoffman-LaRoche, 119, 298
Hokuetsu, 27
Honda, 41, 180, 185, 196, 212
    federalism at, 266
    motorcycles of, 177–179, 206, 209
    strategic intent at, 197, 198
Honda, Soichiro, 116
Honeywell, 89–90
    beginnings of change at, 91–93
    need for structure at, 97–100
    participation amok at, 93–97
    Patton-style management at, 90–91
    relaxing style at, 100–102
    return on investment at, 102–105
    seven principles of managing at, 92
Horton, Robert, 272
Hotel industry, 161, 162
Hughes, Thomas, 121
Hughes Aircraft, 157
Hurdle rate, 61–63
H-Y War, 178–179

Iacocca, Lee A., 29, 214
IBM, 113, 119, 123, 138, 164, 238
    as business ecosystem, 284, 287, 288,
        289–290
    compared with Microsoft, 244
    copier business of, 206
    federalism at, 265
    FS system of, 117–118
    Fujitsu's attack on, 27, 199
    global brand positions of, 212
    laptop computers of, 255
    and Motorola, 297
    personal computer of, 245, 281, 284,
        289–290, 293
    quality improvement at, 202
    shared activities at, 161
    workstations of, 259

Ibuka, Masaru, 112–113
ICI, 275–276
ICL, 259
Illinois Institute of Technology, 237
Imitative vs. innovative product design,
    11–12
Imperial Group, 155
IMSAI, 287
Indivisibilities, 66
Industrial doors, 190–191
Industrial dynamics, 181
Industry, U.S., 25–26
    challenge to management in, 46–47
    and Japanese micromanagement,
        31–36
    and Japan's shrewd use of
        manufacturing excellence, 36–41
    levers of change in, 26–30
    and technological renewal, 41–46
Inflation, 60–61
Information systems, quality and, 75–76
Information technology industry, 197
Ingersoll-Rand, 27
Initial public offerings, 110
Innovation, 107–108
    approaches to competitive, 204–208
    bureaucratic barriers to, 111–112
    encouragement of, 9
    incrementalist approach to, 120–124
    industrial, 15
    in large companies, 112–118
    necessity for advantage through, 29
    process, matching management to, 124
    and productivity, 130
    "Silicon Valley" approach to, 199
    in small enterprises, 108–111
    strategy for, 118–120
    time-based, 186–189
Innovative vs. imitative product design,
    11–12
Integration, backward, 12–14
Intel, 113, 115, 119, 243, 251, 259
    IBM's investment in, 290
    Magnetic Memory Group at, 123
    microprocessors of, 117, 252, 253, 258
    and Microsoft, 295–297
    success of, 252–253
    "20% solution" at, 118
Interdependence, as principle of
    federalism, 272–273, 275, 278,
    279
Intrinsic motivation, 313, 314, 317
Inventor-entrepreneurs, characteristics
    of, 109–111
Ishikawa diagram, 225
ITT, 154

Japan, 264
    air conditioner industry in, 67–83,
        187–189
    appliance exports of, 27
    approaches to competitive innovation
        in, 204–208
    automobile industry of, 28, 31–37, 46,
        284
    capital investment in, 8
    expenditures on R&D by, 5
    innovation in companies in, 116, 117
    laptop computers in, 241, 253–256
    low wages and variety wars in,
        172–179
    managing time in, 171–172
    micromanagement in, 31–36
    productivity growth in, 1
    remaking strategy in, 194
    semiconductor industry in, 82, 247,
        251
    shrewd use of manufacturing
        excellence in, 36–41
    time-based competitive advantage in,
        172, 179–180, 181
    time-based innovation in, 186–189
    time-based manufacturing in, 184, 185
    time-based sales and distribution in,
        185–186
Jidoka, concept of, 40
Johnson & Johnson, 164, 266
Junk bonds, 138, 148
Just-in-time production, 38–40, 177,
    190, 191

Kanban, 38–40
Kantrow, Alan M., 25
Katz, Abraham, 31
Kawasaki (motorcycles), 179
Kawasaki Steel, 250
Kidder, Tracy, 124
Kmart, 284–285, 291, 292, 293
Kodak, 206, 212
Komatsu, 196, 197, 198, 202
Korea, 212, 241, 251, 256
Kyocera, 256

Labor, U.S. Department of, 52–53
Laptop computers, 241, 253–256
Learning
    double-loop, 305–306, 307, 313
    interactive, in large innovative
        companies, 116–118
    single-loop, 305, 306, 307, 316

Leveraging resources, problem of,
    194–195
Limited, The, 180
Lloyd's of London, 274
Loew's, 156
London Brick, 155
Lotus, 290, 295
LSI Logic, 249–251
Lucky Gold Star, 212

McDonald's, 180
McGee, Victor, 114
Machinery industry, 5
Machine tools industry, 27
Macintosh, 244, 245, 246
McKesson, 160
McLane Company, 293
Malkiel, Burton G., 6–8, 60
Management
    American ideal, 15–20
    challenge to, 46–47
    changing career patterns of, 15–17
    creating economic value by, 21–23
    criticisms of, 21–22
    decisions faced by, 11–15
    denominator, 213
    European example of, 20–21
    excuses for decline of, 4–8, 22
    failure of U.S., 2–4
    fast-track, 213
    orthodoxy, new, 8–10, 15
    Patton-style, 89, 90–91
    premium on, 29–30
    style, changing of, at Honeywell,
        89–105
Manufacturing
    flexible, 177, 180, 185, 205
    strategy, 133–134
    time-based, 183–185
Margin retreat, 173–175
Marker, Russell, 109
Market-driven behavior, 10
Market orientation, in large innovative
    companies, 113–114
Marriott, 161–162, 164
Matsushita, 119, 180, 185, 205, 206, 212
    joint ventures of, 207–208
Maturity, concept of, 210–211
Mazda, 33, 202, 205, 208
Mentor Graphics, 243
Merck, 113, 119, 284, 298–299
Merger(s), 53–54, 138–139, 148
    mania, 18–20
Micromanagement, Japanese, 31–36
Micropro, 285, 286

Microprocessors, 252, 253, 258–259,
    285–287, 296
  Sparc, 259
  Zilog, 288, 289
Microsoft, 243, 251, 262, 290
  and Apple Computer, comparison of,
    243–246, 249
  and Intel, 295–297
Ministry of International Trade and
    Industry (MITI, Japan), 79
Minolta, 212
Minorities, employed at Honeywell,
    103–104
MIPS (millions of instructions per
    second), 242
MIPS Computer Systems, 250
MIT, 181, 254
Mitsubishi, 27, 187–189
Moore, Gordon, 113
Moore, James F., 281
Morita, Akio, 113, 274
Motorcycle industry, 177–179, 206, 209
Motorola, 26, 219–220, 239–240, 251,
    258, 271
  and Apple Computer, 284
  attempts at education and training at,
    222–224
  language of quality at, 220–222
  literacy problem at, 228–231, 233
  microprocessor of, 297
  motivating people to learn at, 224–226
  Service Club at, 224, 225
  See also Motorola University
Motorola Executive Institute, 222
Motorola Training and Education Center
    (MTEC), 223–224, 230, 231, 234
Motorola University, 222
  curriculum development at, 235–236
  electrifying present and future
    employees at, 239–240
  events leading to establishment of,
    226–233
  finding and training faculty at,
    237–238
  open-ended education at, 234–239
Motorola University Press, 237
MS-DOS, 243, 287

National Semiconductor, 247
"Natural consequences of maturity,"
    41–42
NCR, 255
NEC Corporation, 167, 180, 197, 212
  laptop computers of, 255, 256
  supercomputers of, 241
Newman, Cardinal, *The Idea of a
    University*, 235, 239

Nippon Electric, 27
Nissan, 37, 203
Northwestern University, 237
Novell, 297

Ohno, Taiichi, 177
Olds, Ranson E., 282
Olivetti, 214, 255
OPEC, 1
Organizational defensive routines,
    308–310
Organizational design, purpose of good,
    18
Organizations, small, flat, in large
    innovative companies, 114

Panasonic, 212
Pareto chart, 225
Pascale, Richard, *The Art of Japanese
    Management* (with A. Athos),
    275
Pepsico, 159
Pepsi-Cola, 269
Personal computers
  as ecological business development,
    285–288
  IBM's, 245, 281, 283, 289–290, 293
Pharmaceutical companies, 297–299
"Phased program planning," 120–121
Philip Morris, 148
Philips, 208, 259
Pilkington, 113, 123
Pizza Hut, U.K., 269
Planning loop, breaking, 180–183
Pluralism, 272
Porsche, 209
Porter, Michael E., 137
Portfolio management, 9–10, 120
  as concept of corporate strategy,
    150–154
Prahalad, C. K., 193
Process development, 14–15
Process yield, focus on, 37–41
Procter & Gamble (P&G), 159–160, 161,
    164, 292
Product design
  imitative vs. innovative, 11–12
  quality and, 76–79
Production
  costs of, 31–33
  just-in-time, 38–40, 177, 190, 191
  and work force policies, quality and,
    79–81
Productivity
  defined, 127
  paradox, 127–135

Product quality, 67–68, 82–83
  contrasts in, 33–36
  measuring, 68–72
  sources of, 72–82
Professional and scientific instruments
  industry, 5
Programs, policies, and attitudes, quality
  and, 73–75
Pseudo-professionalism, gospel of,
  17–18

Quality, *see* Product quality
Quality circles, 92, 94, 215
Quinn, James Brian, 107

Radio Shack, 285
Rappaport, Andrew S., 241
Raychem, 117
RCA, 211
Recession (1981–1983), 118
Reciprocal responsibility, 202, 203
Reinvestment, 58–60, 66
  and cash-generating rate, 60
  decline in, 52–55
  and deterioration rate, 60–61
  and hurdle rate, 61–63
Renier, Jim, 100, 101
Restructuring, as concept of corporate
  strategy, 154–156
Return on investment (ROI), 9
Ringi decision making, 116
Robotics, 131
Rockwell International, 26
Royal Dutch Shell, 147, 266
Rubbermaid, 292

Sales and distribution, time-based,
  185–186
Sam's Club, 293
Samsung, 212
Sanyo, 26, 27, 205
Sara Lee, 138, 154
Schumpeter, Joseph, 11
SCM, 155
Sculley, John, 214
Sears, 289
Seiko, 212
Self-enlightenment, 277
Semiconductor industry, 82, 241, 242,
  247–253, 256
7-Eleven convenience stores, 293
Seven-Up Company, 148
Shareholder value
  and corporate theme, 167
  creation of, through diversification,
    146–149, 163
  use of, to judge performance, 139
Sharp, 180, 205, 255
Shell, 275
Shipbuilding industry, 172–173
Shoot-outs, developmental, in large
    innovative companies, 115–116
Siemens, 207, 212
Signatures on one's work, 276–277
Silicon Graphics, 260
Silicon integration, 247, 248, 253
Silicon Valley, 199, 250, 251
Silicon wafer, 248–249
Simplification, American penchant for,
    18, 19
Six Sigma, 221
SKF, 173, 175
Skills, transferring, as concept of
    corporate strategy, 156–159
Skinner, Wickham, 127
Skunkworks, in large innovative
    companies, 116
Sloan, Alfred P., 47, 283
Soft-drink industry, 148
Sony, 26, 180, 211, 212, 276
  and Apple Computer, 284
  innovation at, 112–117, 123
Southland Corporation, 293
Soviet Union, 272
Sparc microprocessors, 259
S.S. Kresge, 291
Stability vs. fluidity, 43–44
Staff meetings, 99
Stalk, George, Jr., 171
STC, 207
Steel industry, 147, 172
Steering committees, 97–99
Strategic business units (SBUs), 211–213
Strategic fit, maintaining, 194–195
Strategic intent, 196–198
  achieving, 199–200, 204
  and approaches to competitive
    innovation, 204–208
  essence of, 214
  and means and ends, 199, 200
  and strategic planning, 198–199
Strategy(ies)
  for innovation, 118–120
  manufacturing, 133–134
  remaking, 193, 194–208
  technology-driven, 44–46
  time-based, 189–191
  See also Corporate strategy
Subsidiarity, as principle of federalism,
    270–272, 276, 277, 278
Sun Microsystems, 250, 257–259, 263,
    297

"Sunset law," 64
Sun-tzu, 196
Supercomputers, 241, 253
Surrender, process of, 208, 209–210
Sutton, Matt, 91–92
Suzuki, 179
Synergy
  concept of, 157
  rejection of, 160
Syntex, 109, 114, 123–124

Taiwan, 241, 251, 256
Tandy Corporation, 287, 288, 289, 290
Task teams, 92–95, 97–98, 99–100
  career development, 102
  EEO, 103–104
  pay, 102–103
Taylor, Frederick Winslow, 132
Technological renewal, 41
  and fluidity vs. stability, 43–44
  and misperceptions of causes, 41–42
  and technology-driven strategies,
    44–46
Telefunken, 207–208
Television industry
  color, 26, 204–205
  high-definition, 211
Texas Instruments, 251, 255, 259
Textile industry, 117, 172
Textile machinery industry, 26
Theme, creating corporate, 167
Theory-in-use, 307–308
Thinking Machines, 241
Thomson, 208
Thorn, 207
3M, 117, 118–119, 123, 138, 159, 164
Time
  -based competitive advantage, 172,
    179–180, 181, 183
  -based innovation, 186–189
  -based manufacturing, 183–185
  -based sales and distribution, 185–
    186
  -based strategy, 189–191
  and breaking planning loop, 180–183
  managing, 171–172
Timken, 134
Toshiba, 27, 180, 205, 206, 209, 245
  ASICs of, 250, 251
  global brand franchises of, 212
  laptop computers of, 254–256
  and Sparc microprocessors, 259
Total customer service, 215
Total quality control, 177
Total quality management (TQM),
    304–305, 305–307, 313, 315

Townes, Charles, 121
Toyo Kogyo, 33
Toyota, 27, 31, 32, 176–177, 180
  ecosystem of, 284
  joint venture of, 208
  time-based manufacturing at, 185
  time-based sales and distribution at,
    185–186
  SR5 of, 82
Toyota Motor Manufacturing, 185, 186
Toyota Motor Sales, 185–186
Traditions, irreverence toward company,
    100
"Transient economic misfortune," 42
Transistors, 248–249
TRW, 164
Twinheads, 255

Unilever, 266, 272, 275
Unionization, 40–41, 283–284
Unisys, 253
United Auto Workers (UAW), 283
United Kingdom, 154, 235, 250, 269
  See also Britain
United Technologies, 123–124, 164
Unix operating system, 244, 257–258
UNIX Systems Laboratories, 297

Vagelos, Roy, 299
Value, creating economic, 21–23
Value chain, 157–158, 159
Variety wars, low wages and, 172–179
Vendor management, quality and, 81–82
Vision
  effect of obsession with productivity
    on, 131–132, 135
  in large innovative companies,
    112–113
Volkswagen, 37

Wages, low, and variety wars, 172–179
Wal-Mart, 284–285, 296
  evolution of, 290–293
Walton, Sam, 291
Warwick, 26
Weisz, Bill, 238
Weitek, 251
Western Electric, 114
West Germany, 5, 8
Whitbread, 269
Wiggenhorn, William, 219
Wilson Art, 180
Windows operating system, 243, 244,
    245

Women, employed at Honeywell, 103, 104
Wordstar, 289
World War II, 17, 171, 172
W.R. Grace, 19

Xerox, 165, 196, 197, 200, 206–207
Xilinx, 251

Yamaha, 177–179, 209, 211
Yanmar Diesel, 176–177

Zeos, 255
Zilog microprocessor, 288, 289